Read what people are saying!

May Britt, world famous actress of the s[...] my said: "I'm sure that the author's first-hand [...]ded insight into the life of one of the worlds g[...]

Janet Leigh, legendary actress of stag[...]d of Sammy's wrote about this book: "...a real [...]ad' again with Sammy and Arthur...."

Glenn Ford: "*Sammy Davis Jr., Me and My Shadow* reveals many things about a great entertainer that nobody but his best friend, Arthur Silber Jr. could know...it's a fascinating read...."

Liz Smith, gossip columnist for the New York Post wrote: Arthur Silber Jr., a longtime confidant and business manager to Sammy...beating two other upcoming Sammy books to the punch...[gives] inside up-close dish on the entertainer's affair with Kim Novak, his marriage to May Britt and the racial injustices he encountered while building his career."

Jim Bacon, world renowned Hollywood columnist and author said, "One of the best books on Sammy Davis Jr. I've ever read! Arthur Silber Jr. captures everything on paper that made Sammy 'Mr. Wonderful.' It's a heartfelt tribute from someone who knew Sammy very well."

The Globe, 6 /17/03, article covering an entire page written by Rod Gibson entitled "Sammy Davis Jr. and Kim Novak, True Story Revealed At Last:" "Silber writes the inside story of Sammy's life including this forbidden love affair...."

The World Enterainment News Network article posted June 11, 2003: "Beloved crooner Sammy Davis Jr. attempted suicide on his wedding night because racial jibes drove him mad, according to a new biography. The "Mr. Bojangles" singer's former personal assistant Arthur Silber Jr. has revealed the cabaret star's personal pain in a new memoir, *Sammy Davis Jr.–Me and my Shadow*. Silber claims the song-and-dance man was distraught at having to end his secret romance with actress Kim Novak...."

Los Angeles Times, 10/29/03, Hollywood Behind-the-Scenes by Alice O'Neill, **"The truth about Sammy."** Reading Arthur Silber's memoir of Sammy Davis, Jr. is like being a fly on the wall as the life of a famous celebrity unfolds. The singer/actor/dancer who died in 1990, just two years after his father died, is remembered by the man who acted as his personal assistant and shared his life for twenty years. Silber's father was a successful manager of celebrities **Nat King Cole, Mary Martin, Martha Raye, Ann Miller** and **Sammy Davis, Jr.**

Silber Jr., who'd lived with the Davis family when he was a teen, considered Sammy his brother. He knew the inside details of Davis' love life and tells how the superstar met, wooed and lost most of the women he loved, including **Kim Novak** and **May Britt**. This is not a gossipy book but seems to fill in the gaps left by the tabloid stories we've all read about.

SAMMY DAVIS JR.

ME AND MY SHADOW

A Biographical Memoir

by

Arthur Silber Jr.

® ™   © Samart Enterprises • Valley Village, CA

Other works by Arthur Silber Jr.:
The Little Christmas Story Book (CD)
The Christmas Rose (Cassette)
Grandma's Breakfast, Lunch, Dinner & Things (Cookbook)

Editor: Sandi DeSilva
Associate Editors: Ilene Gutierrez & Dorothy (DC) Fontana

Front Cover: art & design–Klaus Ernst, lettering–Matt Rupp
Back Cover & Inside: photo restoration,
page layout and design, typesetting and style–Dawn King

Published by

11543 Addison Street
Valley Village, CA 91601 USA

WEBSITE: www.arthursilber.com
E-MAIL: sammysbook@earthlink.net

Dedication

TO MY FAMILY

NITA, MARK, SHAWN, ROBIN,

STEVE, KAYLA, BRANDON,

MY MOM, MONYA,

MY DAD

&

"THE POOH"

Acknowledgments

The author herewith expresses his gratitude to the following individuals, named and unnamed for their invaluable help and contributions in making this book a realization.

Credit is due and particular mention must be made:
to my wife Nita, whose idea and persistence got me started;
to my family: my mother, Monya; Mark, Robin, Shawn, Steve, Kayla and Brandon; and to my beloved companion "*Holly, The Pooh*;" to my dearest friend Sandi DeSilva and to Ms. Ilene Gutierrez (Miss Red Pencil), and Dawn King for all their able and meticulous work, in the editing of this book, as well as their capable management and contribution to the telling of this story.

A very special credit to my dad, Arthur Silber—without his guidance and friendship this story could never have happened.

Table of Contents

List of Illustrations

Sammy Once Said:

"In the same way that live performance is an impermanent art, a star is an impermanent illusion, who lives only in the memory of those who have seen him and then dies with them. I believe that by keeping our films, video tapes and books in the hands of those who so diligently and lovingly restore and take care of them, the illusion of Sammy Davis Jr. will never die."—Sammy Davis Jr.

It is said that beauty is always a bonus…but it cannot match the bonding of spirits between two people. When it is present…it is just there, and let no man put assunder.

And this is my contribution to his illusion.

Prologue

This is the **real, true** story of Sammy Davis Jr.—the story that has never been told before because there is no one left alive to tell it. During the almost twenty-three years I was with Sammy, no one was closer to him. We went everywhere together, ate together, traveled together, shared women, rooms and later suites as his fame rose, twenty-four hours a day, seven days a week. I even lived with his family, and called Sam Sr. "Dad," Sammy's grandmother "Mama," and Will Mastin "Massey." They were as close to me as my own family, and Sammy the brother I never had, as I was also to him.

This is the story of one of the greatest entertainers the world has ever seen. First though, I need to provide a little background about how Sammy came into my life and how I ended up in this close position with him.

My mother, Monya, was a very well known dancer and later, spent many years in movies. My father, Arthur Silber, was one of the most well-known and respected talent agents and managers in show business. He was President of the Theatrical Agents Association for twelve years and managed such stars as William Boyd (Hopalong Cassidy), Martha Raye, Ann Miller, Nat King Cole, Mary Martin, many more too numerous to name, and yes, Sammy Davis Jr.

I was an only child who traveled constantly with my father. In 1946, when I was fifteen years old traveling with Dad in Hawaii, I met Sammy Davis Jr. and we became lifelong friends. It was then and there that Sammy and I began staging mock fist fights, which we would enjoy doing for many years to come, and which would enhance his career in movies later on.

My first big professional break came when I was twenty-one and Sammy hired me as his personal assistant. Later I became his Production Manager and Lighting Director, a position I remained in for the next twenty years. It would be impossible to measure everything I learned from Sammy about show business. He was the consummate professional, a genius at his craft and one of the most versatile and gifted talents show business has ever produced.

More specifically, we traveled all over the world and went everywhere together. I know firsthand about the prejudice Sammy was

Sammy and me, circa 1950

subjected to as he was the first Black performer to break the color barrier in so many clubs, hotels and theaters. I stayed with Sammy in all the so-called "Black" hotels on the "Black" side of many towns in many States. Being with Sammy, I was also a recipient of all the racial slurs, insults, threats and attacks of one kind or another. Being White and Jewish did not help me either. The hatred and venom directed at Sammy as a human being was ugly and unbelievable and I lived it with him.

When Sammy was learning to be a quick-draw expert, he practiced with me and consequently we both became very, very good at it. He performed quick-draw tricks on stage for years and that was very popular with his audiences and fans. Another thing we practiced for years was sword fighting and hand-to-hand fighting like in the Old West. We had been practicing and staging mock fights since I first met him but never dreamed these games would become so important to his career. We played like kids, but seriously, too, and all these antics, although great fun to us, became vital to Sammy in his movie career and in his live stage performances. I am the only person who shared these activities with Sammy and it illustrates, in part, the special relationship we had.

In the years I spent with Sammy he drank nothing stronger than Coca-Cola, and lots of it. We shared women, we shared our families, we shared our lives, we shared confidences. This book will tell the **real** story of Sammy's affair with Kim Novak, a relationship which, at that time, could have ruined both their careers and their lives. I am the only one still alive who knows the real story besides, Patsy Rees and of course, Kim herself.

This book will tell the **real** story of the devastating auto accident which cost Sammy his eye, and almost cost him his life. The most accurate version was **not** told in Sammy's autobiography, *Yes I Can!* That manuscript was originally over twelve hundred pages long and the publisher made Sammy cut it in half. This is partly because **all** the truth in some of the stories could not be told, even at the time his book was published. It would have been too dangerous for Sammy and those he loved.

This book will also tell other stories that were left out of Sammy's book, such as his two suicide attempts and the **true** story of his first marriage to Loray White.

Some of the professional highlights this book will elaborate on are behind the scenes stories of three Royal Command Performances: for England's Queen Elizabeth, Princess Grace and Prince Rainier of Monaco, and England's Queen Mother. I co-produced many of Sammy's other shows including England's Best Television Show of 1961, called *Sammy Meets the Girls*.

The years I spent with Sammy were some of his best years and certainly some of mine. We formed a company called Samart Enterprises, a compilation of our first names, which I still own today. Samart Enterprises was founded to finance the development of new products and anything else which might interest us. Some of the best stories are of the products we did **not** back when they were presented to us.

Sammy Davis Jr. was the greatest entertainer who ever lived, at least that's what Frank Sinatra and many others used to say. He was talented beyond belief and knew show business inside and out. On the personal side, he was deeply sensitive and caring, funny and generous to a fault. One of my most prized possessions, which I always wear, is a solid gold medallion of Moses and the Ten Commandments, engraved from him to me on the back. Sammy wore the only duplicate.

Some of the other previously incomplete or untold stories this book will tell are the **true** stories of Sammy's relationship with and marriage to May Britt; Sammy's close friendship with Eddie Cantor; the first time Sammy played Miami Beach, and broke the color barrier there, in a club owned by Sophie Tucker and Ted Lewis; inside stories of the Rat Pack and Frank Sinatra; how Sammy ended up with Maurice Chevalier's famous hat; Sammy's first television appearance, and many many more. None of the stories in this book are hearsay, but events I witnessed personally and was part of.

Sammy and I were both camera buffs and this book includes many pictures from his and my personal collections, almost all of which have never been seen before except by family and close friends. For example, I shot the only pictures ever taken of Sammy with Queen Elizabeth II.

It is important for the reader to know a few vital facts about what made Sammy run, and simultaneously dispel many of the myths others have perpetrated about him. As a child, Sammy never played football, baseball, stickball, catch, or even kick-the-can. Sammy never had a pet and never learned to swim. Consequently he had a lifelong fear of water. Sammy never learned to write, never went to school and never did any of the simple things that every other kid did. He taught himself to read and learned everything else by watching and listening to others. Sammy simply never had a childhood.

So many legends, lies and half-truths have been told about Sammy Davis Jr. that I just had to write this book and set the stories straight. Even the bios on Sammy that have run on television are full of inaccuracies. I know, because I was there! I was there for the fun, the hard work, the laughter, the tears, the triumphs and the fears—all before the drinking and drugs entered into his life—**The Good Years**. I was there for the **best** of those years, and this book will tell it all.

Arthur Silber Jr.

Kim
Novak

Royal
Performances

Fund
Raising

Marilyn
Monroe

Elvis

Judy
Garland

Eddie Fisher
Liz Taylor

Comedy

Bill
Cosby

Movies

Shirley
MacLaine

Recording

Sammy Davis Jr.
The Good Years

What can you say about Sammy Davis Jr.? He was the most versatile performer of his generation. His dancing was a study in fine rhythm and agility; his timing precise. He was a human dynamo. People said he was monumental, mammoth, a one-man marathon. He could play drums and a half-dozen other musical instruments. He was a singer, comedian, movie producer and author. He appeared in virtually every major nightclub in the world and guest-starred on nearly every network television variety show from *All In the Family* to numerous soap operas and countless dramatic shows.

He was one of a kind, the world's greatest entertainer. Sammy could transmit unparalleled excitement to an audience with every fluid movement of his body, yet dramatically convey his social consciousness and humanitarianism through his songs, acting and writing. His energy was all-consuming; and his performing would entrance his audience into whisperless, squirmless, coughless admiration. Yes, you could say all that about him, but no one ever knew what really made Sammy run, the man and yes, even the boy, behind all the accolades.

While developing his theatrical talents, one vital aspect of his life was overlooked, and that was schoolbook learning. Sammy never had any kind of a formal education. All he learned during his young years was taught to him at home, first by his grandmother, Rosa B. Davis, a short, stout lady we called "Mama." She was the ruler of the roost, the matriarch of the Davis family; and she ruled it with kindness, love, strength and a big wooden spoon. If you didn't "do right" around her, or in her house, you would get that spoon alongside your head or whatever part of your body was closest. Behind that came the lecture on "what's right" or "what's wrong," then came a hug and a kiss. It goes without saying that if every kid had a grandma like Mama, the youth of today would be in a much better place. I think you could call it respect.

**My mother with "Mama,"
Sammy's grandmother**

**Elvera "Baby" Sanchez,
Sammy's mother**

Mama was Sammy's first teacher; and it was her home that Sammy, Sam Sr. and Will Mastin would live in when work was scarce. With the Trio always rehearsing, Sammy never had the time to learn mathematics or how to write. What little he did learn, aside from what Mama taught him, came from the other performers and the stagehands.

As a child, when Sammy wasn't working his act, he would go into the other performers' dressing rooms and they would teach the little guy as much as they were able. To the end of his life, Sammy could not write or spell very well or do anything but basic math. He taught himself to write "Best Wishes." "Good Luck," a few other phrases and sign his name.

The one thing he did do was teach himself to read. He was a voracious reader and read everything he could get his hands on. This enabled him to talk knowledgeably on almost any subject. But the real driving passion behind this little man was to learn all he could about becoming a performer.

Bill "Bojangles" Robinson was so impressed by this young man and his natural ability that he tutored Sammy. He was the most important influence in the creation of Sammy's own dancing style.

When Sammy first walked on stage in 1929 at the age of three, he wasn't called Sammy. Sam Sr. called him Popa; and "Uncle" Will Mastin, his dad's vaudeville partner, called him Mose Gastin. Sam Sr. and Will Mastin were poor, and steady work was hard to come by. With the color barrier being what it was, Black entertainers could only work in certain places.

"We all have troubles sometimes," Will used to say to Sammy, "but those people out front don't know. No matter how bad you're hurting, leave your troubles in the wings and come out smiling."

While Sammy was dancing, his father would go into the audience and throw a half-dollar onto the stage so other audience members would be prompted to throw money to Sammy during the act. Sammy eventually became the greatest tap dancer in the world, but fancy trick dancing was the first thing he learned. As a young performer, he didn't know how to do a time-step (the first step you learn in tap-dancing). With all the tricks he learned, he never could get the time-step down until later.

Never, ever did Sammy, his father or Will sit down in their stage clothes. Never! It was important not to wrinkle their show clothes. It started with Will Mastin's training. You could be the poorest act in the world and have nothing but tattered clothes; but when you walked on the stage, you were immaculate. In your stage clothes you never walked out of the theater, you never hung out, you never sat around. Sammy was from the old school, unlike many of today's acts who perform in the same clothes they wear on the street. Stage clothes were special and not to be worn for any other purpose.

Sammy spent most of his younger life working in the theater and often stood in the wings watching other performers on stage, developing a feel for the timing. As he watched the other performers, he began to anticipate when a gesture would fail or when an attitude would work or not work; and he remembered everything he saw. This was a part of what made him the ultimate performer he became.

Sammy was about seven years old when Will Mastin took him around to the booking offices. I remember hearing Will say he often told Sammy, "There are two words in show business: 'show' and

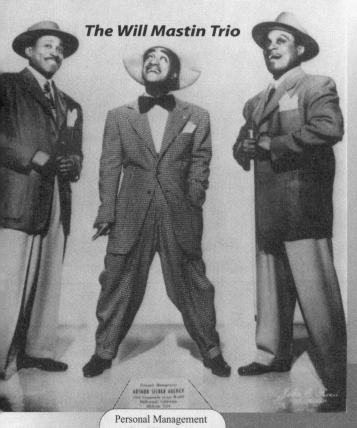

The Will Mastin Trio

Personal Management
Arthur Silber Agency
1554 Crossroads of the World
Hollywood, California
HI-Hillside 7219

My dad and Sammy

My dad, Arthur Silber Sr.

'business'—and one is as important as the other. The dancing is knowing how to please the audience; that is the show. Getting the dates and the money is the business."

Another trite but true saying in those days, quoted often by my father, Arthur Silber Sr., and Will was, "Your handshake is all the contract anybody needs." I was raised that way but, sad to say, I'm afraid those days are long gone. Sammy and I were raised to believe that our word should be like the word of God—our bond, our creed, the code we lived by. We were taught that if you lose that, you lose what you really are.

In show business, during the days of vaudeville, and the days that preceded it, the way of life on stage was different. Unfortunately, it has never been the same.

In the days of vaudeville, it was against the law to have any child under sixteen sing or dance on stage; and the Geary Society was the watchdog for that law. When Sammy was two-and-a-half years old, he first appeared on stage in the Will Mastin revue, "Struttin' Hannah from Savannah." It was his first performance as a dancer. Sam Sr. and Will put burnt cork all over his face and white makeup around his mouth to try and make him look like Al Jolson. They called him "Silent Sam the Dancing Midget."

One of the milestones in Sammy's early life took place when talking motion pictures came into being. Vaudeville, from that point on, was virtually on its way out. Theaters used to use vaudeville acts of singers and dancers to kill time during the eight or ten minutes it took to set up the speakers and films for the feature show.

Sadly, that was the end of Will Mastin's big act. During that time these miniature revues were called flash acts. Some of Will's acts were called: "There's No More Holiday in Dixieland," "Shake Your Feet," and "Hannah from Savannah."

In the audience: (left) Sammy's sister, Ramona, with their mother, Elvera

Sammy and Elvera, New York City, Mayfair Hotel balcony, opening night, Porgy & Bess

The first time Sammy's name appeared on the marquee was when they were called "Will Mastin's Gang, featuring Little Sammy." Will said from that time forward, they would be a trio and split the money evenly, three ways, as they were all partners now.

Will and Sam Sr. would go on stage first and form a strong impression on the audience, then Sammy would go out and keep them going, the essence being to start strong, hold them, and save yourself for the big finish. There are only two things to remember in show business: make an impression and leave them loving it. That is the essence of a real performer; always leave them asking for more. And don't go back and give it to them, just leave them wishing they had it. Too many acts in show business today can't remember that simple rule of the business. Many contemporary performers wear out their welcome and overdo their performances. Sammy never did; he always left them wanting more.

Will Mastin, my dad, Sam Senior, and me

The Will Mastin Trio

Personal Management
Arthur Silber Agency
1554 Crossroads of the World
Hollywood, California
HI-Hillside 7219

Sammy front row center, last row: Sam Sr. far left, Will Mastin, far right

*June 20, 1946, arriving in Hawaii—
the day I met Sammy—
I'm second from left (at age 15).
To my left is Will, then Sam Sr.,
my dad and Sammy. The
others are the rest of the
performers on the bill.*

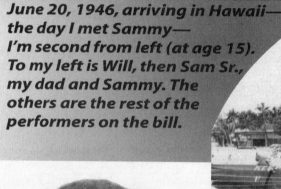

*Above: on the beach
in Hawaii with Dad*

Left: young Sammy

The Beginning

It all started for me in May of 1946. After the Second World War, my father, one of the biggest independent agents in Hollywood, had been asked to put together a show for the 442nd Regimental Combat Team, the WWII all-Nisei Japanese Army unit in Hawaii. Dad asked me if I wanted to come along. I was in high school and summer vacation was about to start; so, of course, I was excited to be able to go. I traveled often with my father as he went about his business, but this would be my first trip on an airplane and my first trip overseas.

We arrived at the airport, and I met the people who were going to perform. Eppie Pearson was the star of the show, and his wife was with him. Eppie, a comedian, was a huge man, almost four hundred pounds. His unique talent was playing a tiny miniature piano, and I do mean miniature. There were only three of these miniature pianos in the world, and Eppie had all three custom made for himself. The female singer on the show was Marilyn Hare. There was a lady sword swallower, whose biggest trick was to swallow a neon tube and light it up. The other comedian on the show was George Tibbles, who went on to become one of the biggest screenwriters in Hollywood, and also, I believe, to direct and produce. Last, but not least, was the Will Mastin Trio.

Will had never been on a plane before, and it scared him. I don't think any of them had ever been on a plane before, including Sammy. In those days, it was a DC-7, which took quite a while to get to Hawaii from Los Angeles. Will sat down in an aisle seat, grabbed the arms of the chair, and he never moved his head one inch from side to side until that plane landed. Then we had to get on another plane, a DC-3, which was even smaller, and fly from Oahu to the island of Hawaii where the first show was scheduled. When we came back to Los Angeles, it was on a red eye. Will was still as frozen in his seat as before; and in the middle of the night, we hit an air pocket. That plane suddenly just dropped twelve hundred feet. Will never stepped on a plane again, ever.

At the time, Sammy, fresh out of the Army, was twenty-one years old. I was only sixteen, but we seemed to hit it off right away. It was on the Big Island of Hawaii where Sammy and I began to hang out together, talking and playing around like brothers. Both big movie buffs, we used to talk a lot about movies and the fighting in them. We started to make up a routine of fake fighting, and we became adept at this very quickly, acting out movie parts at the same time.

From Hawaii, we went to Honolulu on the Island of Oahu. One day while there, we stopped in an open air restaurant to have lunch. Sammy and I decided to have one of our fake fights to see how everybody would react. We started yelling and screaming at each other, and Sammy took a punch at me. Then I took a punch at him. We began fighting all over the restaurant, banging chairs and tables around. Sam Senior and my father broke us apart, and the manager came running over. It was quite a scene. Of course, Sammy and I were in hysterics about the whole thing, but my dad didn't think it was so funny, and neither did Sam Senior. We both caught hell for it.

At that time, Sammy was an unknown performer with the Will Mastin Trio, which was a dance act, opening for other performers' shows. He just danced, did a little patter and a few impersonations. The impersonations were all of White people: Edward G. Robinson, Jimmy Stewart and James Cagney. He also did singer Vaughn Monroe, who had a very distinctive style and voice. But Sammy never really sang then; he never professed to be a singer. Always, his big thing was dancing. Sammy was the greatest tap dancer I ever saw; he was fantastic.

Will Mastin

We became buddies during that trip; and when we came back to the mainland, we remained close friends. Every time Sammy was in the Los Angeles area, he would call me; and I would go down to his hotel on Fifth Street in Los Angeles, which was about two cuts above what it is today, and that is about as low as it gets. He stayed in a hotel called The Williams, a room with just a bare light bulb hanging from a cord in the ceiling. For some reason, I had no qualms about going there and meeting or picking him up. We would walk along Fifth Street, go up to Main Street in downtown L.A., maybe catch a movie. Of course, I was the only White person around, but that never entered my mind.

One time, I invited Sammy to come spend a few days out at our house in the San Fernando Valley, twelve or thirteen miles from downtown Los Angeles. I went down in my car to pick him up, and he spent three or four days at my house. He used to sleep in my room in a sleeping bag on the floor next to my bed. We didn't have an extra bed, so the floor was the only place he could sleep.

While growing up, I lived across the street from the same park I still live across from today. Sammy used to put gravel on the metal park tables and do a sand dance, a sort of soft shoe. He loved to imitate Fred Astaire. Those tables are still there; and every time I see them, the picture of Sammy dancing from table top to table top comes into my mind. Sammy and I also practiced our fighting in this park. For some reason, we were very big on this fake fighting, and we had it down pat. We were as good as any stunt people in Hollywood, maybe better than some.

Sammy was in town when I had a pre-graduation from high school party, so I invited him out. He and I decided to stage a fight during the party.

Sam Davis Sr.

Our plan was that when everybody got there and the party was happening a little bit, Sammy would come to the door. I had picked Sammy up earlier, and he sat across the street in the park for a while until the party got going, then he rang the doorbell. I invited him in and introduced him to everybody. They weren't impressed that he was Sammy Davis Jr. because he wasn't a big name yet, but they were impressed that he was an entertainer.

Sammy went into the kitchen. One of the kids I grew up with, who also knew Sammy, was in on the gag. He put ketchup on a handkerchief and put it in Sammy's breast pocket. The three of us went back into the front room where Sammy and I started an argument. I threw a couple of remarks at Sammy, and we started fighting. We fought all over the front room and into the dining room, knocking chairs around and calling each other names. We really went at it. I knocked him down on the floor, and he pulled out the handkerchief and put it to his face. The ketchup was smeared down his mouth. Then I picked him up and threw him through the kitchen and out the back door into the yard. Sammy, my friend and I became hysterical with laughter.

None of the guests knew how to take this. My girlfriend and a couple of other people ran out to the back yard, where Sammy, my friend and I laid on the grass laughing ourselves to death. Another case of bad timing. We really caught hell from our friends for that because we had frightened them pretty badly. It wasn't a matter of being fun; it was a matter of scaring them. Sammy apologized, turned on his charm, and the party ended up being a success.

Our friendship continued to deepen for the next couple of years. After I spent one-and-a-half years in college and a year in trade school, Sammy asked me to come on the road with him as his personal and production assistant. Thus began my career in show business.

Eppie Pearson's wife, Sammy, Marilyn Hare and me

Diamond Head Oahu, Hawaii

Left to right: **Will, Big John (Sammy's body-guard), PeeWee (Sammy's stepmother), Sam Sr., Sammy and me**

Left: **Bill Miller, owner of the Riviera Club, with Dad**
Below: **This could kill you, as it did him.**

I Go to Work for Sammy

The hotel we stayed at in New York was the Americana on 47th Street and Broadway, where Times Square begins. The hotel entrance was located directly across the street from the stage entrance of the Palace Theater. It was a "Colored" hotel, and I lived there with Sammy —quite an experience for a Jewish, White guy from the San Fernando Valley. In the early years of the Will Mastin Trio, we always stayed at this hotel. The hottest chicks in the world always hung around there.

My father had secured a booking for the Trio at Bill Miller's Riviera in Fort Lee, New Jersey, right across the George Washington Bridge from New York City. At this time, the Riviera was one of the biggest clubs in the East. Sammy was the opening act for Tony Martin, a major singing star at the time.

We became good friends with Tony and everyone else on the show. In those days, all big showrooms had their own chorus lines, and there was a party going on all the time someplace or other, mostly in Sammy's room at the hotel. My job was to set the show each night. I had to make sure the music was there, distributed on the music stands, and that the few props Sammy used were on the stage. He always had a silver mug, filled with Coca Cola, cigarettes, ashtray, matches and a huge prop cigar about a foot long that he used with his Edward G. Robinson impression. I had to insure the lighting they needed for the act was ready. At that time, it was fairly simple lighting—mostly upstage and usually what we call a three-color wash, which generally consists of red, blue and amber or sometimes red, amber and green. There were also spotlights to set.

One thing Sammy was particular about was bounce light. In those days, a lot of stages were made of light maple hardwood floors. If there was an orchestra behind Sammy, a spotlight could bounce off that floor, bounce off the trombones or saxophones, and create a distracting flicker that took the audience's eyes off the performer. If the horn players moved around or talked, which they absolutely are not supposed to do during an act, the light could catch their instruments and cause another distraction. Spotlight setting was both art and necessity.

While at the Riviera, Sammy began to bug Will and Sam Sr., arguing that the Trio had reached the point where they needed their own musical conductor. Will was absolutely against the idea. He was extremely controlling about the money they made and how it was spent. Though the money they made was split evenly between them, Will controlled it all. Sammy and Will used to get in some pretty heavy arguments about this.

The band at the hotel had a young clarinet player by the name of Morty Stevens. We became close friends with Morty, and he began to hang out with us. We soon found out that he was not just a clarinet player, but also an excellent pianist who had graduated from Julliard School of Music in New York City. Sammy asked Morty to write arrangements for a couple of songs. Morty was young and anxious to get his career going. He wrote arrangements Sammy just flipped over.

Sammy went to Will Mastin and literally demanded that they hire a conductor. Will flatly refused, to which Sammy said, "**I'm** going to hire a conductor. Just take it out of my salary." Once Will heard the arrangements Morty had written, he caved in and agreed to hire him for a while and see how he worked out.

New York was kind of home base for us, and we spent a lot of our time there, always in the same hotel. Jess Rand, a young man then too, was a publicist who used to pick up on show business information and run it all over town to the big columnists, such as Walter Winchell. Jess became part of our gang: Sammy, Jesse, Morty and me.

Every night after the show, we would go to Lindy's to get something to eat. Most of the time, we were invited to sit at the Comics Table with the likes of Milton Berle, Johnny Carson, Red Buttons, "Fat" Jack Leonard, Alan King, Buddy Hackett, Jackie Gleason, Myron Cohen, Jack Carter

Morty Stevens, talented musician

and many others. Imagine what it was like to sit with these enormous talents—it was a great honor to be invited to this table to sit with the greatest comics in the world! This was a very special booth, and the first thing you saw when you walked in the front door to Lindy's. Full of Damon Runyon characters, Lindy's was unique.

After we ate, we would play skeetball next door then go to Sam Goody's, which was the record store in New York City. When we left Sam Goody's we would always walk over to the Copacabana, where Sammy and I would stand out in front and he would talk about how he would love to play there. The Copacabana in New York was the epitome of night clubs. I used to say to him, "Don't worry, Sam, one day you'll headline here."

He answered, "No, man, I can't even go in there to watch a show."

Then I would say, "But, one day you will."

After that we would catch a bus or the subway, or if we had the money, we would catch a cab, and go up to Harlem. The Apollo Theater was at 125th Street, and we would hang out there. We used to spend much of our time at the Apollo, as Sammy would go there to learn anything and everything he could from Lionel Hampton, who taught him how to play the vibes and drums. We never missed a chance to hang out with Gene Krupa, Buddy Rich, and the other greats who played the Apollo. We used to stand in the wings watching these fabulous artists, and Sammy's mind, hands, feet and body would absorb everything he saw, heard and was taught. He was like a big sponge, drinking it all in, all the time.

Sam Goody's is to the right of this scene

"Fat" Jack Leonard, at the
Comic's table, Lindy's

Drummers:
Buddy Rich (top)
and Gene Krupa

Sophie
Tucker

Then we would go back to the hotel, either bringing the chicks with us or just finding them waiting for us back at the hotel. We **always** had a party going on and chicks around. We had girlfriends, too; mine was a chorus girl from the club. One chorus girl in particular was not a girlfriend but became a very close friend of mine and remained so until the day she died. Her name was Barbara Constantino, and she later became Mrs. Gary Crosby. Barbara's father held a very high position in the Mob and eventually he was found dead in an apartment, killed gangland style. Barbara was a class act and one of the most wonderful ladies I have ever known.

Another place everyone hung out at in those days was Danny's Hideaway, owned by Danny Stridella. We began going there almost nightly and were seen by "everyone." Jess started getting Sammy's name in the papers, in the columns and everywhere else he could, which was a big benefit to Sammy. We were young, just hanging out together, working on our careers and having a ball. There wasn't a girl safe on the block anywhere near us.

Sammy's next engagement was very successful for him from a publicity point of view because Jesse was promoting Sammy and was really great at his job. It was in Miami Beach, Florida at the Beachcomber, which was owned by Sophie Tucker, who was a huge star, and Ted Lewis, the famous vaudevillian. Sophie and Ted would each perform a couple of nights a week in the club. They invited Sammy down to star in the show. He was just starting to hit his stride, and Sophie and Ted made him the co-headliner along with Myron Cohen, one of America's greatest comedic storytellers.

More important than being billed with Sophie and Ted was that this was the first time Sammy Davis Jr. had ever performed below the Mason-Dixon Line and the first time I had ever been in the deep South. It was also the first time that I, as a White, Jewish young man, traveling with a Black young man in the deep South, had ever run head-on into American prejudices. Sammy had experienced prejudice in the Army, but this time was different. Sammy was scared to death to go down there, and Will didn't want to go at all, but the money was so big for that time they couldn't afford to turn it down.

Sammy and the rest of the troupe were going to take the train, and Morty and I were going to drive Morty's old Plymouth. We had an interesting trip driving down because there was one road that went through the Okefenokee Swamp which was made of crushed coral shells, the basis for all roads in Florida even today. Outside of the Great Lakes, the Okefenokee Swamp is the largest body of water in the United States. We didn't know where we were, and it was kind of spooky for two young guys from New York.

When we reached Miami, we were staying at the Lord Calvert Hotel, something like a poor man's Holiday Inn, but for Blacks. Its clientele was made up mostly of the Black ball players and athletes because they were not allowed to stay in Miami Beach in those days. You should have seen the looks on the faces of the people at the hotel when Morty and I went to check in! It took a lot to convince them we were in the right place and that we were with Sammy Davis Jr. of the Will Mastin Trio. We got a lot of disapproving looks for the first few days. I became friends with many of those people and even have home

movies of us swimming around in the pool with Roy Campanella and his kids and the greatest pound-for-pound boxer in the world at the time, Middleweight Champion Sugar Ray Robinson.

This was Morty's first trip out of New York, and he was definitely not "hep" to show business yet. Even though he had been playing in the band at Bill Miller's Riviera, he had not been out and about, so to speak, like Sammy and I. He certainly had never stayed in a Black hotel.

Later that day, we went to the train station to pick up Sammy, Will, Sam Sr. and Nathan Crawford. When the guys got off the train, we looked for a redcap to help with the luggage, but none would stop. They all passed us by and went to pick up luggage from the White people getting off the train.

World Middleweight Champion, Sugar Ray Robinson

Will said, "Let's just carry our own!"

We all picked up bags and started to leave the platform when a big burly cab driver came pushing his way through the people and bumped into Will, knocking the bags from his hands.

As he passed, he said, " Get outta my way, Niggah!"

Will stood there wondering what to do next. Well, I knew what to do! I dropped the bags I was carrying and made a jump at the cab driver.

Will grabbed me by the arm, turned me around and said, "That won't get us anywhere, and it might get you killed. Let's just get the bags and get out of here!"

Just inside the station there was a big sign that said, "WELCOME TO MIAMI," and right under that there was another sign that read, "BLACKS TO THE LEFT AND WHITES TO THE RIGHT." Yeah! Welcome to Miami! God, I was mad!

At the hotel, we were met by Eddie Compadre, the person in charge of running the club. He sat us down and explained that only White cab drivers could cross the bridge from Miami to Miami Beach, and they weren't allowed to pick up any Colored people, so he gave us a car for going back and forth. Of course, we had Morty's car as well. Eddie explained there was a curfew in Miami Beach for Colored people and that they had to have police cards to be there after curfew hours or be arrested.

I just came unglued at this point and yelled, "Aren't there some kind of laws about that?"

"Yeah," said Eddie, "there are if they want to enforce them."

"Do Morty and I need cards too because we are traveling with Black people?" I yelled.

Eddie said cards were not required for White people, but we had better be very careful.

We went to the club to rehearse for the opening. At this time, and for many years to come, Sammy and I were tremendous camera buffs. We never went anyplace without a camera, and it became a big hobby for us. Next to the club was a camera store and after rehearsal, Sammy and I went into it. That was the first time in my life I sensed something wasn't right. Sammy was talking to the guy in the store who was elusive, cool. It wasn't blatant, but the feeling of prejudice was there.

Nathan Crawford, Will Mastin's man Friday

Nathan Crawford, Will's life-long friend and assistant, had rented a car and took Will and Sam Sr. back to the hotel since Will felt safer traveling around with friends. When Sammy and I came out of the camera store, we saw two drinking fountains in the parkway right in front of the store that were constantly running. It was the first time in my life I ever saw signs that said "Whites Only" and "Blacks." Each drinking fountain had a sign on it. It was like someone took a knife and stuck it in me, and Sammy as well. I think it hit me harder at that time, though, because Sammy had seen this before but I never had. I had only heard about this sort of thing, but it never really sinks in until you start seeing it for yourself. It was not so much the shock of seeing the signs as it was how mad it got me. It was really starting to enrage me every time I saw "Colored" or "Black" posted somewhere.

I started to scream right there on the street. "What the fuck is going on here? What kind of people are they down here? Isn't this what we fought the Civil War for?"

Sammy grabbed me, "Art, just shut your mouth. Keep quiet. You're gonna get us in trouble."

"Let some motherfucker say something to me! Just let them! I'm already mad!"

"If somebody tries to say something to you and you get mad, they're gonna shoot you, and shoot me along with you, just for the fun of it."

I shut my mouth, and we stood there trying to hail a cab to take us back to the hotel. Then a bus came around the corner, and in the lower right hand corner of the bus window was a sign that read "Whites Only." Not thirty seconds behind that bus came another one that said "Blacks." I started to get mad all over again; and Sammy told me to shut up, that it wasn't going to do me any good. "This is the way it is down here," he said. "We both have to live with it."

"I don't have to live with this kind of crap," I snapped.

"Yes, you do," he responded.

We finally caught a cab, and the driver informed us he could not take us to the hotel in Miami because he was not allowed to drive any Coloreds across the Causeway into Miami. Instead, he would take us to the Causeway and drop us off, and we would have to walk across to the other side. Then in Miami, another cab would pick us up and take us wherever we wanted to go. Sammy saw the blood start to boil in my face again and grabbed my arm, telling me to shut up.

It was about an hour before the show, and I had stepped out the front door of the club to see how things were going. There was a man walking out front passing out a small newspaper bearing the headline, "NIGGER ON THE BEACH." The following story was titled, "Stamp out Sammy Davis, Jr.," and read: "The Black people are an un-American disease which threatens to spread all over the beach..."

Talk about going ballistic! I just wanted to beat the shit out of this guy! But I remembered what everyone was telling me, so instead I took the paper in to show Eddie and asked him what he was going to do about it. Eddie said, "Take me out and show me the guy."

As we went out the door, Milton Berle got out of his car to come in the club and heard this guy yelling out his "NIGGER ON THE BEACH" stuff. Milton walked over and knocked the guy right on his butt, then kicked him out into the gutter. The guy got up and ran away as if he had just been shot out of a cannon. That was the last time we ever saw him.

Sammy, and Will Mastin Trio, with entertainer, Milton Berle

When I went back and told everyone what had happened, they just could not believe it. Who would ever have thought that Milton Berle of all people would do something like that. He did what I wanted to do and who would dare to tangle with Uncle Milty?

Sammy's opening night was a smash success. He got three standing ovations and tremendous write-ups in the paper. Every show was jam packed, and the people loved him. Sammy did most of the engagement with Sophie Tucker, who really gave him a big boost. Sophie was as big as you could get, and she packed a lot of weight in the business. She was a show business legend, just loved Sammy and helped him all she could. In my personal opinion, the engagements at Bill Miller's Riviera and at the Beachcomber would be two of the major starting points of Sammy's meteoric rise to stardom.

Morty Stevens

Life at Lord Calvert

left: Pepper and me
above: Sam and
me by the pool
right: Sammy shooting
me shooting him

One evening, a couple of hot-looking chicks came backstage and wanted to meet Sammy. After talking to them for awhile, Sammy called me aside and said, "After the show, these two chicks are going to come over to the hotel so, instead of coming with me, you take them to the hotel."

I sat with them during the second show. They were two "working girls," prostitutes, high class call girls from New York, in Miami Beach on vacation. They were going to go back to their hotel to get some of their things before going to our hotel in Miami. They were driving a Cadillac that was the strangest color I had ever seen, kind of a pinky-brown. I asked one of them what the color was called. She reached down into her scoop-necked blouse, pulled out one of her breasts, pointed to the nipple and said, "It's titty-nipple pink."

I told her I had never heard of that color, to which she replied, "I had this car 'specially painted.'"

She put her breast back in and pulled out a joint, still driving. The other girl was in the middle and I was sitting next to the passenger door. It was hot as hell, but they rolled up the windows, lit up the joint and asked me if I wanted a hit. I said no because I had never done any kind of drugs in my life, (and never have done drugs to this day). I was concerned about getting high from the smoke they were generating in the car because the windows were up. Fortunately, the window on my side was slightly open, and I was able to breathe a little fresh air.

Those days in Miami Beach, the streets had no curbs; they just slanted up and onto the lawns. There were no sidewalks either. Suddenly the car started veering, and the girl driving was half on the street and half up on a lawn. I saw a road sign coming right at me! She was high, driving this car, and I was starting to get concerned, so I grabbed the steering wheel and put us back on the road. I asked her if she would like me to drive, but she said, "No, I'm all right."

While I was doing my thing with the girls, Sammy was so caught up with all the people in his dressing room he forgot about getting a ride back to the hotel. He also forgot that he had sent me with the girls, so he was left there alone. They were locking up the club, and he was stranded, sitting on the curb wondering what to do. He tried to hail a cab, but none were about to stop. After a few had slowed down but would not take him, Sammy finally yelled out that he would pay double. One guy took pity on him and said that he would take him as far as the bridge, but no further.

Sammy got out of the cab at the bridge and started to walk across when a police car pulled up. The officers shined their spotlight right in his eyes. They ordered him, "Stop right there and put up your hands!"

Sammy was petrified—and for good reason. One of the cops patted him down and asked him what he was doing there. Sammy answered that he was Sammy Davis Jr., and he was playing at the Beachcomber Night Club. He added that he had a card and showed it to the officer, who took Sammy over to the police car and asked the second officer what he thought they should do. The second officer said, "Well, if he is working at the club and has a card, let's take him over to the bus stop so he can get a ride home."

One officer asked for his autograph, and Sammy was happy to comply. As they drove away, it was about 5:30 in the morning. Sammy waited another hour before a bus came along to take him back to Miami and the hotel.

When Sammy finally made it back to the hotel in Miami, he came busting through the door and was ready to kill me. He was screaming at me, asking where in the hell I had been and why I just left him at the club with no way to get home. I reminded him that it was **his** idea that I go with the girls and bring them back to the hotel. He thought for a moment, then realized it was all his fault.

He looked around the room, and got a good look at the girls who were still there. They proceeded to calm him down; and they did a great job, too! Sammy, Morty, the girls and I played all the rest of the night and most of the next day. All unpleasant thoughts of the night before just seemed to fade away. The girls hung around with us for a couple of days, then went back to New York.

After we left Miami, we played the Latin Quarter in Philadelphia, Pennsylvania. The Latin Quarter was run by a big Mob boss named Rocky Palladino, and it was the Mob headquarters for that part of the United States. When you worked nightclubs in those days, all the clubs were either owned, run or controlled by the Mob. These were their legitimate businesses. The Mob doesn't necessarily make all their money from illegal activities. For instance, in those days, they controlled the linen services for the hotels and nightclubs, the silverware and dish suppliers, liquor suppliers and a number of other related businesses. This is how they legitimized their activities and, in addition, had tremendous control over the hotels and nightclubs.

There always has been a unique relationship between the underworld and entertainers. The underworld seems to be fascinated by the entertainment industry, and the people in it. You could not work in a nightclub anywhere in the United States without coming into contact with these people. The object was that you had to maintain your own balance between yourself and them. If they asked you to come up and have a drink or sing a song, you did it and didn't ask why. Sooner or later down the line, if you needed a favor, all you had to do was ask. That's the way the world ran then.

Sammy never became involved with any shady dealings or anything like that; most performers didn't. There were rumors about some performers becoming deeply involved with the Mob, but Sammy was not one of them. He worked for them, and many of them became great friends of his, but there were never any shady deals involving Sammy.

The Latin Quarter had been an old church. From the street level, you walked down two flights of stairs, where there was a doorman

Sam Sr., Sammy, comedian Henny Youngman, and Will

dressed like something from the Arabian Nights. He had these funny shoes that turned up at the toes, and you wanted to ask him where he parked his flying carpet. He was the nicest guy in the world. You would go down another flight of stairs, make a right and go down yet another flight, ending up at the bar. Then you'd turn left and walk toward the Club itself. The bar area was on the right, cordoned off with a banister that separated it from the walkway. The Mob guys always hung out in the bar. Being around them over the years, we learned what to say and not say, when to approach them and when not to. I assure you they were well armed at all times.

Several incidents happened during this engagement. Walking down the steps, the first thing we came to was the hat-check stand on the right, with a very attractive hat-check girl who looked Indian. When we came down the first time and were introduced to her, I was the last one in line. When I was introduced, she looked up at me, grabbed me by the chin, pulled me right to her face, said, "You're absolutely gorgeous!" and planted a big kiss on me.

"Well, so are you, baby," I replied. "Hey," I thought to myself, "here's my girl for this town."

The hat-check girl really fixated on me; she just wouldn't leave me alone and ultimately became a tremendous nuisance during this engagement. She followed me around the club, and it was bothering the hell out of me; she was like a little puppy dog. In spite of her initial introduction to me and her subsequent flirtations, she turned out to be a virgin and wanted to stay that way. During that time in my life, I wasn't used to dealing with virgins. I tried to be nice, but she was in love and that was that, as far as she was concerned.

In the evenings, we used to eat dinner at the club. They would serve us our meals at the tables along the back wall next to the hat-check stand, near the bar area. The second or third night we were there, I was eating dinner when a commotion started at the bar.

A guy got off a bar stool, roaring drunk, and bumped against a table where two of "The Boys" were sitting having a drink. This man really slammed into their table and said something caustic to "The Boys." One of them told him to get on out of there and pushed him away. The drunk turned around and got belligerent. Everyone began reaching inside their coats, getting ready just in case, and I thought, "Oh, God! Something's gonna happen, and I'm sitting right here!"

These guys weren't looking for any trouble, but the drunk was looking for a fight and didn't know when to quit. "The Boys" finally got up, and I'll never forget it; one guy hit the drunk in the jaw, and the other guy hit him in the stomach. When the drunk doubled over, the man who hit him in the stomach grabbed him by the nape of his neck and smashed his knee into the drunk's face so hard it pushed his nose pretty near to the back of his head. Bang, boom, bang—then "The Boys" literally picked the drunk up, threw him over the table and the rail onto the floor in the walkway. They jumped over the rail, picked him up again and threw him into the staircase—not up it, but into it, face first. This guy's face was pulverized. "The Boys" called the doorman who picked the drunk up by his belt, dragged him up the steps, and put him in a cab. Then "The Boys" calmly returned to their table, ordered two more drinks and continued drinking.

The amazing thing was that no one else in the bar moved while this incident was happening. Everyone stayed where they were, including me, and kept out of it. We learned fast that one didn't want to start anything in this club.

During one of the shows a couple of nights later, I was sitting in the back of the showroom, which was quite large, as it used to be an actual church. Evidently somebody made a racial slur that I could not hear from where I was sitting, but was definitely heard on the stage. Sammy was in the middle of performing; and, for the first time ever, I saw Sam Sr. shoot a look down at this guy. The man must have repeated what he'd first said, but I still couldn't hear. Sam Sr. started to leap off the stage and go after him, which is absolutely unheard of. It was never done by Sam Sr., Will or Sammy. They were too professional to ever do that, but it must have been so bad that Sam Sr. couldn't take it. At that time, Sam Sr. was a big strapping man right out of *Gentleman's Quarterly*, and he was going to go after this guy. When Sam Sr. started to make the move to go off the stage, the waiters in the club grabbed hold of the heckler, and he was out of the club in two seconds. You don't want to do anything like that in a club owned by the Mob.

In Philadelphia, we stayed at the Bellevue Stratford, a first-class hotel, downtown near the statue of William Penn. To the best of my memory, this was the first time we stayed in a so-called White hotel. Obviously, it was because the reservations were made by Rocky

Palladino. Nobody was going to tell him who could and couldn't stay there.

Now we went to Boston. At this point, living life with Sammy Davis Jr. had become quite something. When we started out together and were on the road, we shared one room. Now, we had two bedrooms in a suite. Sammy partied continuously until all hours of the night, and it was really interrupting my life. Sammy could go for two or three days with no sleep, without the aid of drugs. He drank nothing but Coca-Cola then, and he just wanted to party, party, party all the time— always tons of girls—hanging out with me or Morty, or both of us. Life was one big party. Sammy and I were also always practicing quick draw, or sword fighting down the halls of the hotels.

Actress, Mamie Van Doren, photographed by Sammy

Playing Monopoly was another big thing with us, and we used to play for hours. In Boston at that time, there was a group playing called The Vogues—three White guys from Canada who had a couple of big records out. I remember one night in particular, we were all sitting around with The Vogues and a couple of chicks when there was a knock at the door.

Sam Sr. was all dressed up like Dapper Dan yelling, "Let me in, let me in!" He had a good-looking White woman with him and said, "They're after me, man; they're after me! They're gonna kill me!"

Sammy said, "What are you talking about?"

"I got one of the guys' chicks with me." He was referring to one of the mobster's girls. That was about as big a no-no as you could pull. You simply did not do that! But here was Sam Sr., scared to death.

You entered Sammy's suite directly into the front room. Off to the left was a bedroom which had another entrance to the hall. Sure enough, there was another knock at the door. I took Sam Sr. and this lady into the bedroom. As these guys came into the front room, I let Sam Sr. and her out of the bedroom into the hall. The men were definitely looking for him. God was shining on Sam Sr. that night because he got out of that hotel before they found him. They were going to kill him, pure and simple.

We were worried about something happening to Sam Sr. while we were still in town, so Sammy made a call to Rocky Palladino, and he got the situation straightened out. The girl was wrong to go out with Sam Sr. under the circumstances, and the relationship ended that evening. The pressure was removed from Sam Sr., but it was a pretty scary incident.

Once we were staying in Philadelphia playing a club called the Latin Casino in Cherry Hill, New Jersey, just across the Ben Franklin Bridge. Sammy was now an established star, not playing second bill to anyone else, unless it was a huge star. He was the headline act in Cherry Hill. As usual, lots of chicks were hanging around, and Sammy got something going with one particular girl he knew was a Mob girl. He knew better, but he was always pushing it to the edge.

One evening we were all up in Sammy's room, and it was late. By then, I had my own room, across the hall and just down from Sammy's suite. Sammy always slept in the nude. The only thing he wore to bed was a handkerchief tied across the top of his head because, as most Black performers did in those days, he used Pomade on his head, which looks and feels like Vaseline. He tied the handkerchief on his head to keep the grease from getting all over the pillow.

I left Sammy alone in his room and was in bed just falling off to sleep. Sammy was always big on security, and everything was locked up tight. It couldn't have been more than thirty minutes later when I got a phone call from Sammy. He was absolutely panic stricken, "Oh, Christ! Get over here right away!"

I jumped into my pants, grabbed his key—I always had a key to Sammy's room—and ran across the hall. He was sitting on the couch and exclaimed, "Oh, God! You can't believe what just happened! They almost killed me!"

"What the hell are you talking about?" I asked.

"I was in the bed, just dozing off, when all of a sudden two guys grabbed me by my skin, literally." Then he showed me the fingernail marks where they had torn his skin. "They hung me out the window and were gonna drop me!"

"What?"

"They were gonna kill me! Jesus Christ! We've gotta get out of this town!" Then he told me the girl he had been seeing was a mobster's girlfriend.

"I told you not to fuck around with her," I said. "You know better than that."

Sammy didn't have any fat on his body; he was all muscle. The two guys had actually picked him up by his skin and hung him out of the tenth-floor window of his suite, over the street. He begged and pleaded to make a phone call, and somehow convinced them to let him make that call. He called Rocky Palladino, but was unable to reach him. Then he called Sam Giancana in Chicago, but was able only to reach Donjo Medlivine, who talked to the guys on the phone and convinced them to back off.

Donjo Medlivine was one of the owners of the Chez Paree in Chicago, an after-hours key club, run by himself, Dave Duschof and Jack Schotz. Of course, they, too, were members of the Mob. Donjo was one of the finest men I have ever known, a true diamond in the rough. He was one of the best friends Sammy and I ever had. He saved Sammy's life on more than one occasion, and Donjo certainly saved Sammy's life that night.

Sammy was playing Pittsburgh, Pennsylvania at a place called the Twin Coaches; and we went to an after-hours club after his show. The club was getting ready to close, and all the Mob guys were taking off their jackets, getting comfortable at the blackjack and dice tables. It was quite a sight, seeing their guns and hardware. Sammy and I were in the office talking to the boss, and three or four other guys were in there with us when Sammy and I overheard a hit being ordered on someone. When we left the club, I asked Sammy, "Who are we going to call about this?"

Sammy said, "We're not going to call anybody."

"What do you mean? We have to call somebody and tell them what we know."

"No, we don't," he answered. "Because if we do tell somebody, we're gonna be dead. Just keep your mouth shut. We didn't hear anything."

In all honesty, that has worried me for over forty years. I don't know who the person was, or even if it happened, but it's always bothered me tremendously that I overhead something like that but couldn't do a thing about it, or I would die myself.

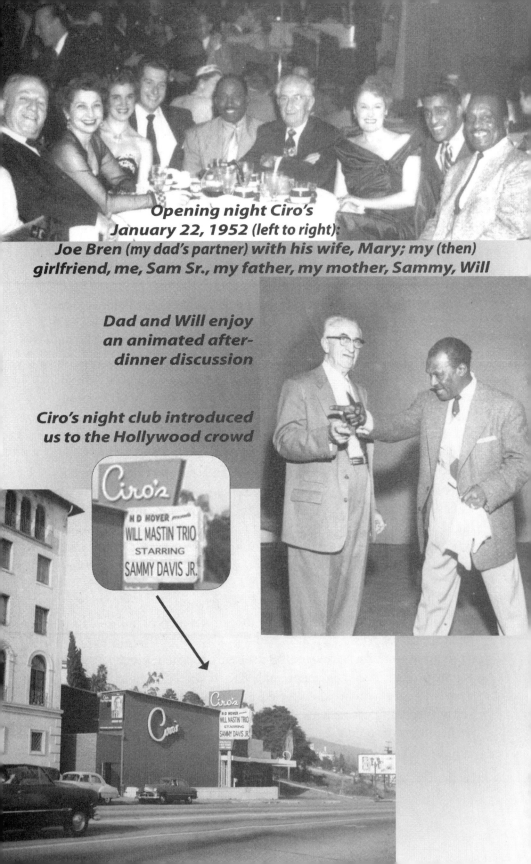

**Opening night Ciro's
January 22, 1952 (left to right):**
Joe Bren (my dad's partner) with his wife, Mary; my (then)
girlfriend, me, Sam Sr., my father, my mother, Sammy, Will

**Dad and Will enjoy
an animated after-
dinner discussion**

**Ciro's night club introduced
us to the Hollywood crowd**

Ciro's
H D HOVER presents
WILL MASTIN TRIO
STARRING
SAMMY DAVIS JR.

Sammy Goes Big Time

Leaving Pittsburgh, we returned to Los Angeles. My father, still the agent for and manager of the Will Mastin Trio, had an offer for the Trio to open at Ciro's. One of the biggest night clubs in Los Angeles, Ciro's was a very important engagement for any act in show business. Herman Hover, the owner of the club, wanted the Trio to open for Janis Paige, the headliner. However, the offer was for five hundred dollars a week, and Will Mastin told my father he would not accept anything less than five hundred fifty.

My father said, "Will, are you crazy? This is the biggest break of your career! You can't tell a man like Hover that you won't work for the money offered! Don't you realize that this is one of the most important clubs in the country?"

But Will held his ground. He felt that, since they had previously been paid five hundred a week playing another club in Los Angeles called Slapsy Maxie's, a step up into the big leagues should mean more money. Reluctantly, my father went back to Herman Hover with what Will Mastin had said. Before Mr. Hover had a chance to say a word, my dad offered to pay the difference out of his commission, as long as Mr. Hover didn't tell Will. Hover replied, "If you think that much of them, then I will pay the difference. Is there anything else we can do to make them happy?"

"No," my dad said, "There's nothing else you can do. They will do the rest."

And that they did. On opening night, Sammy did everything he could possibly do on a stage within the time allotted. The stars and big Hollywood names in the audience were spellbound by the Trio, and especially by Sammy. This little black man was more than anyone could imagine; Sammy exploded on stage. Tinsel Town had never seen anything like him before.

I was backstage in the wings just to the side of Janis Paige while she was waiting to go on. She was absolutely livid, stamping her foot and saying, "Damn it! Damn it! How in hell am I supposed to follow that?"

When the Trio walked off stage, they got a riotous standing ovation, went back, took their bows and the audience clamored for more. Sammy was smart enough to know that they were just the opening act and not to overdo it. Janis Paige was furious and told Mr. Hover that from that point on, she would open the show and let the Trio close. Mr. Hover agreed.

The next day, *Daily Variety* said, "The Will Mastin Trio was a walloping success;" and the *Los Angeles Times* said, "The Will Mastin Trio, featuring the dynamic Sammy Davis Jr., were show stoppers, and Janis Paige has relinquished her closing spot to them."

Mr. Hover called my dad and told him that he was giving the Will Mastin Trio equal billing on the marquee, which, of course, made Janis Paige (who was going with Errol Flynn at the time) even madder. Regardless, that show became the hottest ticket in town.

Every night, for the next two weeks, Sammy's dressing room became the who's who of Hollywood. Well-wishers kept trying to give this diminutive new star advice, although Sam had already forgotten more about show business than most of these people ever knew to begin with. From this point, some of Sammy's and my closest friendships were formed. I vividly remember the days spent hanging out with Barbara Luna, Rod Steiger, Harry Belafonte and Jeff Chandler, one of the greatest, most genteel men I have ever known. Some of our dearest friends, and the two who knew Sammy the best in the beginning, were Janet Leigh and Tony Curtis, who were great fun. We hung out at the corner of Laurel Canyon and

Sunset Boulevard site of famous Schwab's Drug Store (the spot in which Lana Turner was discovered). During those days in Hollywood, Schwab's was a magnet for every would-be actress or actor and the place to go to be discovered.

I had moved out of my family's home in North Hollywood to live at the hotel with Sammy. The Sunset Colonial Hotel turned out to be the place to be, and became our Hollywood home for the next few years. I could go on and on naming the stars both big and small that we spent time with; we were having the time of our lives.

From Ciro's, the Trio went to San Francisco to play at the popular Bimbo's 365 Club. By that time, the word had gotten out through the media about Sammy and the Trio, so the club was packed every night. Ben Swig, owner and president of the Fairmont Hotel chain, sent his son, Dick Swig, to catch the show. In San Francisco, the Fairmont is as good as it gets, and as high as you can go (the Fairmont sits atop Nob Hill). One night after the show at Bimbo's 365 Club, Dick Swig came back and spoke to Will about playing the Fairmont. Will told him to call my dad and to make the arrangements. The date was set for a few months down the line so as to not repeat San Francisco too soon.

After closing Bimbo's 365 Club, we headed for Chicago and the Chez Paree, which had just begun featuring performers. Sammy and the Trio were the first live act to play there. Boy, did that joint jump then!

One night, Sammy and I were sitting with Donjo Medlivine, one of the owners of the club, in his private booth. It was after Sammy's show, and the Chez Paree, one of the most popular after-hours spots

in town, was getting quiet. However, one customer at the bar began causing quite a commotion.

Donjo was short in stature, stocky and muscular. He had the face of a wrestler, but with kind lines. He talked tough but would do anything in the world for you if you really needed him. It was no secret that Donjo was well connected with the Sam Giancana Family.

Actors: (left) Jeff Chandler and Charles McGraw

Now, the man at the bar was really getting loud, and Donjo excused himself and went to the bar to try and quiet him down. I was sitting at the end of the booth, and Donjo was just off my right shoulder. He walked up to the man, a big-ass Texan about six-feet-four to Donjo's five-feet-five or six, and said something to him. This made the guy get even louder and more belligerent. Donjo hit him, and I've never in my life seen anyone hit that hard. When Donjo hit the Texan, his whole forearm went into the man's stomach, and he doubled over and sank to the floor. The security guys, already at the scene, picked him up and put him in a cab. A couple of days later, we learned the big Texan was a good friend of Donjo's and was in the Chez Paree all the time. He was a very wealthy man who had just gotten out of hand, and Donjo quieted him down.

While in Chicago, we were invited to the beautiful home of a multi-millionaire. Our host pushed a button in the wall, and it opened to reveal an entire room filled with every conceivable kind of pinball machine ever invented, as well as a variety of slot machines. We learned that our host was the manufacturer of pinball and slot machines used by much of the underworld. This was a tremendous source of the Mob's income. Sam Giancana and Donjo were there, as well as a number of other well-known underworld figures and their women.

As Sammy and I stood next to one another playing pinball games, I looked around the room at all the big money and big Mob people and couldn't help but think to myself that this night was a turning point in Sammy's and my life. I turned to Sam and said, "Can you believe where we are, and who we're mixing with? Just look around, man! Think of who we were hanging with just a few months ago, and look at us now."

A few days later, my dad called Will and told him that the Trio had been booked into the Venetian Room of the Fairmont Hotel in San Francisco.

Will takes a break

Bimbo's 365 Club—Watching the show— Morty Stevens and Sammy at far end of the table

Under the Sunset Colonial Hotel's fringed canopy, at the heart of Sunset Strip— Sammy and I lived here; this was my first home away from my parent's house. Right: Dancer, Juliet Prowse

Now Appearing

Will Mastin Trio

Venetian Room

Ernie Heckscher and his orchestra

the Fairmont Hotel

Sammy Davis Jr.

Foster and Kleiser

Shopping at Sy Devore's

The Fairmont

About a week or so before we were to leave to go to the Fairmont Hotel, Sammy called me into his room and asked me what kind of clothes I thought he should wear in San Francisco. I said I wasn't sure, but I knew that San Francisco was called the New York of the West Coast. Sammy said that maybe we should go over to Vine Street in Hollywood and see what Sy Devore had in his store. Sy Devore had one of the upscale men's stores that catered to many of the male stars in Hollywood.

I said, "Great, but you know his things are very expensive."

Sammy replied, "Well, we'll be way up there on top of Nob Hill, so why not look as though we belong there?"

"So, what are you going to do to get the dough to buy all this new stuff?" I asked.

Sammy asked me if I thought my dad would give him an advance against his salary. We walked down to my dad's office, which was about five blocks away in a very well-known place called Crossroads of The World, and talked to him. Dad thought it was a good idea that Sammy and the Trio make a good-looking impression off the stage as well as on, so he advanced Sammy the money he needed, and Sammy and I went to Sy Devore's.

Sammy got a couple of men's suits, some ties and about ten dress shirts, five with plain cuffs and five with French cuffs. Of course, the shirts had to have Sammy's initials on the pockets. He also bought a different set of cuff links to go with each French cuff shirt. Later, these shirts and cuff links would play a big part in our lives. And last, he bought a couple of pair of men's high-top dress boots.

Armed with new clothes, new band arrangements and a newly acquired taste for the better life, Will Mastin, Sam Sr., Sammy and I arrived to the Fairmont Hotel.

Mugging for the camera

Upon our arrival at the Fairmont, we were met by Dick Swig, who managed the hotel for his father, Ben Swig. Dick could not have been nicer, as was everyone else in the hotel. Remember this was a major five-star hotel, and the first premier-class showroom the Trio had ever played. It was also our introduction to living in this kind of style. However, the first couple of trips to San Francisco after we started playing the Fairmont, Will was more comfortable staying in

the Fillmore District (the Black section of San Francisco), instead of using his room at the hotel, and would come to the Fairmont to change just before the show. Old habits are sometimes hard to break, but the good times and the big times were starting there and then, on top of the hill—Nob Hill.

Sammy took my picture on the roof of the Fairmont Hotel

Sam photographed Ava Gardner

At that time, in the lobby of the hotel was a restaurant called The Camellia Room. It was a very upscale coffee shop/restaurant. Many mornings I had breakfast there with Dick Swig. We became good friends and remained so for many years to come.

This was a very important milestone in Sammy's life and the first door of so many to come that he himself would open.

The Venetian Room was as sophisticated and high class as any nightclub in the world. When people came to the shows, the women would be wearing evening gowns or formal cocktail dresses and the men tuxedos or dark suits. The tables were set with crystal stemware, and on each table was an elegant crystal vase with a single red rose. The dance and show music was played by Ernie Heckster and his Society Band. This was a wonderful time for a little Black dancer from Harlem and a White Jewish boy from the Valley. I guess what I am saying is that Sammy and the Trio had taken San Francisco by storm, and Sammy was the king of that hill. These people had never before been subjected to what came to be known as "The Sammy Experience."

All that being said, what do two young men find to do during the day in the City by the Bay? They could either go to Fisherman's Wharf, the movies, or take the cable car downtown and window shop.

Reading his reviews in **Variety**

We window shopped. As we walked along, we came upon a store called Abercrombie & Fitch, which had just about everything you could possibly imagine, and then some. This was a unique store; one could find anything from fishing poles to pool tables, and all that was needed to outfit a full safari in Africa. They had clothes and cuff links (of which Sammy bought a few pair) and even a department that supplied everything one needed to start fencing—we called it sword fighting.

There were masks, gloves, outer protective wear and all the accouterments. Sammy just could not get any further in this store without buying a couple of fencing swords so we could practice playing Errol Flynn and Douglas Fairbanks Jr. This started a new activity for us. Since we already had the fist fighting thing down pat, we decided: "Why not do it with swords?" and stupidly, we proceeded without any kind of protection. However the question now arose: "Where does one sword fight at the Fairmont Hotel?"

It started in Sammy's room, but that did not last long as there was not enough room to play Zorro there! So we moved to the roof of the hotel and the halls, where Sammy and I could jump around. As with everything else we did, Sam and I became so good at this, we could call out the moves to each other as we dueled.

"En Garde!" I challenge

You would think we had spent hours and days learning a set routine, but not so. Just like our fist fights, it was spontaneous and on the spot. It must have been a strange sight to have the Fairmont elevator doors open and the guests inside look out to see a short Black guy and a tall, White guy sword fighting down the halls of the hotel, with our swashbuckler's dialog and all.

Once while fencing down the hall, I got too close and cut Sammy by mistake. In true *Corsican Brothers* style Sammy, exacting his revenge, insisted on drawing my blood as well. He decided we should rub our wounds together and become blood brothers—and so it would be for the rest of our lives.

After a few comments from the guests got back to Dick Swig, we were told to keep it on the roof. Mind you, no one complained; they just commented on the sight. As a matter of fact, frequently they would get off the elevator and watch us. Sammy and Arthur had found a new home. Sammy was like a magnet. People flocked to the hotel to see him, and we both started to make many new friends, especially chicks.

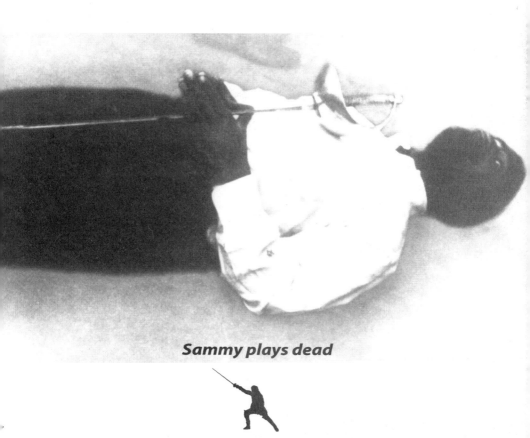

Sammy plays dead

Dancing on the Fairmont rooftop, our playground

My surprising friendships

Sammy with Eartha Kitt, actress, dancer, and multi-lingual singer

The Fairmont Experience

This will cover years of experiences in the 1950s while performing at the Fairmont Hotel, condensed into one chapter.

The Fairmont is a magnificent hotel that sits atop exclusive Nob Hill in the beautiful City by the Bay, San Francisco. One could not help but be impressed by the opulent entrance to the hotel and its splendid staircase leading from the mezzanine to the lobby floor and to a restaurant called the Camellia Room. In one corner was a candy and ice cream shop called Blum's. Down the hall was the entrance to the Venetian Room, (the main showroom and formal dining room of the hotel). In front of the Venetian Room was the Le Ronde Bar, which turned very slowly like a merry-go-round. Next to the Venetian Room was the banquet room, called the Cirque Room. In the hallways of the lobby floor hung pictures of the 1906 San Francisco earthquake. The Fairmont Hotel, thankfully, was one of the structures spared from that earthquake and subsequent fire.

Downstairs from the lobby floor was a wonderful restaurant, Al Williams' Papagallo Room, a popular place to go after attending the shows in the Venetian Room and the theater. On the California Street side, in the hotel, was a small movie theater that seated about fifty people and ran movies during the day. Then there was the Tonga Room, a superb Chinese restaurant built around a full-size Olympic swimming pool. Floating in the center of the pool was a raft where live musicians played dinner music. The restaurant was decorated like a Chinese garden, and every fifteen minutes it would thunder and lightning and rain real water. The rain also fell on the pool area where the band float was covered so the musicians would not get wet.

Sammy and I had many wonderful experiences at the Fairmont in addition to our sword fighting. On our first trip to there, some of my high school friends came to San Francisco to see Sammy's show.

Joe Louis held the title of World Heavyweight Boxing Champion longer than any other man in history

We did two shows a night; and one night after the first show, I was leaning over a table with my hands on it talking to my friends when I felt a tap on my left shoulder. It was Sammy. Still leaning on the table, I turned to look over my left shoulder at him. He said, "There's someone here I want you to meet."

Still leaning on the table, I turned to look over my right shoulder and instead looked straight into a large gold belt buckle like cowboys wear with the huge initials "JL" embedded in diamonds. As I continued to look up, I saw a giant of a man standing just in front of me. Sammy said, "Art, I would like you to meet Joe Louis."

There stood the legendary Heavyweight Champion of the World! As I went to shake his hand, it was like trying to hold onto a huge ham. I was a pretty big guy myself, six feet tall and about 185 pounds, but this man was a mountain. My God, I was meeting a living legend! We talked for a short while, but people were gathering around trying to get autographs; and Sammy wanted to get Joe out of there. What a moment for me—one I'll never forget!

Whenever in San Francisco, Sammy and I would go window shopping. Sammy just had to keep buying things. As his paychecks got bigger, so did his habit of spending money. The spending began during the first Fairmont Hotel engagement, and it never stopped until the day he died. Sammy was generous to a fault, and the spending was not just on himself, but for everyone he cared about—always.

One day we wandered into a camera shop and before we left, it was obvious that photography was to be our newest favorite pastime. Sammy bought us both very good cameras and all the great stuff that went with them. This began a serious lifelong hobby at which we both became extremely good. Neither one of us went anywhere after that day without a camera.

This hobby opened up new doors of experience for both of us. For one thing, it was a great way to get chicks up to our room. It was much better than saying, "Come up and see my etchings."

The new line was, "Come up and let us take some pictures of you." Another popular line of ours, thanks again to Sammy's new-found interest in shopping, was: "Come up and see my cuff link collection." By this time, his collection had increased considerably and was growing larger by the day. What better prize for a young lady than to be able to put on a new shirt with the initials "SDJr." on the pocket? It wasn't planned; it just worked out that way, and it worked well, I might add.

We made many friends during our frequent stays at the Fairmont Hotel, one in particular was the young man who was heir to the Coro Jewelry fortune. At that time, it was the largest costume jewelry company in the country making very expensive, high-end costume jewelry. He had a lady friend for me to meet because he was sure we would hit it off. I was never one for blind dates, but he assured me not to worry.

I had taken my car to San Francisco this trip and drove to the lady's place filled with a certain amount of trepidation. I rang the bell and when the door opened, standing before me was a Marilyn Monroe clone. She was wearing a black cocktail dress with a low neckline that left absolutely nothing to the imagination and a black hat with a little black veil that just barely covered her eyes. She was stunning, and this was one of those moments that comes along just a few times in a man's life. We looked at each other, and the only words spoken were, "Hi, Arthur. I'm Sonja."

My ever-present camera

Sonja Miller

At that moment, a new world opened up for me—no doubt about that. It was love at first sight; a kind of all-consuming thing that was sexual beyond belief and would eventually be devastating for both of us.

On the way to the Fairmont we didn't talk much, just kept looking at each other, excitement so thick you could cut it with a knife. It was hard to breathe.

I couldn't wait to see Sam's face when I walked in with this lady. As we approached the suite which Sammy and I shared, I asked Sonja to stand clear of the doorway, out of sight. I did not use my key, just knocked on the door. Sam called, "Who is it?"

"It's me."

"Come on in; I'm having dinner."

I told him I had left my key in my room. He exclaimed, "Damn, Silber. Can't you even remember your own door key?"

He opened the door wearing nothing but a pair of white boxer shorts and held the door open by leaning against it with a knife in one hand and a fork in the other. I stepped in and said, "Sam, I'd like you to meet Sonja Miller."

Sonja stepped into view; "I'm very pleased to meet you, Mr. Davis."

Sammy took one look at her and breathed, "Oh, fuck!" then slid down the door to the floor with the door wide open, still holding the fork in one hand and the knife in the other.

Sonja suggested, "Mr. Davis, maybe you should shut the door. Someone might walk by."

"Yeah, I guess you're right," Sammy answered. Then he realized the only thing he had on was a pair of boxer shorts, jumped up, grabbed his white bathrobe and began apologizing all over the place. I was having the time of my life watching him fall all over himself trying to get control, which was a hard thing to do with this "Every Man's Dream Woman" standing in front of him. Sonja was great about it and took it with great humor and dignity. For Sonja and me it was the beginning of a very serious romance.

When Sammy did his show he would walk around the dance floor and work the audience. One night during the first show, sitting ringside was a gorgeous woman I'll call Virginia. She was dressed in a purple evening gown, and she had very short hair. She had the kind of haircut that almost looked like a man's cut, slicked back on the sides and sprayed silver with silver sparkle dust all through it.

Virginia could not take her eyes off Sammy; she was transfixed. After the show Hans, the maitre d', gave me a note for Sammy with a rose from Virginia. Hans told me Virginia was the daughter of a well-known San Francisco socialite. Her note thanked Sammy for the show and asked him to join her party at their table for a drink.

Sammy asked who she was and I told him. Still, he was hesitant because he didn't want to say or do anything that might offend the San Francisco gentry. I told him it couldn't hurt. He said, "I don't know, man. This chick was burning holes through me with her eyes the whole show."

"Do you want me to go over and make your apologies?" I asked.

"No," he said. "I'll go, but you'd better come with me."

"She invited you, not me," I said.

He said, "If you don't go, then I won't go."

I knew how badly he wanted to meet this woman, so I said, "Okay, I'll go, but just for a minute or two."

Virginia, her date and another couple were introduced. Sammy had his usual Coca-Cola, and I my usual ice water. Virginia monopolized Sammy shamelessly in front of everyone, including her date. She made sure Sammy sat beside her and, as dignified as she was, couldn't keep her hands off him. She managed to put a note into Sammy's pocket, gave him her phone number, said that she was coming back for the second show alone, and she wanted to talk to him more after the last show.

Sammy did not read her note until we had reached our suite. He asked me what I thought he should do. To be honest, Sonja was with me, and I had my mind on much more important things; but Sammy really wanted to follow through on Virginia's invitation. I asked Hans to hold a table for three in Virginia's name for the second show and told Sammy that Sonja and I would sit with Virginia during the show. Virginia was nice as she could be, and the three of us really hit it off.

After the show Sammy suggested we all go to the Papagallo Room to eat. Virginia said she would prefer that we go to her apartment instead. Sammy was getting concerned about being seen alone with her (remember this was in the 1950s, and interracial couples were still taboo); so instead of all going together, the girls went to Virginia's place in a cab, and Sammy and I left in my car twenty minutes later.

What a night that turned out to be—candlelight, soft music and mad, unadulterated sex. When daylight came, I knew I had to get Sammy out of there, so I knocked on Virginia's bedroom door and told Sammy that we had to go **now**—it was starting to get light outside. When he came out of the room I almost died laughing.

The silver spray and sparkles from Virginia's hair were all over Sammy's face and in his hair. He had so much Pomade in his hair that the silver sparkles would not comb out; he was going to have to wash it out, not an easy chore for his thick hair. By the time we got back to the hotel, about six in the morning, it was light outside. We had to walk through the lobby, trying to be as inconspicuous as possible. Picture this: one tall White guy and one short half-black, half-silver guy. We did not go unnoticed. Ain't love grand?

"Virginia,"
Sammy
and Sonja

My romance with Sonja lasted for about two years before it faded away. So much happened during the years we played the Fairmont that it would be impossible to tell all the stories. Sammy, never one to stand still, kept learning new skills. He taught himself to play the trumpet, bass fiddle and piano. Whenever we played the Apollo Theater in Harlem, Lionel Hampton taught Sammy the vibraphones and the drums. Drums were his best instrument. Most tap dancers can play the drums, since what they do with their feet is primarily what a drummer does with his hands.

Sammy became so good at playing drums and vibes that he added them to his act. He would roll out a complete drum set on a platform and go at it, a big hit with the audience. Sammy was great at the drums.

During one of our engagements at the Fairmont, there was a combined big jazz band which was touring the United States and also happened to be in San Francisco. It was comprised of some of the greatest musicians in the world. One night the whole band came in to see Sammy's show. Buddy Rich and Gene Krupa, two of the world's premier drummers, were in the group. Of course, Sam introduced them and invited them to sit in. He bantered back and forth with Buddy and Gene and taunted them playfully, saying, "You were pretty good in your day."

Buddy and Gene retorted, "Do you think you can do better?"

"Well, I guess we'll just have to find out whether you two guys have anything left," teased Sammy. With that, Sammy called for his drum set to be brought on stage, and he began to play. This became a challenge between the drummers.

Sammy drumming

Sammy and me with Eartha Kit

Gene Krupa came up first and just buried Sammy! Then it was Buddy Rich's turn. He said, "Well, that's pretty good, but let me show you how it should be done!" He took over the orchestra's drum set and did his thing. Then the two great drummers just went crazy.

Sammy laughed, "I guess I'll just have to show you guys a thing or two," and called for his vibes to be brought on stage. It turned out to be one of those great show business nights when all that can be said is that you really had to be there. The spontaneous artistry was at its best and a joy for everyone lucky enough to have been there. The Fairmont rocked that night.

A day or two later Eartha Kitt, a good friend of Sammy's, visited the City by the Bay and stayed at the Fairmont. Sammy and I spent a lot of time with Eartha taking pictures and playing Sammy's favorite game, Monopoly, which he played with a vengeance. Monopoly money was like real money to Sammy. He loved buying and selling property, and he **really** hated to lose. One night during Monopoly, Eartha asked Sammy what kind of property he owned.

"None," he replied.

Eartha, always brutally frank, was shocked. "Well what do you do with all of your money? You seem to have enough to buy all that jewelry and all the other things I see around your room." She gave Sammy a long lecture about what to do with his money and made more than a lot of sense. If Sammy had only listened to Eartha and taken her advice to heart, he would have been a very rich man. But that was not to be; it just wasn't Sammy. He made a lot of money in his career and spent it all.

San Francisco is home to a world-famous North Beach nightclub called Finocchio's, which culturally is about as far as you can get from Nob Hill. The show at Finocchio's is made up of drag queens, transvestites and female impersonators. This became one of our favorite spots to hang out, and we became friends with the performers.

Not thinking of the culture shock to the Fairmont guests, one night Sammy invited all of Finocchio's performers to join us at Al Williams' Papagallo Room for dinner. They all showed up in drag. I know that the Papagallo Room and the Fairmont Hotel will never be the same. It was quite a party!

Eartha Kitt, photographed on the Fairmont's rooftop

I'm sitting with Christine Jorgenson, a big personality in the 1950s and 1960s —the first man to have a successful sex-change operation

Sammy leaps above the San Francisco skyline, while dancing on the roof of the Fairmont Hotel

From the opulence, dignity and elegance of our first engagement at the Fairmont Hotel, the Trio was booked into the Last Frontier Hotel in Las Vegas, another major culture shock, to say the least. This would be the first time the Trio was to headline in Las Vegas; in the past they had been just an opening act at the El Rancho Hotel.

As we were preparing to leave San Francisco, Will, Sam Sr. and Sammy told me they wanted me to go back to Los Angeles for a couple of weeks. They preferred that I did not go to Vegas. I couldn't believe my ears. I turned to Sammy and said, "What in the hell is this all about?"

He said, "Man, like this isn't my decision alone. You gotta under-stand that in Vegas we've got to stay at Mrs. Shaw's Rooming House on the Black side of town, and we all agree that it would be very uncomfortable for you. Besides that we can't even go into the Fron-tier by the front entrance. We gotta go in by way of the kitchen."

I was fit to be tied and screamed back, "When has it ever bothered me being or staying in the damn Black side of town? It sure never mattered in Los Angeles, Miami or New York, and plenty of other places I can't even think of now. You're as much my family as my own mom and dad. I go where you go, and fuck 'em all!" I was so mad, I was shaking.

Then Will walked over, put his arm around my shoulders and said, "Arthur, you're as much a part of this family as we are, and always will be, but this time we're right, and your dad agrees with us."

"What in the hell does that mean?" I yelled.

Will said, "You know, Arthur, your dad and I have known each other and worked together long before you and Mose were born. It's for the best, and in a couple of weeks we'll all be together again in Arizona."

I was so mad I could hardly speak. "Yeah," I said, "who ever heard of Apache Junction, Arizona, anyway? You mean to tell me there ain't no Black side of town there?"

I was still roaring mad at all of them, including my dad and the rest of the world. I could not believe that this Black and White thing kept popping up in my face. I was not brought up that way. I never thought that way. And now my own family was throwing this ugly issue at me.

Sam Sr. came up to me, cupped my face in his hands, kissed me smack on the mouth and said, "Son, we understand your feelings and we love you for it. This has nothing to do with you. It's our way of showing our love and concern for you. What'ya gonna do—just sit in some hotel room and read the papers or watch TV for two weeks, and only spend a few hours a night hanging around the dressing room? You know, we're not even allowed to walk into the casino or anywhere else in the Frontier."

I turned to Sammy with a jerk and yelled, "Well...you just standing there with your big mouth shut. You got nothin' to say about this?"

His head was hanging down, and he was staring at the floor. He raised his head and said, "I know you better than anyone in the world, and I damn sure know how you feel, but this is the right thing to do."

With that, I pushed all of them aside and screamed, "None of you know how in the hell I feel! More to the point, I guess I can say for the first time in my life I really know how you must feel about this damn Black thing! If you're good enough to headline at the Frontier, a major hotel in Las Vegas, but you're not even good enough to walk into the hotel, let alone stay there, then no, I don't feel good at all, and all I can say is fuck 'em all, the whole fucking bunch! Well, I'll do what you ask, like I have a choice. But rest assured that as of this moment, no one will ever come between my family and me again!"

And they never ever did!

Sammy & me being Cowboys

Cowboys and Indians

I arrived in Apache Junction, Arizona, wondering what new challenges awaited us here. I was still pissed off about Vegas. It didn't matter, though, because just like always, when Sammy and I were together all was right with the world. Once again in a new town, this time in the Old West, we were wondering what to do with our time when we weren't working. We thought of a new and exciting idea—we went window shopping.

Cowboys and Indians danced in our minds as we walked down the main street, taking in all of the Native American garb, jewelry and decor. I told Sammy we should go horseback riding. I grew up riding horses and had always enjoyed it.

Sammy looked at me like I was crazy saying, "I don't do horses, and I damn sure don't ride 'em! The closest I want to be to horses is betting on them at the racetrack."

I kept insisting, but he would have no part of it. Sammy was scared of animals, including cats and dogs, and had been all his life. We walked, looked and window shopped until we happened upon a gun store. What a surprise—Sammy had to go in! Going in to look around usually meant Sammy was about to buy something.

Sure enough, an hour later we came out of the store with a new hobby. Sammy bought three Colt .45s (two for himself and one for me), holsters, saddlebags, lots of live ammunition and blanks and a scabbard for the Winchester 30/30 I had bought for myself. We had grown up staging fistfights, had fought with swords, and now we were going to play cowboys and Indians. Guns and ammunition were our new toys, but dangerous ones. If not handled properly, they could kill. Now we could learn to fast draw and stage mock gunfights like at the OK Corral. We were cowboys now!

I told Sammy, "Now that we're going to play cowboys, you gotta ride horses!"

"No," he said. "First we'll go out in the desert and learn to shoot."

Target practice

"Then why did you buy the saddlebags?" I asked. "Are you going to strap them on me and ride off into the sunset? I think not!"

Sammy told me to check around and see if there was someplace we could go to practice with our new guns. The club owner where we were playing said he had a friend who would be happy to take us out; and the next morning Joe Lightfoot called to take us out to where we could shoot. I thought to myself, "Joe Lightfoot. Is this guy for real?" I woke Sammy up and told him that Joe Lightfoot was waiting for us in the lobby.

"Yeah, sure!" he said. "I'll bet he's a real Apache Indian too, huh?"

That's exactly what he was, and we climbed into Joe's station wagon with our guns and ammunition and headed for the mountains. As we got closer, Sammy asked Joe what they called this place, and Joe responded, "The Superstition Mountains."

Even though Sammy and I weren't well versed in the Wild West, we had heard of the Superstition Mountains. Sammy got very quiet, then said, "Aha! That's where that lost gold mine is, isn't it?"

"Sure is!" said Joe. "The lost mine of the Apache gold."

Sammy's demeanor was changing; you could see it in his face. We were just below the foot of the Superstition Mountains when Joe pulled into his ranch. What a kind and wonderful man this was. His wife and family had prepared lunch for us and after we ate, we were going to try out our new guns. During lunch Joe told us stories about his family from way back and about the mountains and their many legends. Sammy and I lapped it all up, and Sammy could not stop asking questions, one after another; he was hooked.

After lunch, Joe took us out to his barn where his kids had saddled three horses for us. Sammy took one look and said to Joe, "No, man. I can't ride, and I don't ever want to try."

Joe replied, "I swear to you the horse I have chosen for you is so calm and gentle you won't even know you're riding."

I said, "Come on, Sam. If I can do it, so can you."

But Sammy stood fast; I could see him thinking. Through all of our lives, whenever I challenged Sammy he could not stand it. It was the same as playing Monopoly with him; he just could not stand to have someone beat him. He always had to live up to a challenge, and that was what really made Sammy run! It was the secret I knew about Sammy that nobody else knew: put up a door in his face and he would find a way to go through it, around it, or even make a new doorway. Arthur had the little key to his best friend's guts. No matter how scared he was, there was no way Sammy was going to let me show him up or beat him out; sibling rivalry, just like brothers.

With a little help and a great deal of trepidation, Sammy overcame his fear and got on this animal that terrified him. Joe's kids had put Sammy's saddlebags and ammo on the horse. Joe had one of his sons walk Sammy around the corral a few times on the horse. After about fifteen minutes of walking, Sammy became Hopalong Cassidy, the Lone Ranger and John Wayne all rolled up in one. He said, "Hell, this ain't no big thing! Gimme my guns and holsters and let's get out of here!"

We trotted along the trail and Joe pointed out places of interest in the mountains and told us more stories. Sammy and I ate it all up.

We were no longer in show business; we were in the cowboy business. By the time we reached our destination and took our first shot, Sammy had become the Black Scourge of the Wild West. Inspired by Joe's stories and his insatiable curiosity, Sammy bought every book he could find on guns, the Old West and especially, on how to fast draw, do tricks and handle a gun in a showy, flashy manner.

From that time on, Sammy and I spent at least two or three hours a day standing in front of a mirror or facing one another practicing our fast draw. I was never one for fancy gun tricks like Sammy; I was just fast, very, very fast. When we got back to Los Angeles, we had special fast draw holsters custom made for us by the man who made holsters for nearly every cowboy star in Hollywood. The holsters were made of leather and steel, which caused them to stay open when the gun was drawn out. We had our guns tweaked for fast draw by having the spring in the hammer filed down so it could be cocked easier. The top of the hammer was bent out just a little so you could catch it with your thumb as you drew the gun from the holster. In fast draw the gun is cocked in the holster before it is drawn. More new toys for us to play with, and Sammy became so proficient at gun handling that he put it into his act.

Soon, we were back in Hollywood with new worlds to conquer. One afternoon Sammy and I were sitting around talking and he said to me, "Don't you think it's time you taught me to drive a car?"

I gave him a kind of sneaky look and said, "You want me to do what?"

"Teach me to drive," he answered.

"So let me get this straight," I said. "You want me to take you out in my customized car and teach you how to drive. You just learned how to drive one horsepower, and now you want me to give you three hundred horses to drive. You can barely handle a sword, for God's sake!"

With that he jumped up, grabbed his sword and said, "Sir, you have insulted my integrity, so I have no choice but to challenge you to a duel to the end!"

God, how I loved to dig at him! He was so easy. All I ever had to do was put it to him in that way, and he would predictably react. "Sir," I answered, "I would love to take you on, but I would not like to spill your blood all over this nice carpet. So instead I will try and teach you how to drive."

The best parking lot to teach Sammy to drive on would have been at the Sports Arena or the Forum in Los Angeles; but since they had not been built yet, we ventured onto the large parking lot on the corner of Beverly Boulevard and Fairfax Avenue where the CBS Studios are today. Now, on that lot was a big coliseum-shaped structure made of wood with a football field in the center, around which was the best red clay midget auto race track in the world. This was Gillmore Stadium, named for a line of gas stations that were all over Southern California at that time. Next to the stadium was a huge building called the Pan Pacific Auditorium, where the Ice Follies and many other large conventions were held; it was the Los Angeles Convention Center of that time.

Between Gillmore Stadium and the Pan Pacific was a huge unobstructed parking area shared by the two venues, which was a great place to teach someone to drive a column shift; and believe me, we needed a lot of unobstructed room. We bumped, ground and jerked our way all over that parking lot; and finally Sammy got it down well enough to get a driver's license. But it's a good thing he only had to make check marks on the written test, as he still could not write much more than his name. This was a wonderful accomplishment for Sammy. He got the license, but thank God he never asked to borrow my car!

Our circle of friends in show business began to grow bigger and became more famous, as did Sammy. We spent a great deal of time at Universal Studios where Tony Curtis, Janet Leigh and Jeff Chandler were under contract. They were some of our closest friends. We spent a lot of time at Tony and Janet's house. Tony started painting works of art around that time and became a successful artist as well as an accomplished actor.

Sammy could not get enough of the movie life, and one of his greatest dreams was to win an Academy Award. God, how he wanted to be an actor, but he never thought it would happen, so he just taught himself to impersonate some of his favorite actors. Impressions and impersonations came just as easily to Sammy as everything else in show business did. Sammy had an uncommon ear and was extremely observant. That's why he learned everything so fast, such as all the instruments he played. One of his favorite games was to call up restaurants and hotels and order food to go or room service, using the voice of some big star. You could not tell Sammy from the real Cary

Grant, Jimmy Stewart, James Cagney, or anyone else he put his mind to impersonating. It was another way to get into the wonderful world of make believe where Sammy loved to live and play.

Originally Sammy couldn't sing a note; he was a hoofer, the best there was. Doing impressions was the way Sammy broke into singing. In those days, doing impressions allowed Sammy, as a Black performer, to do things on stage as other people, that he could never have gotten away with on the street. Sammy was a perfectionist in his impersonations, as he was at everything else he did. When he was learning to impersonate someone, he would get all the moves and mannerisms down pat. He did Jerry Lewis better than Jerry did, and many others as well. Every day Sammy would play music in his room, impersonating the famous singers of the day and their styles; and that's how he became the great singer he was.

The first singer impressions he developed, after Vaughn Monroe, were Billy Eckstine, and Billy Daniels. Sammy played around with the trumpet, so he also did a little bit of Satchmo-Louis Armstrong. However, one of the strangest things is that, as much as Sammy was around Frank Sinatra, and as close as they were, Sammy could not impersonate Frank. He had Frank's attitude; he would put on the hat, throw the jacket over the shoulder and walk off the stage; and everyone knew it was Frank. But he could never really get his voice. No one could.

As he learned more voices, talking as well as singing, Sammy put them into the act. This was really starting to upset Will, as he just wanted to do their dance thing and that was it. It was hard for Will to finish his dance numbers and then just stand there on the stage while

Sam took off doing all these other things. Sammy was aware of Will's discomfort and tried to keep him and Sam Sr. involved in the act.

20th Century Fox— Marilyn Monroe, Sammy and me

Once a new car named a Singer (not a sewing machine on wheels) was being introduced at Twentieth Century Fox Studios. Sammy was invited over by a photographer friend to have his picture taken standing next to the car. The photographer forgot to mention that the picture would also include Marilyn Monroe. She was in the middle of filming *How To Marry A Millionaire*.

Though Sammy and I had already met Marilyn at another friend's engagement party, this was still a very pleasant surprise. After all,

"To Art, Love and Kisses, Marilyn Monroe."

looking at Marilyn Monroe in a strapless evening gown definitely was not the worst way to spend a little time.

After the brief shoot the photographer took a picture of all three of us standing and sitting on and around the car. Sammy and I each had been given pictures of Marilyn and we asked her to autograph them for us. While she was doing that, the photographer took a picture of her signing them. Those pictures are on the wall in my office to this day, one of them signed "To Art, Love and Kisses, Marilyn Monroe." They are among my most prized possessions.

We were to go back to the Chez Paree and arrived in Chicago feeling all was right with the world. From opening night the place just jumped.

At the Chez Paree, Sammy started doing fast draw tricks with guns in his act and demonstrated some of his gun tricks to the audience. The Chez Paree was a big room with a stage. The entrance to the club where the people entered was through a short but fairly wide hallway. On either side of the hallway (back of the wall on one side and up about three steps), were the dressing rooms. Across the hall were the club's offices.

One night, Sammy's friend Joe Louis had come in to see the show; and I took him and his party to visit Sammy in his dressing room. Sammy and Joe were talking about guns and fast draw and Sammy showed Joe some tricks. Sammy had several Colt .45s; some he used on stage and others just for practice. Colt .45s come in different barrel lengths: 6-inch, 7-inch, and a Colt .45 Buntline that was used by Wyatt Earp in the old West. It had a barrel that was nine or ten inches long. That is very long for the barrel of a revolver, but the longer the barrel, the more accurate the gun. Wyatt Earp used to pull it out and knock people over the head with it, rather than shooting them.

On stage, Sammy used 3/4 load blanks. A 3/4 load blank shoots fire out of the barrel quite a distance, and you have to be very careful when you do this. He used to only shoot it toward the end of his show, and it would scare the devil out of the audience. When he fired it, he had to aim at the back of the stage because the blank shoots out a wad, called the packing; and it also shoots out powder. A 3/4 load is a very heavy load; the only thing heavier is a full load of blank. With such a load, if you're standing within five or six feet, you're going to get hit by the powder, and maybe by the wad, and feel as though you've been shot. Fire comes out of the gun about a foot-and-a-half; it's very effective. Sammy never used a full load on the stage because it was too dangerous.

So, he was showing off to Joe, pulled off a fast draw with the Buntline, and all of a sudden, bang! To this day, just as it happens every day in this world, Sammy didn't know there was a real bullet in this gun. How it got there, he and I never knew. A .45 caliber bullet went off just as people were leaving. The bullet passed through the wall of Sammy's dressing room, right through the crowds who were exiting the club along the hallway, and through the wall on the other side of the hallway. It crossed the office and imbedded itself in the third wall.

Sammy was extremely lucky that night. God was looking down on him and all those people walking through that hallway, because he could easily have killed more than one person as the bullet passed through the wall at the head level of the people leaving the club. Somehow it missed, but scared everyone to death. When a .45 goes off you can't miss the sound; people went running and screaming, but no one was hit.

Sammy, who always wore a white bathrobe offstage, came running out of his dressing room and out the front of the club in his robe to see if he had killed anybody. It was a very scary moment. The incident was written up in the papers, and Sammy got a visit from the Police Department restricting him from using any more large load blanks on the stage. That was probably smart, considering the club we were in, because if the gun ever went off in the wrong direction, somebody could get hit with the wad and be blinded or seriously hurt. Yeah, I would say everything was all right with the world on that occasion.

After our shows at the Chez Paree we would go over and hang out with the Mob guys, and there were always lots of women around. Hanging out with Sammy Davis Jr. for most of my young life put me pretty high on the list for great looking women.

I have been asked all of my life from day one with Sammy, "What is it that chicks see in him? He's ugly, he's short..." and more. What stars don't have a lot of girls and women hanging all over them any time they snap their fingers? Don't Mick Jagger and Dennis Rodman have their choice of dozens of women on any given night? And they don't exactly have classic leading man good looks either. Any star, be they actor, musician or athlete, can hand pick any one of hundreds, or even thousands of women who want to be with him. Maybe it's personality or magnetism, a sort of magic. Whatever you call it, some people just have an unexplainable aura and others are drawn to it.

I got used to people asking the question. It happened every night. After setting the show, which was my main duty, I would take care of Sammy's friends and his other guests. I had to make sure they got the right seats, the right bottle of wine or champagne, and whatever else they needed or wanted. I also had to juggle the women. Not a bad day's work if you're looking for a job. Once my duties were done, I would sit down to watch the show with the guests, who always included gorgeous girls, show girls, call girls, and regular beautiful women; and there was always one who would ask me, "How could anybody go to bed with him? He's so ugly!"

Then I would bet myself a hundred bucks, "This is the one who will be in bed with him tonight." When I finally stopped counting I was millions of dollars ahead of myself; and, if it had been real money, I could have retired at thirty.

It's hard to explain what Sammy had that made him such a magnetic personality, as a performer and as a person. His dynamics and charisma on stage overcame and overshadowed any racial barriers or physical looks. His personality transcended all dimensions. There are few performers who have had this effect on people. Sinatra, of course; Al Jolson and Judy Garland were bigger than life. Seeing Sammy Davis Jr. perform was like watching a live performance of Sir Lawrence Olivier doing Shakespeare.

Sammy also had many liaisons with beautiful women the public suspected but never really knew about. Ava Gardner, Lana Turner and Marilyn Monroe were close friends from way back in the beginning of their careers, as were many more of the world's most gorgeous women.

Around 1951, we were scheduled to play a couple of benefit shows in New York, one up in the Catskills, the other in New York City; and we had been given rooms in the Waldorf Astoria Hotel Towers. After the benefit in New York, we went to Lindy's and then the Apollo Theater where Billy Eckstine was the star that week.

We arrived back at the hotel about two-thirty in the morning and entered the Tower elevator. A tall man with a hat in his hand stepped in ahead of us wearing a scarf, gloves and a camel hair overcoat. When he turned around, we were face to face with a show business legend, Maurice Chevalier. What a wonderful moment for us.

Mr. Chevalier recognized Sammy and spoke first, introducing himself. When the elevator stopped at his floor we were still talking to him so we got out to continue our conversation. Mr. Chevalier told us he had seen Sammy do impressions of him and he thought Sammy impersonated him very well.

"The only thing you're missing," he said in his own inimitable voice, "is my straw hat." At that point, he gave Sammy the straw hat he was holding in his hand. Sam really flipped. He used that hat in his act for years until it was literally worn out.

Maurice Chevalier was a most gracious man and certainly a show business icon. I have never been easily impressed with big stars as I have spent all my life around them, but meeting this man made a huge impression on me.

Billy Eckstine had invited Sammy and me to play golf with him the following week, and Sam asked where and when, not letting Billy

Jazz singer, Herb Jeffries

Entertainer, Maurice Chevalier— Sammy holds the trademark straw hat

Singer, Billy Eckstine, one of Sammy's first impersonations

know we had never played golf in our lives. We were very big at miniature golf, but that's a whole different game.

The next day Sam and I went…guess where? Window shopping! We found ourselves back at Abercrombie & Fitch where, as usual, Sammy bought us the whole ball of wax. Now the only thing left to do was learn to play golf, which, of course, was to be our **new** favorite pastime.

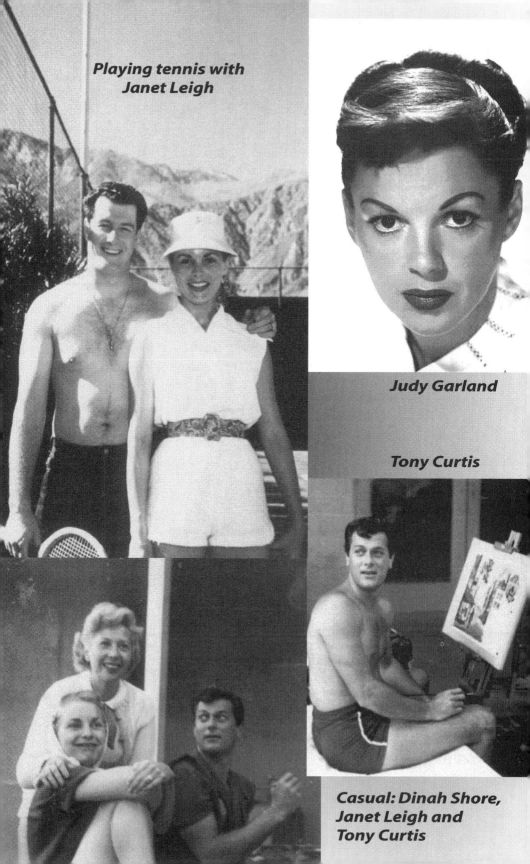

Playing tennis with Janet Leigh

Judy Garland

Tony Curtis

Casual: Dinah Shore, Janet Leigh and Tony Curtis

Moving to California

Once the golf equipment was sent to the hotel, Sammy told me to find someone who could teach us something about the game. I called the sporting goods department at Abercrombie & Fitch, and they set us up with a golf pro in New Jersey. We hired a limo and were off to the golf course.

Talk about laughing. The two of us trying to learn the game of golf was a scream. By the time we played with Billy Eckstine, we sort of had the rudiments down, but mostly spent the entire time laughing. Soon Sammy and I began to take the game seriously, and we played about four or five times a week. Years later Sammy had his own golf tournament, the Sammy Davis Jr. Greater Hartford Open.

The funny thing about Sammy and me is that no matter what we did we were very closely matched, and golf became a big challenge between us. Whenever we played, there was an additional incentive; we played for fifty to seventy-five cents a hole. Sammy took these bets very seriously. You could borrow five hundred bucks from him and he'd never ask for it back, but if you owed him fifty cents from a bet, he would bug you every day until you paid him. Naturally, I would return him the favor. Sibling rivalry was always alive and well between Sammy and Arthur.

We set up golf times as we traveled all around the country, and playing golf on certain courses became a big problem for Sammy. Most of the golf courses throughout the United States were still restricted, and that meant Blacks and Jews were prohibited from play-ing. Of course, Sammy refused to let that stop us. As we became better at the game, Sammy made a point of asking celebrities he worked with who happened to be White to join us, thus using their name power to get us onto the courses. The result was that these golf clubs and courses were literally forced into breaking down the wall of prejudice that had existed just to let Sammy Davis Jr. play on their courses, thereby making it much easier for the Black golf-lovers who came behind him. Sammy was, again, opening doors where there were no doors.

On one trip to San Francisco Jack Benny asked us to play golf with him. Can you picture Jack Benny, Sammy Davis Jr., and yours truly playing a threesome on the most prominent course in San Francisco in the late 1950s? The laughter and the antics on the course that day would have made a great television special today. Jack Benny, in person, was just the way he was on stage—his dry sense of humor and the faces he would make. The banter between him and Sammy was hysterical; and when Sammy got off a sharp remark or joke, Jack would practically roll on the ground. He was the best audience in the world.

It was around this time, 1952 or '53, that Sam Sr. and Will decided on a big change: move out West and make Southern California their permanent home. Rosa B. Davis, the family matriarch we all called Mama, was Sam Sr.'s mother. He asked her what she thought about moving to California. Mama was taken by surprise, as she had lived in Harlem just about all her life. She was very hesitant at first about leaving all her friends, but the whole family was most insistent. Sam Sr., Sammy and Will promised to buy Mama a house of her own, where Sam Sr. and his significant other, Peewee, would live with her as one big family. Sammy hoped to be living nearby. They also promised that Mama would always have someone to take her around whenever and wherever she wanted.

Mama finally relented, and soon she was in sunny California, living in a nice little house on Orange Grove Ave. When you really wanted soul food, that was the best place in town to find it. It was great having Mama around as she was one of the finest women I have ever known—a woman with a heartfelt knowledge of real life and how one should really live it.

My mother, Sammy (in his make-up robe) and Peewee, his step-mother

She was a kind and gentle woman, and I spent a good deal of time talking with her and enjoying her wonderful sense of humor. God would have been hard pressed to put a finer woman on this earth.

Will Mastin was old school. He still lived in Harlem at that time, and he didn't move until much later. He bought a large motel in Riverside, California, and had it for many, many years. After he retired and wasn't involved in show business at all, he lived at the motel.

It was also at that time that Will brought Nathan Crawford with him as a permanent employee. Nathan was another very kind and quiet man with a good heart who once was in Will's flash act and was Will and Sam Sr.'s very good friend. In previous years, when times were slow for the Trio, Nathan often loaned them money to keep them afloat financially. Now he was out of a job, but the Trio was doing well and working steadily. So Sam Sr. and Will offered to partially repay Nathan for his loans from those early difficult years. Nathan would not take any money and, instead, asked if they knew someone who would give him a job.

"Of course!" said Will. "Pack your bags; you're coming with us. We need an all-around man like you to help us." Nathan became Will's personal assistant, confidant and driver since Will never did learn to drive.

About the same time, Sammy decided that he needed a personal valet to help set up his dressing room and take care of his tuxedos and the rest of his clothes. He hired a young man named Charlie Head to work for him.

Sammy was also desperately looking for a house to buy in the Hollywood Hills that would overlook Hollywood and Beverly Hills. We started looking everywhere, driving up one street and down another. There were lots of places for sale with real estate agency signs in front. Sammy was keen on one place in particular. He told me to make the call, acting like I was the prospective buyer instead of him so we could get in and see the place. The house was located at 8850 Evanview Drive on a hillside almost directly behind the Sunset Colonial Hotel where we always stayed. This house had a garage and foyer at street level. Very secluded, the house went down the hillside with three levels. The real estate agent told us all the furniture would stay with the house. He also said Judy Garland was the current owner.

That did it! Sammy was a huge Judy Garland fan. As we walked through the place the real estate agent recognized Sammy, but didn't say anything. We finished the tour and were preparing to leave when the agent called me aside and asked me if I was really the person interested in purchasing the house or if it was Sammy. I said it was Sammy and was promptly told that Sammy could not purchase any home in that area because it was a restricted neighborhood; Colored people were not welcome as homeowners. I told the agent not to mention that to Sammy, that I would break it to him my own way.

Sammy loved the place and just couldn't get over the fact that Judy Garland owned it. He especially loved that it overlooked the rainbow city of Hollywood. No other place would do for him; he just **knew** it would soon be his house and he would be sleeping in Judy Garland's bed.

Recessed front door of Sammy's new house— at street level— it is between the foliage and the garage door in the bottom picture

God, how was I going to tell him that his dream house would not be his first real home? I decided to just come right out with it. "Sam," I said, "they ain't gonna sell it to you, and you know why!"

He looked at me with tears in his eyes and said, "They just won't let me live, no matter how hard I try to have a decent life." He instructed me to find Judy Garland's phone number, no matter who I had to call to get it. "I'm not gonna let them get away with this, if I can help it. It's time I stop letting people walk all over me just because my skin is a different color. Man, I'm sick and tired of having to bend to the White man's world! From now on, I'm gonna do whatever I can to stop this stupid way of thinking!

"You can bet the next time we go into Miami there will be limousines driving us around everywhere and we'll be staying in the same hotel I'm playing in Miami Beach! The next time Sammy Davis Jr. goes to Florida it will be first-class or I won't go, so help me God!

"Whenever they close a door in my face from now on, I'm either gonna bust through it or make a new door for the rest to follow me through!"

And so it was from that time on! This was the real beginning of the attitude that would carry Sammy through the rest of his life—the *"Yes I Can!"* attitude. And it was the same attitude that got him in so much trouble. Whites were offended, and Blacks thought he was trying to be White. Little do the people of color today know how many prejudicial walls Sammy Davis Jr. broke down for them in his lifetime.

I finally got Judy's phone number, and Sammy called her personally. It turned out she was as big a fan of Sammy's as he was of hers. Sammy told her what the real estate agent had said about Colored people not being welcome in the neighborhood and his not being allowed to buy her house. Judy got mad as hell and said she would take care of the matter herself because she thought it was about time attitudes changed. Her exact words were, "Let's knock Hollywood on its ass!"

And that she did! She called the real estate agency and told them that if they didn't sell her house to Sammy, she would pull the deal away from them and sell it to Sammy herself. Boy, did things start to happen then! Soon Sammy was out buying black satin sheets for what used to be Judy Garland's bed, and I ended up with two of her couches. It turned out that, the sheets were so slippery, anyone trying to sleep on them found themselves on the floor. But, Sammy just thought it was funny.

**A home at last:
the pool,
dining room, and
view of the house from
a lower terrace**

Piano practice

**View of Hollywood
from the balcony**

Eddie Cantor

Now good things began to happen for Sammy. To begin with, he just loved Judy's house. It's an important event in anyone's life when they buy their first car or home. But along with a house comes new responsibilities, the first of which is accessories. Sammy found out quickly how expensive this was going to be. By the time he actually bought the house, he had run out of cash on hand. I guess God was smiling on him, though, because an offer came in for Sammy and the Trio to do a major television show.

One of the biggest stars in show business at that time was Eddie Cantor. He was the star of *The Colgate Comedy Hour*, the forerunner many other variety shows that would follow. Eddie was a show business icon from the days of vaudeville, the Ziegfeld Follies, radio, movies and the fledgling industry of television. There was hardly anyone more famous or important in the entertainment industry at that time.

At the production meeting, the Trio was told by the production staff that a minimum performance would be all the Trio needed to rehearse for because Eddie Cantor wanted Sammy to do a whole dance number by himself. This request was troublesome to the Trio, but Mr. Cantor had a meeting with the group and explained that he wanted Sammy to do a dance number much like Fred Astaire or Gene Kelly.

This presented another problem for Sammy, since he always danced freeform and never used any type of choreography. He was a hoofer, and danced from his head and heart as he was feeling it at the moment. Mr. Cantor suggested that Sammy try to choreograph his own dance numbers. Sammy bit on that challenge like a duck goes to water.

He began to practice, and his choreography became more involved as he tried to dance more like Fred Astaire and Gene Kelly with a lot of Sammy Davis Jr. thrown in. He was having a ball with this new idea, as he had never danced this way before. In fact, Sam kind of thought he had become Fred Astaire and Gene Kelly both rolled up into his little body. From this beginning, he became the great dancer the world learned to love.

When it came time for Sammy to dance in front of the television cameras, he was petrified. In those days all television shows were live, and performers did not have the luxury of video tape and the opportunity to re-shoot if a mistake was made. If you goofed, everyone in the country saw it. But Sammy was Sammy; when it came to performing, he made no mistakes. Television audiences were supposed to be calm and simply applaud when prompted to do so by the applause sign. But at this show, when Sammy performed they all jumped up and screamed. He brought down the house that night.

Sammy was still on camera taking his bows and sweaty from the vigorous dance number when Mr. Cantor walked on stage, pulled out his handkerchief and wiped Sammy's brow. Today one might think this was merely a nice gesture, but not in those days. The folks watching the show on television in the South thought this simple little gesture was the signal for the Civil War to start all over again.

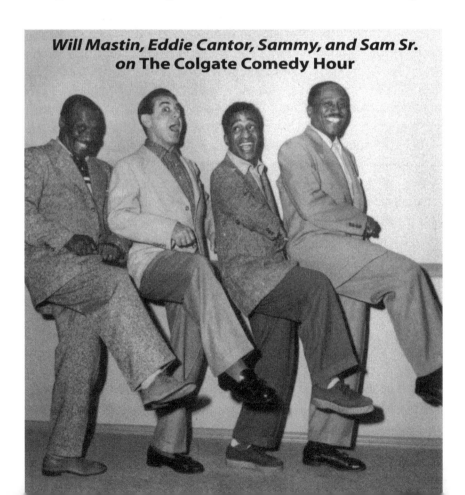

**Will Mastin, Eddie Cantor, Sammy, and Sam Sr.
on The Colgate Comedy Hour**

The phone calls and telegrams immediately started coming in to the television station and later to the Colgate-Palmolive Company. By the next day all hell had broken loose, and hate mail telegrams poured in from the South saying things like, "How could Eddie Cantor wipe the sweat off that Nigger's face?" This kindly little gesture made broadcast news and was in all the papers.

Sammy was mortified by the thought that Mr. Cantor would be called on the carpet by his sponsor, Colgate-Palmolive. But Eddie Cantor was a big star. With all the power and stature that a big star commands, he told Colgate-Palmolive that this was his show, and he would wipe the sweat off anyone's face he wanted to. He told Colgate-Palmolive that if they didn't like it, they could take the show and shove it right where the sun don't shine; and he said it in those very words. Furthermore, he told Colgate-Palmolive he was going to have Sammy back on the show the following week. Then he issued the strongest ultimatum possible. Either he would run his show his way, or there would be no more Eddie Cantor on *The Colgate Comedy Hour*.

The phone calls and telegrams were still pouring in to the television station about Sammy, and this scared Will and Sam Sr. They told Sammy, "See what happens when you step out of your place?"

Sammy jumped up and screamed, "I'm getting sick and tired of everyone telling me what I should, or should not do. I am who I am, and I don't need you telling me that I should stay in my place! What in the hell is my 'place' anyway? Just because I'm Black, do I always have to walk a fine line? People have to either like me or hate me for **myself**, not for the color of my skin!" With that, he left the room, slamming the door behind him.

Eddie Cantor, and Sammy act up on Eddie Cantor's variety show

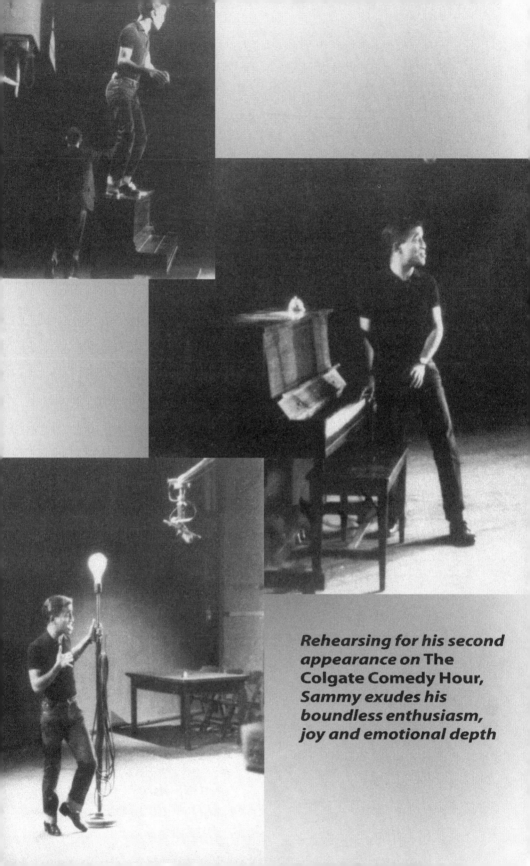

Rehearsing for his second appearance on **The Colgate Comedy Hour,** *Sammy exudes his boundless enthusiasm, joy and emotional depth*

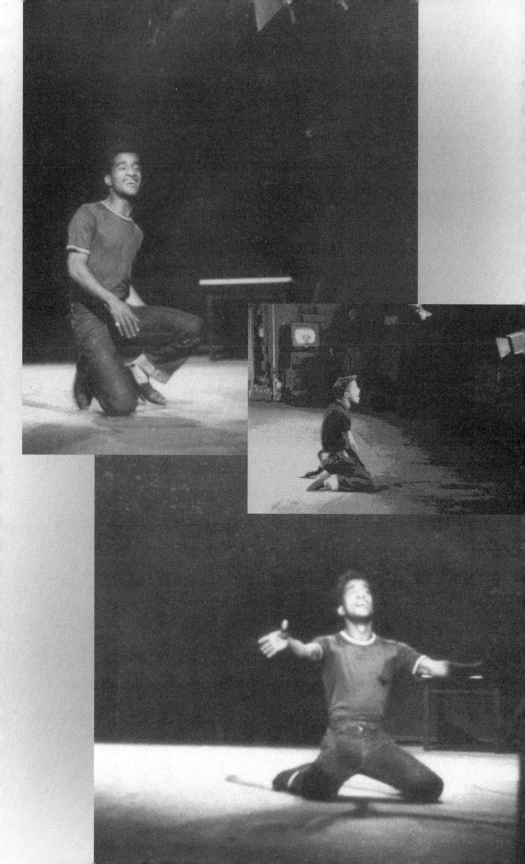

Will and Sam Sr. could not believe what Sammy had just said, but I was not surprised at all. I said, "What do you expect of him? He's human, and he's hurting bad right now. I'll go and talk to him."

I found Sammy outside leaning up against a wall crying. I put my arm around his shoulder and said, " Come on, Sam. Let it go. This will all work out."

Sammy was so upset that all he could think about was that he should call Eddie Cantor and apologize for the trouble. I said, "Apologize for what? You only did what Eddie Cantor asked you to do, and he's the one who wiped your brow."

Sammy said, "Just get him on the phone!"

When Sammy began to apologize, Mr. Cantor stopped him cold and asked Sammy to come right over to his house so he could speak to him in person.

The maid answered the door and led Sammy and me into Mr. Cantor's den where he was waiting for us. There is no way for me to explain what it was like to walk into the house of a living entertainment legend and sit with him in his den sharing conversation. He was a kind man who was comfortable with his place in life, a man who had seen and done it all. He offered us refreshments, and we sat down to talk.

Sammy couldn't wait to make his apology for putting Mr. Cantor in such a spot. But when he started to speak, Mr. Cantor said, "Sammy, stop right there. You have nothing to feel sorry about. I wanted you on my show so the television viewing public could see just who Sammy Davis Jr. is and how much talent you have; and you showed them even better than I thought you would! You are quite a talented young man and will go a long way; you have so much to give. You cannot and should not be stopped by anyone. In fact, I want you on my show again next week.

"Sammy, you must realize that, as a Jew, I know the feelings you have and can understand how upset you are. No one is taking my show away from me. I told Colgate-Palmolive to either take me, my show and the guest stars I choose or I'm gone. I also told them that only some people from the South were offended by what I did; and if they didn't like it, they could go and buy another brand of toothpaste. We got hundreds and hundreds of other phone calls and telegrams from around the rest of the country that were positive. So don't you worry any more about it.

"Let me tell you a story of something that happened to me back in my vaudeville days, when I was just one of the opening acts in the Ziegfeld Follies. You probably know there was a great Black singer, comedian and dancer named Bert Williams who was the first Black person to star in the Follies. One night between shows, we went up the street from the theater to a little bar. We were the only customers in the place and sat at the bar. Bert and I both ordered a whiskey. As the bartender set my drink down in front of me, he said, 'That will be fifty cents.'

"As he set Bert's drink down he said, 'That'll be a hundred dollars.'

Bert Williams, only Black Ziegfield Follies headliner

"Without batting an eye, Bert pulled out his wallet, laid down four one hundred dollar bills and said, 'I'll take three more.'

"The bartender was dumbfounded. I called the bartender aside and told him that Bert Williams was the star of the Ziegfeld Follies just down the street. Embarrassed, he walked back to Bert and apologized, saying he didn't mean it.

"Bert said, 'That's okay—just remember my face the next time I come in here.'

"We downed our drinks and started walking back to the theater, not saying anything to each other. I looked over at Bert and saw a tear rolling down his cheek. I asked him why he was crying. 'The hardest thing of all,' he said, 'is that I can still hear the cheers and applause in my ears.'

"We just walked on, not speaking, but I never forgot those words. Sammy, don't you ever forget them either. Always remember the cheers and applause. The people with hearts will take you for what you are, not what color your skin is or what your religion is. As long as there is prejudice, you will just have to keep knocking the doors down or blowing on the houses until they cave in, which someday, God willing, they will."

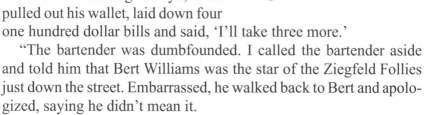

Then Mr. Cantor said, "Sammy, the other day at rehearsal you asked me what I was wearing around my neck and I told you it was a Mezuzah. I want to explain to you what it is and what it means; it is a very holy Hebrew charm. The Hebrew people attach them to, or around, the front door of their homes. We also wear them around our necks for good luck, good health and happiness. Inside is a small piece of parchment paper with several verses from Deuteronomy—a prayer for the protection of the home. When you wear it around your neck, it's supposed to protect you and bring good luck."

Sammy asked, "Do you have to be Jewish to wear one?"

"No, Sammy. I don't think God minds too much which floor you shop on as long as you go to His store."

With that, Mr. Cantor took his Mezuzah from around his neck and handed it to Sammy saying, "I want to give this to you. Wear it in good health, and may it always bring you happiness and inner peace of mind, as it has done for me."

Sammy asked Mr. Cantor if there was some kind of prayer he should say. "No," he answered. "Any prayer that comes from your heart is the right kind of prayer. It is our belief that every person should have the freedom to talk to God in his own way."

"Mr. Cantor, I promise you that I will wear it with pride and never ever take it off."

We continued chatting with Mr. Cantor and left a short time later. Sammy never said a word all the way home, but I knew inside he was at peace with himself.

Sammy relaxing, as usual, in his boxers, Eddie Cantor's Mezuzah visible at his throat

Jeff Chandler and I, long time friends

Morty Stevens, talented musician, arranger and Sammy's conductor

Below, left to right: Sammy's publicist, Jess Rand, Sammy, Jess's fiance, Bonnie, Jeff Chandler, me

Frank Sinatra called Sammy "a great, and good friend"

"We Three" filming (above), and (below) the cast with
Sam Sr., Sammy and Will Mastin (front and center)

Movies and the Copa

It wasn't long before 8850 Evanview Drive became one of the most popular addresses in Hollywood. The house had a built-in projector with a screen for showing movies, so naturally our **next** favorite pastime became watching movies every night. To say that Sammy's house became the "in" place to be every night is putting it mildly. Just about every young and rising star would show up, along with many of the biggest names and celebrities in Tinsel Town.

And guess who had to run the projector every night? Yours truly, of course; and after a while this became a real pain in the ass. Rest assured that right along with teaching Sammy to drive, teaching him to run a 16mm projector was right at the top of my list of my least favorite things to do.

What was fun, however, was hanging out with the major stars and celebrities of that time. People like Barbara Luna, Jeff Chandler, Tony Curtis and Janet Leigh, Harry Belafonte, Rod Steiger, Peter Brown, Steve McQueen and his then wife, Neile Adams, just to name a few. Many of these people became lifetime friends of Sammy's.

One memorable day Steve McQueen took me out in his brand new racing Ferrari up to the top of Mulholland Drive, which is a very curvy, bumpy road running along the top of the Hollywood Hills for miles. Steve decided to show me how fast he could drive that Ferrari on Mulholland Drive and successfully scared ten years off my life. It goes without saying that I never got in that Ferrari with him again.

Sammy's passion for the movies went far beyond just watching them. He loved all of them, but his favorites were horror, science fiction, detective stories and Westerns. He was a movie buff and could tell you the most detailed trivia information—for example, who played Charlie Chan's number six son, or who played the butler in any movie ever made. Sammy had a photographic memory for who played any part, large or small, in any given movie; and later this became a favorite game with our Hollywood circle of friends. Whenever a group of celebrities got together they would try to see who could best or outdo the other in naming the actors who had played small and bit parts in the movies.

Universal Studios had been known for making most of the big American horror films and their sequels, like *Frankenstein*, *The Mummy*, *The Wolfman* and *Dracula*. Sammy's affection for horror movies would play a bigger role in our lives in later years to come.

Another favorite pastime at Sammy's house on Evanview Drive became the Sunday brunches that he would throw. Hollywood wanna-be cowboys would come over to see who could outdraw the other. Now, there were some pretty fast quick draw guys in Hollywood, but Sammy and I could hold our own with the best of them; and in most cases, they would be trying to play catch up with us. We were both fast, and once I even won a fast draw contest in Las Vegas.

Not everything was fun, however. One night when Sammy's step-mother, Peewee, and Sam Sr. were living in Sammy's house they had a quarrel. Life in general wasn't treating Sammy very well just then —career, family difficulties and other personal problems got him down. Sammy drove up the road in his Thunderbird to a point above Sunset Strip where the hills are very steep. At the time there weren't all the houses there are now, and the drop-off was very sharp. Sammy decided to drive off the cliff. But the mound of dirt forming a shoulder at the side of the road was too high, and just the front wheels went over. The frame of the car hung up on the hump, and he couldn't go forward or back.

Sammy suddenly realized the enormity of what he had almost done and got scared. He got out of the car, went to a house and called me. I drove as fast as I could from my house in the San Fernando Valley up to the point above the Strip where the car was hung up. We managed to free the car and get him home safely. It was an intentional suicide attempt; but only because the pressures of life had come down on him, as happens to all of us, and he hadn't been equipped to deal with it just then. When he realized what he had nearly done, he called me to come and help him.

At least things on the career front were about to change, dramatically. My father got a call from Jules Podell, owner of the Copacabana Night Club in New York, with an offer for the Trio to play his club.

The money was good, but not the best, and especially not what Will thought it should be.

However, Sammy just flipped out, he was so excited. He asked my dad if Frank Sinatra had something to do with the offer. Dad explained that Copa owner Jules Podell had been told by Frank Sinatra that he just had to put Sammy and the Trio in his club. My father offered Jules that if the Trio did not go over well they would play a week at the Copa for nothing.

Sammy could not contain himself. He explained to Will that Frank Sinatra had always said he'd get Sammy an engagement at the Copa, since he knew that playing there was one of Sammy's biggest dreams.

Frank was a big star then; and although Sammy was not unknown, he wasn't Frank Sinatra. One day in New York, Sammy had gone to the Paramount Theater to see Frank, and they had an instant rapport. All through the years, even in Sammy's major career, Frank was responsible for Sammy getting into important club dates, and certainly the Copacabana. Frank would just make a phone call, saying, "Well, if you want Frank Sinatra, you'd better get Sammy Davis or you're not getting Sinatra." Then my father's office would get a call from a club asking for Sammy and the Trio.

Sammy was so excited about playing the Copa he told Will he didn't care if they didn't get paid at all; he was going to play the engagement anyway. He turned to me and said, "Man, can you believe it? We've spent so much time outside that place looking at it, wanting to play there, and how many times have you told me, 'Someday, Sam; someday.' Now, here we go!"

To say that Sammy and the Trio took the place by storm would be an understatement. Everybody who was anybody in New York came to see the show, the new sensation; the place was packed every night. Frank Sinatra came too, and that made it all the more special. Frank had given his word to Sammy; and, as always, he kept it. Sammy was on top of the world. The Copacabana became the place in New York to see Sammy Davis Jr. for many years to come.

Sammy's friends from the Uptown and Apollo Theaters came to see the show in droves, including Joe Williams, Dinah Washington, Ella Fitzgerald, Lionel Hampton, Billy Eckstine, Billy Daniels, Lena Horne and Louis Armstrong. The great jazz musicians of the time came to see Sammy at the Copa, as did many of our friends, both Black and White.

And can you imagine the girls? They were there—from the famous Copa Girls to high-class call girls and plenty of wealthy ladies. Talk about hog heaven! This was a big change from the Copa's usual crowd; the floodgates had opened, and once again, Sammy was the reason.

Early in 1954, while we were at the Copa, my dad had been in contact with the television networks, trying to get the Trio a television special. A producer at ABC had an idea for a sitcom star-

"We Three" production meeting I'm far right, next to Sammy

ring Sam, Will and Sam Sr. and a young lady named Frances Taylor who was very attractive and quite a dancer. The show was to be called *"We Three."* ABC went way out on a limb on this one; no one had ever thought of doing a television sitcom starring Colored people before. They made me assistant to the producer, and I took to it like butter on popcorn. What a challenge that was!

Sam and I, his conductor Morty Stevens, and Hal Belfor (one of the best choreographers around) worked like crazy to make the pilot come off. It turned out extremely well and we thought we were on our way to new careers in television, but that was not to be. This country, in 1954, was not ready for a sitcom starring Colored folks, no matter how hard ABC tried to make it a reality.

"We Three" production—
Frances Taylor (left) and above with Sammy

I consult with Dad—"We Three"

I give ABC the credit for being the first network to try, although it didn't work at the time. Take a look at television today and the numbers of Black performers in shows about and including Blacks.

Nineteen fifty-four was not the best year for any of us. Shortly after returning from the Copacabana triumph in New York, my father unexpectedly passed away. He was the best of dads, and I took his death very hard. He was more than a father to me; he was my pal. I was an only child; and from the time I was eight or nine years old, my dad took me everywhere with him. I caught the last part of the vaudeville era and had the unique opportunity to meet many of the old time great burlesque performers. I grew up running around dressing rooms and backstage.

Frances Taylor, talented singer-dancer co-stared with Sammy in "We Three" for ABC

I guess one could say I grew up just outside that proverbial old trunk everyone in the entertainment business talks about.

Some strange and difficult times followed for me. The day of my dad's funeral, someone broke into his office (the only time ever) and tried to get into his safe where he kept all his contracts. My father had just signed a new contract with Sammy and the Will Mastin Trio. We always thought whoever broke in was after that contract, but they were unable to find it.

To illustrate the integrity of Sammy, Will and Sam Sr., at my father's funeral they took my mom aside; and Will said, "Mrs. Silber, don't you worry. As long as you are alive, you will never lack for money. You will always have a percentage of this act."

My mother lived to be eighty-five years old, and until the day she died she received a percentage of Sammy and the Trio's earnings, although nothing was ever on paper. That allowed her to live in relative comfort and security. The Trio never forgot. These days I'm afraid that kind of loyalty just doesn't exist.

I had to take a leave of absence for a while from Sammy and the Trio to close up my dad's office. He was a very prominent, busy personal manager and talent agent with many clients, and there was much to do after he passed away.

You wouldn't believe the number of vultures that came to feed on Sammy and the Trio after my dad died. Managers, accountants, lawyers and shysters of all kinds came to get a piece of them. Dad had always taken care of everything for the Trio and protected Sammy, Will and Sam Sr. from unscrupulous professionals who might try to steal from them after he died. Dad had accountants who kept the Trio's money in the right places, paid all the taxes on time, and more important, kept a check on Sammy's spending. Dad didn't have control over Sammy's money; but he did have Sammy's ear, and Sammy respected his advice.

After things settled down a bit, Sammy bought Mama a big Chrysler Imperial so she could get around town; but Mama didn't drive, so Sammy hired Rudy Duff to take care of her and to also care for Sammy's house. The people with whom Sammy surrounded himself in the early years of his entertainment career were wonderful, honest, trustworthy people like Rudy, who was as nice as he could be, and others like Murphy Bennett, Charlie Head, Jess Rand, David

Landfield, Nathan Crawford, Jim Waters and Big John Hopkins, who were more like family than employees.

Professionally, the first people to join Sammy were Morty Stevens, his conductor, then Jess Rand, who took care of press relations. Then there was Charlie Head, who was Sammy's valet. When he left, Sammy called upon his favorite waiter, Murphy Bennett, who always used to attend us when we ate at the Garden of Allah in Hollywood. Murphy was probably one of the finest human beings I've ever known—sweetest, kindest and he did everything that needed to be done for Sammy.

Big John Hopkins was just that—huge, about six-foot-six and three hundred and seventy pounds, an immense man. He was Sammy's bodyguard for quite some time. He had three sons who look exactly like their father, and I still correspond with Lorraine, his wife.

David Landfield was a young man who hung around all the time, so Sammy hired him as a kind of go-fer. Sammy hired a lot of people he didn't really need from time to time because they were friends and he wanted to help them out. He'd give them a title and a job. I hate the term "go-fer," but David did what had to be done, running here and there as needed. He went on to work for Jerry Lewis a while later, then became an actor himself.

Nathan Crawford was really Will Mastin's driver and valet and did everything else that had to be handled for Will. A funny thing about Nathan—he was dark skinned and looked enough like Will to pass for him. It was an inside gag among us that sometimes Nathan would go outside after a show and sign Will's autographs.

After Sammy and I formed a production company, Jim Waters and Jean Fleming came into the picture. Jean was our secretary, and Sammy hired Jim, an actor and a friend, to run the office. He took care of all the bills that came in and saw that they were paid if they were personal, or sent on to the bookkeepers if they concerned company business. He would answer Sammy's phone line while Jean answered the main line. If it was something concerning Sammy directly or if someone wanted an interview without going through the press agent, Jim would handle it.

Some people only stayed a short while, and others were with Sammy for a long time. But within a period of two to three years, all these people became the nucleus of Sammy's "family."

David Landfield, me
and Sammy, Burbank,
California Airport

Sam Sr. with Sam's
bodyguard,
Big John Hopkins

Sam's valet,
Murphy Bennett

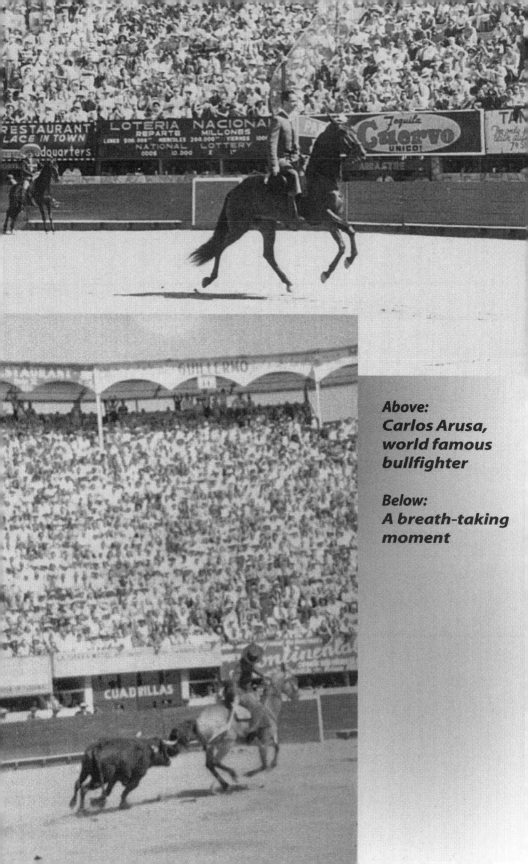

Above:
Carlos Arusa,
world famous
bullfighter

Below:
A breath-taking
moment

OLÉ! OLÉ!

It was summer in Los Angeles and we were closing the show that weekend. One night after the performance I stuck my head out to get an idea of how many people I'd be bringing backstage to visit. I saw a crowd of celebrities gathering around one particular table. Back in the dressing room I said, "Guys, I don't know what's going on out front, but there seems to be some kind of a celebrity out there being mobbed by the other celebrities."

Sammy used to do a tap dancing routine using a black and red cape and dancing in the style of Jose Greco, at that time the world's greatest flamenco dancer. In the dance, Sammy was the bullfighter. He looked every bit the part, thin and muscular, wearing tight pants and the flowing cape,

Two of the greatest bullfighters of the day were Manolete from Spain and Carlos Arusa from Portugal. Manolete fought the bulls in the traditional manner, but Carlos Arusa did most of his bullfighting on horseback. It was very much the "Hollywood society thing" for major celebrities to go down to Tijuana, Mexico on Sundays to watch the bullfights. Bullfighters the caliber of Manolete and Carlos Arusa almost never came to Tijuana to fight the bulls because they felt Tijuana was beneath them. As luck would have it, Carlos Arusa would be fighting on the following Sunday after our closing. To the Mexicans, this amounted to the Queen of England coming to tea at your house. This event was huge!

The crowd in the club was greeting Carlos Arusa, who wanted to come backstage and meet Sammy. He had been very impressed with the show, especially Sammy's flamenco dancing. When I told Sammy that Arusa wanted to meet him, he was delighted. "God!" he said. "Of course I want to meet him! Can you imagine standing out in the middle of a bull ring with thousands of people yelling at you to fight the bull to his death, or yours? My God! Talk about a rush!"

"No, man, I can't," I answered, "and I don't plan on finding out how big the rush is either."

I went out and invited Arusa backstage. He looked just as you'd expect one of the world's greatest matadors to look. Clark Gable or Errol Flynn would be hard pressed to match Arusa's good looks; and of course, he had the attitude as well. We had a nice visit, and Sammy was impressed. Arusa invited Sammy to come to the bullfights on Sunday as his guest and to bring five friends. Of course, Sammy jumped at the invitation and said to me, "Silber, make all the plans and see if there is anything special we need to do. Find out who wants to go besides you."

Our dear friend, David Landfield, was there and said he wanted to go, which left three more invitations; but nobody else spoke up. When we got back to the house where everyone else was waiting, Sammy threw out the invitation. Right away, two of our favorite girls jumped up and said they'd love to go. Sammy said, "Just work out the details with Arthur."

Both the women had been to bullfights several times before, so I arranged for Sammy, Dave and me to take a limo to the Mexican border, walk across and take a cab to the bull ring. The two girls, Kathryn and Robin, were to drive across the border in Kathryn's Thunderbird, as they knew where to go and what to do. They followed the limo down to the border where there was a special place for the limos to park on the United States side. Sammy told me to go with the girls and take his briefcase with me. Sammy wore a very tight, light gray mohair suit; and his pants had no pockets; the jacket had only one pocket, and that was where he carried his money. The rest of Sammy's personal items were in the briefcase, which I placed in the trunk of the T-bird.

Sammy said, "Wait a minute; I need to get something out of the case." I popped the trunk; he got what he needed, and off we went.

I hopped into the T-bird with the girls, and Sammy and Dave went off in a cab. We arranged to meet at the gate where we were to pick up our tickets. I wore a sport shirt and Levis, and Dave had on a sport jacket and slacks, while the girls were both dressed in short shorts and halter tops, which showed off their attributes to the fullest. They were beautiful girls, Kathryn with long blonde hair and Robin with dark shoulder-length hair.

At the arena, the electricity in the air was so thick you could cut it with a knife. The noise from the crowd was deafening. I turned to Sammy and did my best to be heard. "Man, do you believe this crowd and the noise? I can barely hear myself think."

"Yeah, man," Sammy answered. "It's unbelievable!"

Then a gate opened, and the parade began. Everyone involved in the bullfight entered the arena marching in all their regalia. They were quite a sight to behold. I asked Kathryn to explain everything that would happen.

She said, "It's like you have seen in so many Hollywood movies, except there is a lot more blood. I hope you're not squeamish. First, the bull charges out of the tunnel and through the gate into the arena. He becomes mad as hell," Kathryn went on to tell us, "because he gets wounded first by the *picadors* on horseback with lances and then by the *banderilleros*. These brave men on foot thrust *banderillas* into the bull. These are sticks about two-and-one-half feet long with a very sharp steel pointed barb on the end. It is used to make the bull mad when it is plunged into him, and I am sure it also hurts like hell. This is very dangerous, as the bull is charging at each of them while they are running straight at him. At the last minute, the man plunges the *banderilla* into the bull's shoulder and steps to the side, hoping the bull doesn't get him first. The *banderilleros* work their capes in front of the bull so the matador can see which way the bull is hooking his horns and will know how best to work the bull. They come so close to the bull it is absolutely fascinating. Sometimes they get too close and are gored or even killed. [Fortunately nothing like that happened on this day.]

"After the bull has been killed there is a panel of judges who rate the matador on his performance. If they do not feel the matador did well, there is no prize. If the judges feel the matador performed well there are three possible prizes: one ear, two ears, or both ears and the tail, which is the highest honor. When rewarded, the matador walks around the ring sharing his prize with the people, then has the option to present his prize to a special person."

When Carlos Arusa entered the ring, the crowd went crazy! It was as if God had walked in. All you could hear was *"Olé! Olé!"* and cheering. Then the gate was flung open, and the bull charged into the arena; he was upset and looking for something to attack.

One of the most dangerous things for a bullfighter to do is get on his knees in front of the gate to the tunnel from which the fresh bulls run into the ring at full speed. Arusa had gotten on his knees and faced the half-ton of dynamite coming right at him. He gave a twirl of his cape, and the crowd went crazy. Arusa stepped back and watched the picadors work their capes. He was not dressed like the other matadors, but wore a pair of tight gray pants, a bolero-type jacket and a flat cowboy hat with a string under his chin.

After the *banderilleros* finished working the bull with their capes, Arusa removed a beautiful shawl called a *rebozo* from the wall that surrounds the bull ring. He walked over to Sammy and draped the *rebozo* over the front of our box. This meant that on this day his kill would be dedicated to Sammy. The girls knew what this was all about; and when they explained it to us, Sammy could not believe it. This was truly a great honor.

At this point, Arusa's horse was brought out, and the crowd exploded. He mounted this magnificent animal and directed him to run right at the bull where he placed his own *banderillas* into the bull's shoulders. He made these difficult moves controlling the horse with only his body and his knees, and without touching the reins. The sight was unbelievable. I have never seen anything like it in my life, and never expect to again. It was just Arusa and his horse against a bull that would love to kill them both. Training a horse to charge the bull takes months of hard work. As each pass was made thousands of people yelled, "*Olé! Olé!*" God! What a sight to see!

When Arusa had set his *banderillas* into the bull, he dismounted and began to fight the bull in the traditional manner. The second most dangerous thing a bullfighter can do is to work the bull while walking around the bull ring on a ledge that is one foot high and one foot wide and runs inside the entire ring. When the bull charges the matador while he's walking on this ledge, the matador has no place to go as his back is against the wall of the bull ring. He must work the cape so the bull will miss with his horns. Arusa worked himself halfway around the huge ring, and it was "*Olé! Olé!*" the whole time so it almost sounded like one huge roar.

The end finally came to the bull with one quick thrust of Arusa's sword. The bull dropped to the ground like his feet had been cut from beneath him. A perfect kill!

Everyone went crazy, including us. Then the arena became silent as everyone awaited the judges' decision. The award: both ears and the tail.

Arusa walked around the ring holding up the two ears and the hairy end of the tail for all to see and share his win. Then he came over to our box and gave the tail to Sammy. Arusa bowed to Sammy and shook his hand. Then he strutted from the arena almost deafened by the cheers of the ecstatic crowd. If you are a bit squeamish about what these men do, the killing of the bull—the *Duel in the Sun* battle between man and beast—you might have second thoughts about attending a bullfight. Just keep in mind that the bull could have just as easily killed the matador or any of the other men in the ring.

We left the arena all hyped up. Sammy told me to ride again with the girls. He and Dave would take a cab back to the border and walk across to where the limos were parked, and we'd all meet. I jumped into the T-bird convertible with these two gorgeous babes and drove across the border, then sat there for a while waiting for Sammy and Dave to show up, but they never did.

After about twenty minutes I was starting to get concerned, so I walked back to the border on the U.S. side and looked around the station, but did not see them. I approached the desk and asked one of the U.S. Border Guards if anyone had seen Sammy or Dave come through the gate.

The guard said, "Who?"

"Sammy Davis Jr. and a friend." The guard just looked at me. He had no clue who I was talking about. I tried again, "A little Black man dressed in a gray suit and a White guy in blue slacks and a dark blue sport coat."

He jumped up and yelled at me, "Are you the guy in the white Thunderbird with two women?"

"Yes," I said. "Is there some kind of a problem?"

He got up in my face and told me to go over and sit on one end of a long metal bench. It was where they put the luggage when they were inspecting it. "Now, just sit there," he ordered, "and don't open your mouth!"

"But, sir," I asked, "what's happened?"

"Just sit down and shut up!" he repeated.

I couldn't do anything except what I was ordered to do; but I was really getting scared; and no one had answered any of my questions. About three or four minutes later, a door across from me opened, and out came Sammy and Dave led by two Border Guards with a third one carrying Sammy's gun. I looked at Sammy, and he looked straight back at me, shrugging his shoulders as if to say, "I don't know what's going on, but do something."

Evidently, when Sammy had gone back to the car to get something before the bullfights, unbeknownst to me, he had removed his gun from the briefcase and tucked it into the back of his pants. Tired of sitting on the gun all day, he had later taken it out and given it to Dave to carry in his jacket pocket.

The guards walked Sammy and Dave into another room with a window I could see through. The guard I had been talking to yelled at me, "Where is the car with the two women?"

"It's just up the street," I answered, "where they park the limos. Please, sir, will you tell me what's going on here?"

"Your friends are in lots of trouble."

"Trouble? What trouble?"

"You just sit there and be quiet."

Then he told a couple of other guards to go pick up the car and the women and bring them back there. About five minutes later the girls came in, and they were also told to sit on the bench where I was, but on the other end. They were also told to keep quiet.

The girls were terrified and looked at me for some kind of explanation. All I could do was shrug my shoulders. Robin suddenly remembered she had two Benzedrine pills in her purse, and she was scared one of the guards would search her purse and find them. She managed to get them out of her purse without anyone noticing and put them in her mouth. No one was the wiser.

One of the guards yelled to the man who had the T-bird keys to go open the trunk and bring in the briefcase, if there was one. When he got the briefcase, he handed it to someone who appeared to be the head honcho. Then one of the guards asked if the San Diego Sheriff's patrol car and paddy wagon had arrived yet. Another replied they would be here in about five minutes.

The guards came out of the office with Sammy and Dave and made them sit in two chairs. Each of them was then handcuffed to the chair by one wrist.

When Sammy sat down, I said, "What in the hell is going on?"

He started to speak, but the same guard who had been on my case looked straight at me and said, "You open your mouth one more time, and I'll lock you up!"

"Lock me up for what?" I asked. "I ain't done a damn thing but sit my ass on this bench!"

"I'll think of something!" he answered.

I got mad, but there was nothing I could do. About that time, the Sheriff's car arrived and a Sergeant stepped out, then walked into the room. He took one look at Sammy and said, "Hey, Sam, what in the hell is going on here?"

With that, Sammy yelled, "Thank God! Someone who knows who I am!"

The head Border Guard said, "You know this guy?"

"Christ, yes. That's Sammy Davis Jr.!"

"Who?"

"Sammy Davis Jr.," said the Sergeant. "What's wrong with you guys down here? Don't you watch TV or go to the movies? That's Sammy Davis Jr., one of the biggest stars in show business!"

I glanced at Sammy and saw him heave a great sigh of relief. A guard opened the briefcase and found Sammy's wallet and all his papers, an honorary L.A. police badge and a gun permit. He made a quick call to someone and told the head guard, "The badge is real, and so is the gun permit; they're legit."

"Okay, okay, but get the matron to search the girls."

Kathryn went in first; but she had on almost nothing, not a hard search at all. Then it was Robin's turn. Suddenly from behind the closed door of the room, the matron screamed at the top of her lungs and ran out of the room. When Carlos Arusa presented Sammy with the bull's tail, Sammy had handed it to Robin to put in her purse as he had nowhere to put it himself. Robin wrapped the still bloody tail in a tissue, and everyone had forgotten it was there. When the matron was searching Robin's purse, she said, "What's that?"

"A tail," answered Robin.

Thinking it was a pony tail hairpiece, as it was the same color as Robin's hair, the matron took it from the purse then screamed when she saw the bloody end. Sammy explained to everyone's satisfaction. It seemed all this had begun as Sammy, small and Black, started to go by the U.S. inspector at the gate and was asked to empty his pockets. He only had one breast pocket in his jacket where he had placed all his cash, about five hundred bucks. The Border Guard said, "Where did you get all this money?"

"I earned it," replied Sammy.

"That's a lot of money," said the guard.

"I earn a lot of money!"

Accompanying Sammy was a well-dressed White man with a gun in his pocket. Right away the guy had to think, "Drug people!"

Sammy asked him, "Don't you know who I am?"

"No, sir, I don't, but both of you are being held until we work this out."

Now we thought it was finally over, as the U.S. Border Guards had let us all go, so I asked Sammy if he wanted me to go back with him and Dave in the limo or go with the girls. I turned around to get his answer and saw him and Dave being put into the paddy wagon. The iron doors clanged shut, and they were locked in. I turned to the Sheriff's Sergeant and asked, "Now what's going on?"

He replied that the Sheriff in San Diego just wanted to talk to Sammy and not to worry because the worst was already over. "Nothing is going to happen to anyone," he said. "About two blocks from the station Sammy and his friend will get out of the paddy wagon, get into my cruiser, and we'll go in the back door of the station. You see, the Press is all around the front entrance to the station house. They've heard that Sammy's been arrested, and they are waiting for him."

We went in to see the Sheriff and he was very nice, but warned us that if Sammy's gun had been discovered on the Mexican side of the border, Sammy and Dave would have been put in jail and God knows what would have happened to them. That's the one thing the Sheriff was most concerned about since it's against Mexican law and a U.S. Federal crime to carry a gun across an international border. "No matter how legal your permits and badge are in the U.S., it would not have carried any weight in Mexico," he cautioned.

We had a short chat, and he bid us good-bye. The Sheriff's deputies took Sammy and Dave to the limo, which was parked several blocks away, and I went on with the girls. *Olé! Olé!*

Sword in hand, Carlos Arusa prepares for his final approach to the bull—his beautiful horse is very well-trained, and courageous

Above:
Virginia & Charles Conlin, friends of my parents, with Sammy and my mother

GOLDEN NUGGET GAMBLING HALL

Taking on Vegas

In 1954 the Trio went back to Las Vegas to finish out their contract at the Frontier Hotel, and that meant back to the same old rules: "Stay in your place and toe the white line."

Sammy, however, had made up his mind that the days of "toeing the White line" were over for him. The Trio had kept their promise to me, and I had a room at the Frontier during the engagement. Sammy just loved to bounce in and out of my room at all hours. One night he said, "Let's go out to dinner."

"Okay by me," I answered.

Sam declared, "We're going to walk straight through the casino."

"Oh, sure," I chided, "and what's that going to prove?"

"It's going to prove that I'm as good and equal as the next guy. After all, half the people in the casino are here because they came to see my show. Well, here I am; they're going to see me tonight."

I didn't disagree with him; however, I did point out that he should expect the hotel/casino management to go crazy and jump all over him. He made me promise I would not tell anyone, especially Will or Sam Sr. He just wanted to see what would happen.

Off we went to the lobby and gaming floor of the Frontier Hotel casino—big as life. So, what do you think happened? Not one damn thing! People asked him to sign autographs or wanted to shake his hand. It was great, and he was eating it up. Oh yeah, we got the evil eye from the pit bosses, dealers and security, but no one **did** anything; and the customers loved seeing Sammy in person.

After dinner, we went to the dressing room backstage by way of the hotel lobby and still no one said a word; but Will and Sam Sr. were fit to be tied, especially Will. He jumped all over Sammy and all over me, too, but it was Sammy who caught the brunt of Will's wrath. I had never seen Will that mad. His words sounded like they were coming from someone I didn't know.

"Listen, you little Nigger boy," he spat at Sammy, "who in the hell do you think you are? You ain't supposed to be out there mixing it up with all those White folks! You know they don't like it! The head of entertainment was back here yelling at me and Sam!"

Then he turned to me. "How could you let Sammy walk out there with all the big gamblers? Arthur, you know better! You should have stopped him!"

"But Will," I said, "you should have been there. Sammy didn't drive anybody out. Quite the opposite—they couldn't get enough of him."

"I don't care what you all say," Will yelled. "It ain't gonna happen ever again!"

Sammy had been sitting there taking it all in, but then he had enough. He jumped up and began screaming back. "Don't you ever call me 'Nigger' again, Massey! My skin may be black but it's my talent that brings the people in here! I've earned the right to go anywhere in this place I want, and if this hotel don't like it, fuck 'em! I can go back to New York, Chicago, Hollywood and many other places now where I can walk in like a man. Massey, if you and my dad want to sleep on the other side of town and kowtow to these people, then go on and keep being your Black self.

"I live in a big house in Hollywood and have many White friends who accept me for myself. I don't care if this act breaks up. No more coming in through the back door of the casino and staying out of sight until I walk out in front of fifteen-hundred people who have paid lots of money to see me, and who give me standing ovations when I finish my show. No more, Will; no more!"

Then Sammy turned to me and said, "Let's go to your room. I have to get the hell out of here!"

Back in my room, Sammy just sat there with tears streaming down his face. Over and over he sobbed, "No more; no more."

I reminded him that he had another show to do. His response was, "Like hell I do! Not till someone talks to me."

"Who?" I asked.

"Management," he replied.

"Well, what do you want me to do?" I asked.

"I don't know. I just don't know." Then with a jerk he said, "Get the Entertainment Director down here."

I was able to get the man on the phone, and told him Sammy wanted to speak to him. Boy, was he ready for that! He came back at me with, "Yeah, well I want to speak to him, too!"

I told him Sammy was in my room, and he said he'd be right there. When I opened the door three people marched in: the Entertainment Director and two people from Hotel and Casino Management. They spoke first. They did not yell, but spoke in firm voices, telling Sammy about hotel policy and why they thought what he had done was not in the best interests of the hotel. They said he knew the rules and that they would not encourage him to make another appearance in the casino or hotel lobby.

Sammy sat and listened to what they had to say without speaking a word. Then he stood up and said very quietly, "Gentlemen, I respectfully decline to do the next show or any other shows for that matter. I am sure that Will and my father will be happy to do their parts in the shows for you, but not me."

You could see the shock on their faces. No one had ever called their bluffs before. You just didn't do that in Las Vegas in the 1950s, or you might end up in a small hole out in the desert. After a long quiet minute one of the hotel managers stood up, stuck out his hand and said, "You've got a lot of guts, little man. Do what you feel is right and safe for you. Just don't overstep your bounds too much, or we'll have to step in and stop you. Walk through the hotel when you need to. Now just go out and do your shows and all will be well."

We all shook hands, and Sammy thanked them for taking the time to talk to him. "I understand what you said, and I will do my part," he assured them.

As they were going out the door, one of the hotel management staff turned directly to me and said, "See to it that he does what he's supposed to."

Sammy said, "Well, he would anyway, 'cause he's my shadow."

They left, and I said to Sammy, "What in the hell have you gotten me into now? We're talking to the Mob here, and this guy has put it to me to watch after you. That's a laugh! You get out of this, and I end up in the bottom of Lake Mead."

"Arthur, man, don't you realize what just happened here?"

"Yeah! You damn near got us both eliminated!"

"No, no!" he said, "We won the battle!"

"What do you mean, 'we'?" I asked. "All of a sudden you and me are 'we'?"

"Yeah! Right!" he agreed. "You and me are now 'we'!"

"I love the way you dragged me into this thing," I scowled. "Well, don't you think that 'we' should go and tell Massey and your father what just took place in my room?"

"Sure," said Sammy. "Let's go; and won't they be surprised?"

"Surprised would be putting it mildly," I replied. "I know they will really want to learn that they'd better not go too far—whatever that means—or they will simply disappear."

"No, man," exclaimed Sammy. "They'll dig it."

When we went into the dressing room it was cold; I mean you could cut the tension with a knife. Will was extremely upset because Sammy had never talked to him or Sam Sr. like that before. Sammy started to tell them that all was cool and right with the hotel, but Will turned to me and said, "Arthur, tell us what really happened."

I told Will and Sam Sr. what had taken place. Will looked at Sammy and said, "Mose," (the name he called Sammy when he was really serious) "do you really understand what you've done? You know what kind of people we're working for? Do you know what can happen to us just because you and Arthur went into the casino?"

"Yeah, Will," answered Sammy. "I damn sure do know. I made it so we can be treated as the people we are. After all, we're the ones bringing in the business; and if they don't understand that, then we won't work here any more, plain and simple!"

Will and Sam Sr. just looked at each other, knowing the ball was in Sammy's court and nothing they could say or do would stop Sammy. No more would be said on the subject.

A few days later, with his new-found power, Sammy decided to push it a little bit farther. He went into the casino again, bringing me with him just to play it safe. I think "to play it safe" might be a poor choice of words. Let's just say I was expected to go with him. We walked around the casino, and people kept coming up to Sammy just to see him, shake his hand and ask for his autograph.

We wound our way through the casino and passed a craps table where a few people were playing. One man asked Sammy to throw the dice for him for good luck, and Sam said, "Sure, why not?"

I reached out and grabbed his arm to stop him. "What's the matter?" he asked innocently.

"Sam, don't push your luck here."

"Push? Hell!" he said. "The customer's always right!"

He strolled over, picked up the dice, gave them a toss onto the craps table and rolled a seven. He had won for the customer, so he turned to me and said, "See? This is easy. I think I'll give it a try myself."

People began to gather around the table, and again Sammy was having the time of his life. He started throwing the dice non-stop. Before he was finished, he had lost five thousand dollars, a week's salary for the Trio.

Let's just say next that Will and Sam Sr. weren't too happy to hear about that. Although the Mob hadn't killed Sammy, Will and Sam Sr. were ready to do so.

Sammy stood in the dressing room crying like a baby and trying to explain to them what had happened; but no matter what he said, it just wouldn't come out right.

The only solution Sammy could come up with was a promise to pay them back the following week. Once he got to Hollywood, he was going to make good money by recording the title song for the new Tony Curtis movie entitled *Six Bridges to Cross*. Sammy had never recorded a title song before, but Tony had insisted he wanted Sammy to do it, and the studio had agreed. Will and Sam Sr. accepted Sammy's proposal.

The next day I returned to Hollywood to deal with some of my late father's business, and Sammy promised me he would not do a single controversial thing while I was gone. He promised he would just do his shows, then sit in his dressing room and play cards with his valet, Charlie Head.

Jess Rand, Tony Curtis and Sammy

The Cadillac Sammy was driving when he had the accident

David Landfield, me, Sam Sr. and Will Mastin in front of the Caddy

The Accident

It was a cold and crisp November morning right after Sammy's Las Vegas show. He and Charlie Head got in Sammy's new Cadillac and started out for Universal Studios in Los Angeles. Sammy was going to record the title song for Tony Curtis's new movie, *Six Bridges to Cross*. They decided Charlie would drive the first half of the trip so Sammy could catch some sleep.

Charlie had driven over half way, about 160 miles, when he started getting tired and pulled into a gas station at Victorville, California. After fueling the car, he woke Sammy to continue the drive. They were about 125 miles from Los Angeles, and the sun was up.

At that time, Interstate 10 ran from San Bernardino to Los Angeles, their destination. On the outskirts of San Bernardino there is a "Y" in the highway, where I-15 from Las Vegas meets with famous Route 66. Sammy was approaching the "Y" and saw a big Chrysler up in front of him that had taken a wrong turn at the "Y," staying on I-15. The lady driving the Chrysler had really wanted to go onto Route 66, so she decided to drive across the dirt median to get over to Route 66; but in order to do this, she had to back up, so she did.

She backed up directly across the road in the lane Sammy was committed to, thereby blocking him from missing her, and forcing him to pull into the oncoming traffic lanes. There were two cars coming right at him and no place for him to go, so he tried to get in between the car that was blocking him and the first oncoming car. Unfortunately, his Cadillac was too big to accomplish this; and he plowed into the rear end of the Chrysler, then careened off and between the two oncoming cars.

Many of the homes beside that area of the highway had stone walls instead of fences around them. There was a house with a stone wall next to the highway that had two large, rock columns, one on either side of the driveway. Each of the rock columns had been cemented together.

The Cadillac hit one of the cemented rock columns head on. This drove the engine of the car clear into, and then past the front seat. If Sammy hadn't been sitting off to the side, with his arm out the window, he would have been crushed by the engine.

That model Cadillac's steering wheel had a large bullet-shaped cone protruding from it. The doctors surmised Sammy's eye was injured by hitting the center part of the steering wheel. Cadillac discontinued that part of their steering design partially because of this accident. Sammy was thrown against the steering wheel with such force he also broke his nose and cracked his left kneecap on the emergency brake handle.

The back part of the front seat had a solid steel frame about six inches wide all the way around it. At the time of the crash, Charlie was asleep on the back seat. Upon impact, he was thrown forward. his face and mouth hit that steel frame. It broke his jaw and knocked out all his teeth.

Once the car stopped, Sammy climbed out and tried to reach into the back seat to pull Charlie out, but he was blind. His left eye was hanging down on his cheek. The force of the impact had blackened and shut his other eye.

On this day God was really watching over Sammy. There was a young serviceman standing just across the road in a gas station trying to hitch a ride back to his base. He saw the entire accident. He yelled to the station attendant to call an ambulance and ran to Sammy's car to see if he could help. When he got there, he found Sammy trying to push his eye back into his head, holding his hand over his left eye, screaming "I can't see! God help me! I can't see!"

The young serviceman tried to calm him down. At the same time he pulled Charlie from the car. The two oncoming cars stopped, and the occupants got out to help. They ran to the Chrysler that had caused the accident and found two older women lying on their backs in the rear seat with the front seat on top of them. The impact was so great the bumper jack that had been in their trunk was driven through the roof of their car. They were badly hurt, suffering broken legs, ribs and internal injuries.

Charlie was conscious, but soon his lower lip began to swell up so much that by the time the ambulance arrived, he was literally holding his lip with both hands. It looked like a gigantic growth on his face. People who came upon the scene did all they could to help them. It was one of those horrific accidents that you hear about but hope never to see.

The ambulances rushed everyone to San Bernardino Community Hospital, and Sammy and Charlie went into surgery immediately. God certainly had these people in the palm of His hands that day; no one died.

While Sammy and Charlie were in the hands of God on the operating tables, the rest of the world didn't know what had happened. I had returned home a day or two earlier to continue closing my father's business and planned to meet Sammy and Charlie at Universal Studios. I was going to drive back to Las Vegas with them after the recording session.

When I walked into my house, after picking up some laundry, the phone was ringing. It was my father's secretary, Amelia crying hysterically. She managed to ask me if I had heard the news on the radio. "What news?" I asked.

She said Sammy had been an auto accident, and was in San Bernardino Community Hospital. She said he was not expected to live. After the recent loss of my father, this was an extremely terrible blow. It was as if someone reached inside my chest and yanked out my heart. I thought I would throw up! I wanted to go there and be with my best friend, my brother. I wanted to die. I had all these feelings at one time.

I asked Amelia, "What happened? Where? How? When?"

All these feelings—all these questions—the only thing I knew is that I had to get there as fast as I could. I jumped into my custom, hopped-up car and took off for San Bernardino. It was as if I were driving some kind of a jet plane. My car just could not go fast enough for me, even though I was pushing the speed limit by about thirty to forty miles. I drove that eighty miles in under an hour, and to this day, can't figure out why no one stopped me. I guess that same God was looking after me as well, knowing that I just had to be with Sammy, to take care of him and see that no more harm would come to him. It was my job to look after him, and try to keep him out of harm's way; but I had not been with him on that drive—not been where I should have been.

I was the first one to arrive at the hospital, followed shortly thereafter by Will, Sam Sr., Mama, and Nathan. We stood there together in that empty hallway just staring at the "Staff Only" door, and looking at one another. We didn't say much—just waiting for someone to come and tell us something. We knew, only a short distance away Sammy and Charlie lay on operating tables with doctors feverishly working over them.

It was like a doctor movie. All of us were looking down that hall when a tall, thin figure of a man came from the operating room. He walked towards us, a surgical mask hanging from his neck. As he approached, he asked who was family. I answered, "We all are."

"I mean who is the next of kin?" he asked.

Sam Sr. spoke up and said, "Well, I guess that would be me. I'm Sammy's father; but we are all family."

"I understand. My name is Dr. Hull, and I am the surgeon who operated on Sammy. I must tell you that he is okay and he will live. However, we had to remove his left eye."

With that, Mama almost fell over, "Oh, my God, my poor baby!"

We all felt as if someone had hit us with a sledge hammer. We started to cry. Sam Sr. repeated what Dr. Hull had just said, "But you said he is okay and will live—that's right?"

"Yes, Mr. Davis. He will live. But it is still touch and go with his remaining eye. Let me explain. The damage to his left eye caused by the blow can affect nerves in the other eye. I feel the right eye will be fine. However, we won't know for sure for about three days. In addition, his nose is broken and his kneecap was cracked. We took care of these injuries with no problem.

"He is a very lucky person to have survived such a terrific blow to his face without permanent damage to his brain. It is miraculous that he lived, for that matter.

"His companion in the car has lost all his teeth and has a broken jaw. But, he too, will be fine given a little time to heal.

"I am so sorry to have to give you all this bad news. But the best part is that they are both in stable condition, and will recover."

Then the questions started: Are you sure he will be okay? Will he be able to dance? What can you do about the eye? Will he have to wear a patch for the rest of his life?

Dr. Hull put up his hand saying, "Wait! Wait. As I said, he will be okay. And, of course he can dance and do whatever else he did before. Yes, he will have to adjust to certain things, but he will adjust in time.

"As far as his eye is concerned, once it heals, we will give him a glass eye to replace the one he has lost. As a matter of fact, he was very fortunate—we were able to save the muscles that move the eye. They are now attached to a small ball, and when he moves his eyes, the ball moves with them. When we put in the glass eye, the eye socket, which is shaped like a cup, lies around the ball, and the glass eye moves with the other one. From time to time, we will have to replace the glass part as the eye heals and begins to settle; but soon that will all stop, and he will be as close to normal looking as he can be."

Dr. Hull then excused himself, stating he had to get a little rest— he had been on his feet for many hours. He assured us that he would talk to us again later, after Sammy had come out of the anesthesia and he had a chance to speak to him.

We all thanked the Doctor and turned to walk out of the hall where we had been standing for a few hours ourselves. I went outside and sat in my car, crying for my best friend and brother, as well as my father. But I must admit to thanking God that I had not been in that car.

Sam Sr. —a few minutes alone

Medallion back, and front (below left)

TO
ARTHUR
FROM
SAMMY JR.

The two young men, brothers by choice, and by destiny— Sam had two identical, custom pendants made, one for each of us— I still wear mine to this day

The Recovery

The next morning we had our first chance to visit with Sammy and Charlie at the hospital. What can you say when your best friend is lying in a hospital bed with bandages covering both eyes and most of his head, and his friend and valet is in the next room with his mouth wired shut? I walked into Sammy's room, sat down beside him and said, "How's it going, Sam?"

"Damn!" I thought to myself. "What a stupid thing to say!"

He answered, "I don't know, man. I'm really scared to Hell...and back!"

"Sam," I offered, "the doc says you're going to be all right."

"Yeah! All right—with no eyes, a fucked-up knee and a broken nose?"

"But, Sam, think of all the things that ain't broken." I was trying to make light of a very serious situation. Silently I chastised myself, "Damn! Another stupid remark."

I can't say I was at my best. I reached out, took his hand, and said, "God, Sam, I just don't know what to say."

"Hey, man, you don't have to say anything. Just be here when I need you."

"Sammy, I've always been there. Do you think this is going to change anything?"

I just sat there holding his hand and not saying much. The tears came real easy. Sammy seemed to sense my despair at that moment, so he jumped immediately to another place in our conversation.

"Well, first of all, how's Charlie doing?"

"About as well as you are."

"Is he gonna be all right?"

"Yeah, as soon as they give him a new set of teeth. It'll just take time."

"God, I'm sure glad to hear that, because I thought he'd be crippled for life. Hey, man, while on the subject of life—who do you think came in to see me late last night?"

"Who?"

"They told me that the hospital chaplain came in to speak to me, and guess what? He's a rabbi!"

"A rabbi chaplain in a San Bernardino hospital?"

"Yeah, and we had a long talk. Some of the things he said helped me; and for the first time in my life, a religion started to make sense to me."

"Oh, I see," I said. "So being Jewish is going to be your new thing?"

"Maybe, maybe. The rabbi said he would bring me something to read as soon as I get this damn patch off my eye."

"There you go—a Black, Jewish Sammy Davis Jr. Ain't you got enough problems?"

We both laughed, and that seemed to take the tension out of the air. He reached over with his other hand. While holding my hands with both of his, he asked, "How're you doin'?"

"I'm hurting a little," I said. "No, I'm hurting a lot. Not like you and Charlie. But it's kind of hard to sit here and look at you with all these tubes in you, and these bandages around your head and face, not being able to do one goddamn thing to help you. It really tears at my guts. I know lots of people will be upset by this accident, but they don't understand how you and I feel about each other. No one else understands our relationship and that we're like brothers to each other. Guns, fencing, golf; it's as if we're the same person, yet two guys who love and care for each other."

"I know," he answered. "Something no one else will ever understand is that we're family."

"Yeah, I guess. But speaking of family, they're all just outside this room; and I can tell you they're all worried about you. But like Mama said last night, 'My little Sammy is in God's hands, and God will take care of him.'"

"I know," he said. "She told me the same thing."

"Yes, but did you also know that Tony and Janet were here and placed a medallion in your hand that had Saint Christopher on one side and a Star of David on the other? You were holding it so tight that it had to be pried out of your hand.

"By the way, Eddie Cantor called and told me to let you know he will be here to see you."

"Eddie Cantor is coming all the way out here to see me?" he asked.

"That's what he told me; and I might add that Walter Winchell just wrote another one of his famous 'open letters' in his column, and read it on his radio show. It was to you! He said, 'This is your New York correspondent winding up another edition with a word of advice to a young Sammy Davis Jr., in a hospital somewhere in San Bernardino, California. If you can hear me—never forget that behind every dark cloud, a brilliant star is shining! Remember, no champ ever lost a fight by being knocked down, only by staying down!'"

"My God!" Sammy whispered. "Winchell?"

"Yes, Winchell. You've made the news all over the world, and it's starting to get real busy around this hospital. The world is beginning to find out what's happened to you. There are calls, telegrams, flowers, gifts; and all your friends want to visit. But for the first few days at least, Dr. Hull has limited the visitors you and Charlie see. He wants you both to get all the rest you possibly can until he is sure your remaining eye is going to be all right, and Charlie's mouth is on the mend."

In those first few days following the accident, many of Sammy's closest friends, Tony Curtis, Janet Leigh and Jeff Chandler, to name a few, visited him at the hospital. Many wonderful things happened, and Sammy's closest friends were really there for him. In fact, Jeff offered one of his corneas in the event that it was needed to save Sammy's sight in the other eye. Thank God that was not necessary,

Sammy with Walter Winchell, news columnist and radio commentator

but can you imagine a movie star of Jeff Chandler's magnitude even making an offer like that? Or anyone, for that matter?

Jeff stood in for Sammy at the Frontier Hotel and Casino in Las Vegas the night after the accident, even though he could not dance, play any instruments or do impressions. He could sing a little, though not very well. But there he was, on that stage at the Frontier, telling stories, singing a few songs and talking to the audience. Jeff Chandler was some good friend, the best you could ask for.

The next night Billy Eckstine played for the Trio; and later Betty Hutton, another big movie star, came out of retirement to stand in for Sammy. Soon the Frontier was able to arrange for another act to play out the rest of the Trio's contract.

Jess Rand, Sammy's publicist, had his hands full taking care of the Press. The King of Entertainment was down, and everyone wanted to help. I just about wore out my car going back and forth from North Hollywood to San Bernardino every day. But I felt I had to be there in case Sammy needed me for anything.

During this time, some of the most significant changes in Sammy's life took place. A few days after the accident while Sammy and I were talking, he began to panic. He grabbed my arm really hard and said, "What in the hell am I going to do now? What's going to happen to me?"

"What do you mean, 'What's going to happen to you?' You're going to get better, and keep right on doing what you've always done."

"No, man. I've been lying here thinking. I've only got one eye, and I don't know if I can dance any more. I might be out of balance."

"Sam, what in the hell are you talking about? Did someone come in and hit you along side your head last night?"

"No," he answered. "I really mean it! What's going to happen? The only thing I know how to do is dance, sing and do impressions."

"Okay," I took a deep breath. "You're having it bad right now, but do you really think all your fans are going to stop coming to see you? Do you think your feet and legs have forgotten how to dance just because you only have one eye now? I think not!

"Remember what Winchell said about not staying down just because you've been knocked down. Ain't nothin' changed. We're all here; no one is going anywhere. As a matter of fact, judging by all the mail, calls, telegrams and people trying to see you, this hospital ain't big enough to handle it all.

"And when Eddie Cantor comes in today, you'd better not talk like this. Feeling bad about your situation right now is understandable; but for God's sake, don't dwell on it."

"Yeah, I guess you're right, but it's really tough not to."

"Sure it's tough, but remember that the Sammy who has pushed his way through so many closed doors is not the Sammy who would stop fighting. That ain't Sammy Davis Jr., and you know it!"

"Okay, Silber. Enough already!"

I smiled. "I'm glad to hear it. Whenever you start to talk like that, I'm going to jump all over your ass!"

That afternoon, the nurse came in and told me Eddie Cantor was in the hospital lobby asking for me. I jumped up and said, "Sam, he's here. Now don't start any of that, 'I'm sorry for myself' shit."

"Silber, I thought you were going to get off my back."

"Yeah, you're right, Sam. I'm sorry."

I went to the hospital lobby to get Mr. Cantor, and as I approached him, he held out his hand and asked, "How are you, Art, and how is our little giant?"

"Mr. Cantor," I started to answer.

"Eddie," he said. "That's what my friends call me."

My God, here I was, standing with one of the greatest stars in the world, and he was telling me to call him Eddie! "Okay," I answered; "Our little giant is just down the hall, and he's so excited that you would come to see him."

"That's what friends do when a friend is in the hospital," he said.

I kept thinking how all my life my father told me, "The bigger the man the bigger the person." For the first time in my life, I understood what that meant.

I ushered Mr. Cantor into Sammy's room and said, "Eddie's here."

"What's this?" Sammy said. "Now you're on a first name basis with Mr. Cantor?"

Mr. Cantor reached for Sammy's hand and said, "And I'm Eddie to you as well."

At that point, I wanted to leave the room so they could have some time alone, but Mr. Cantor asked me to stay. He sat down to talk and started by making a few jokes. Then he said to Sammy, "I see you're still wearing the Mezuzah I gave you."

Sammy kind of jerked and said, "You know, the night of the accident I jumped in to take a quick shower after the show and placed the Mezuzah on the dresser. When I was about a half hour out of Las Vegas I realized I had forgotten to put it back on. Oh, my God! You don't think that if I had been wearing it…Oh, my God!"

"Sammy," said Mr. Cantor, "don't even think of that kind of thing. It will drive you nuts." Then he quickly changed the subject. It made me stop and wonder.

They continued to talk for a while longer. Then Mr. Cantor said he ought to leave and give Sammy a chance to rest.

"You know, Mr. Cantor, I mean Eddie, everyone in the hospital knows you're here. If you don't mind me imposing on you, could you stop in and say hello to my valet, Charlie, who's just down the hall? And could you maybe stick your head in and give a wave in some of the wards as well, before you go?"

"It's not an imposition at all; it's a privilege."

Again I thought of my recently deceased father and what he had told me so many times. This man was certainly that man my father had described, and indeed, much more.

Mr. Cantor got up to leave, cupped Sammy's cheeks in his hands and said something I will never forget. "Sam, you have a tough time ahead of you, but you have great inner strength. Never forget the talent God has blessed you with. Take care of it as it is a rare and precious gift. Protect it and use it well. It will carry you to wherever you want to go."

"Thank you Mr.…I mean Eddie, that means a lot to me coming from you; and I will always remember it."

I put out my hand to Mr. Cantor. "I want you to know, Eddie, you are one of the most wonderful people I have ever met. May I add my thanks to you for coming, and for what you said to Sammy? He really needed that today."

Mr. Cantor patted me on the cheek and left the room. Outside he grabbed a nurse by the hand and said, "Let's you and me go visiting this place."

Everyone able to drop in on Sammy at the hospital did so. Of course, that included Frank Sinatra. Sammy spoke with Frank about his fear of going back on the stage. Frank wasted no words and jumped on Sammy, just as I had done. He simply said, "When you get out of this place, you will come to my place in Palm Springs until you are well enough to go back to work."

"Go back to work where?" Sammy asked.

"Doesn't he know about the offer?" Frank asked me.

"I thought Mama told him," I answered.

"What the hell are you guys talking about?" Sammy asked.

"Sam," I said, "a couple of days after the accident an open offer was wired here for the Trio to open as the headline act at the Sands Hotel in Las Vegas for twenty-five thousand dollars a week, as soon as you're ready to go back to work. It was signed by Jack Entratter himself, the general manager and part owner. Why do you think we're all over you about you thinking you have no place to work?"

"Frank, is it really true?"

"Yeah, buddy; it sure is."

"My God, the Sands! Well, I guess I'll just have to get better real fast. But, when I am ready, I want to go back to where it really all began for us. I want to open at Ciro's first. Arthur, Chicky Baby (one of Sammy's nicknames for me), check into it for me. Then tell Massey and Dad, to see if it sounds good to them."

"It sounds just right to me, Sam. I know my dad just smiled down on you and nodded his head in approval."

Frank thought it was a great idea as well.

Just then the rabbi came in, as he had been doing a couple of times a day since the accident. Sammy could not get enough information about Judaism; and after the patch came off his good eye, he read everything he could on the subject. I could see and hear a subtle change coming over Sammy. He had been so close to death. That, and thinking about Eddie Cantor's Mezuzah had sunk deep into Sammy's soul. He began to find another place within himself. It was subtle, but it was there. Sammy had found God—in his own way, of course. That was what he did best: Sammy's way.

Then one day Dr. Hull asked, with a smile on his face, "Don't you think you've used this room long enough? I've got to kick you out of here tomorrow."

Sammy jumped out of bed and ran down the hall yelling, "They're letting me out of this place of dumb food and Jello!"

The nurses and the rest of the hospital staff and patients who were in the area began to applaud. Sammy ran back to his room where

Dr. Hull was also applauding. "Thanks Doc," he said. "I really love ya, but I'll really be happy to go."

Once the hullabaloo died down, Dr. Hull told us to sit down because he wanted to explain what Sammy should expect while recovering, and what he could and could not do for awhile. Dr. Hull turned to me with a serious look in his eyes and said, "Arthur, it's up to you to keep a rein on him. As he gets better and better, he will want to overdo it."

"Okay, Doc, I'll do whatever it takes."

"Yeah, Silber," laughed Sammy, "you'll hold my hands, won't you, Bubby?"

"Yeah, the Vegas guys want me to keep you in line, or I'll end up in a hole in the desert. And now the Doc will probably castrate me if you get out of line. You're really getting a kick out of this, aren't you?"

"Well, who better than you?"

Sammy, with tears rolling down his face, put his arms around Doctor Hull and really started to cry. "Doc," he said, "how in the hell can I ever thank you for saving my life?"

"Sammy, there is no need for thanks. You're a wonderful person and a great star. We need you Sam; we all need you."

"Doc, I swear to you that when I get back on my feet, I will do a show out here and raise enough money to build a new wing on this hospital. You can take that to the bank."

Sammy was as good as his word. Months after he was released from the hospital, Sam set up a charity concert at the San Bernardino County Fairgrounds to benefit the hospital. I made phone calls to a lot of people, and we were able to get a good many to promise an appearance or to perform. Jeff Chandler made an appearance as did James Garner and Sidney Poitier. Judy Garland and Danny Thomas were also there to perform with Sammy. That night, they raised a lot of money for Dr. Hull and the San Bernardino Community Hospital.

When Charlie left the hospital, he went home to his family to finish recuperating. Although Sammy offered him a lifetime job, Charlie never returned to show business.

The day of Sammy's release, he went to Frank's house for a couple of weeks of recuperation. I went back to Hollywood to get Sammy's house ready for his homecoming, and to take care of a lot of other business.

Tony Curtis and Janet Leigh

Sam Sr., Jeff Chandler, Will Mastin

Jess Rand, Sam, Jeff Chandler, Marilyn Monroe and me

Rehearsal

With Morty on clarinet

Another Opening of Another Show

Finally, no more daily drives to San Bernardino, but there was still plenty for me to do in Los Angeles. Will got in touch with the William Morris Agency (now the booking agency for the Trio). He advised them that once Sammy had recovered enough to return to the stage, he wanted to do his comeback show at Ciro's. Herman Hover, the owner of Ciro's wanted nothing more than to have Sammy and the Trio back where it had all started for them. Meanwhile, the Morris Agency had also responded to Jack Entratter at the Sands Hotel in Las Vegas and accepted their generous offer.

Sammy was finally able to record the title song for *Six Bridges to Cross*. Universal had finished filming the movie, and normally, the song would have been recorded by then as well. However, Tony Curtis was adamant that Sammy do the song. At the time, he had enough clout to keep the studio from signing someone else. They held off for a month or so until Sammy was recovered enough to do the recording.

No one, including Sammy, knew how well he was going to be able to dance now that he was blind in his left eye. He was going to have to learn new ways to keep his balance when dancing and moving to his left. While remaining aware of the audience, he still had to avoid bumping into Will, who danced at Sammy's left side. I felt that would be Sammy's greatest concern until he actually got up on a stage and worked it out.

Just before Sammy was ready to end his stay at Frank's house, he called me to request that I rent a rehearsal studio in Los Angeles where he could practice. For Sammy, this would just be another obstacle to overcome, another barrier to kick down. How I admired his courage.

I'll never forget the first day that Sammy, Morty and I went to the little rehearsal studio. Sammy carried his dancing shoes in a paper sack so no one could see them. Sammy was particular about his tap shoes. He would adjust them before every single show, not just at night. He had a little bag in which he carried extra taps and screws, as well as a screwdriver. He would sit there with his little screwdriver and adjust the screws to the right space between the tap and the sole of the shoe. It wasn't screwed tight to the shoe. There was a space which modified the sound, and he knew just what sound he wanted to get. It was a "chink, chink, chink" kind of sound. I have been around a lot of tap dancers all my life, and Sammy was the only one I ever saw who had a little play between the tap and the shoe.

Now Sammy was about to see if he could still dance. He sat down on a chair, kicked off his street shoes and put on his dancing shoes. Morty began tinkling the piano keys and without getting out of the chair, Sammy's feet began tapping like a machine gun.

He may have had doubts—we all did—but his heart, body and feet never had a doubt. Sammy's talent wasn't gone; it had just been forced on vacation. After a minute or so, Sammy stopped tapping and began to cry. Then he asked Morty and me to leave the studio for a minute or two so he could try some real dancing in front of the large mirrored wall that all dance studios have.

Standing outside the room, Morty and I heard Sammy start to dance. We could not see him; we could only hear him. Morty and I gave each other a big hug of relief and gratitude—a tender moment between two men who had tremendous love and affection for the guy on the other side of the door. He was doing what no other dancer in the world could do—and he was doing it with one eye!

We heard Sammy stop, so we went back into the room where the three of us grabbed each other, hugging and crying. This was a giant step for Sammy, probably the single most important obstacle he ever had to overcome. As always, this little man's will just pushed him on.

There were many other adjustments he would have to make, but, after a time, Sammy became so comfortable with his disability, people would forget, or never even notice, that he was blind in one eye. Sometimes even I forgot. We would be walking together talking, with me on his left side. He'd just say, "Silber!" and point with his finger, meaning I should walk on his right so he could see me.

I always baited Sammy whenever I could; it was a game between us. Years later, when it was no longer a sensitive issue, I'd say to him, "You're older. You can't see out of your left eye. You can't see to swing a golf club." He'd always yell, "Murphy! Find a golf course —get me a time!" He'd always react the same way, taking me on; but he never gave in to the fact he couldn't see out of his left eye.

Besides going back and forth to the dance studio, and running around town doing all the errands, I spent a lot of time with Sammy and Morty at the Garden of Allah Hotel and Restaurant. Being around his friends at this popular Hollywood hangout made Sammy feel better about himself and closer to the business he loved. Sammy even kept a small apartment at the hotel where he stayed much of the time, rather than going to his house.

There was a waiter who worked at the Garden of Allah who, on his time off would run errands for Sammy. It wasn't long before Sammy asked him to come to work as his personal dresser, taking care of the things Charlie Head used to do before the accident. Thus Murphy Bennett arrived on the scene, never to leave until Sammy's death.

Murphy Bennett, Sammy's valet

How does one describe Murph? He was the kindest, most thoughtful man I have ever known in my life. Murphy was always there when you needed him, and had an uncanny way of not being around when you needed your own personal space. He was not a diamond in the rough, but a true gem.

Life started to get good again, and Sammy was preparing for one of the biggest nights of his life: his comeback to show business. He had begun rehearsing with Sam Sr. and Will and was getting used to having them on stage with him without looking awkward.

As opening night grew closer, we all actually began looking forward to it—all but Sammy, who was still scared to death. No matter how we tried to encourage him, it didn't help very much. All the friends, all the chicks and all the king's men couldn't help Sammy come to grips with his stage fears. Try as he did to relax, New Year's Eve was just around the corner—opening night.

Can you picture opening at Ciro's in Hollywood on New Year's Eve? That would be a frightening thought, even for anyone who was not facing Sammy's latest challenge. Santa Claus and Christmas came and went, leaving only seven days to go.

Late in the afternoon of December 31st, Sammy, Morty, Murphy and I went to Ciro's where the maitre d', George Schlatter (later producer of *Laugh In*), was getting the room ready for that evening's performance. We went into the dressing room and sat, while Murphy set up all Sammy's things.

Morty, Sammy and I tried to make small talk, but it wasn't working. Sammy finally said, "Okay, guys, let's go out on the stage and try this thing out. I've just got to get a feel for the stage and the room again 'cause I'm still scared shitless."

"Aw, come on, Sam," I said. "You've been rehearsing this for months. You think your feet have forgotten all the dancing you've done and your voice has forgotten how to talk and sing? Damn, man! You've gotta pull it together!"

"Fuck you, Silber! I'm the one who has to walk out on that stage, not you!"

"That's right, Sam. It's your night, and every friend and fan you have in the world is pulling and praying for you. Get your shit together!"

Morty jumped in, "You guys cut out all the arguing. It isn't doing anyone any good. Art, you're just getting Sam mad."

"Damn right you are!" Sammy chimed in.

"That's the whole idea," I answered. "I want to get Sam good and mad so he'll forget about feeling sorry for himself, and put his thoughts somewhere else, even if it means getting mad at me."

"Okay, okay, Silber. I'm mad," Sammy said, "but I still love your little Jewish ass, so let's get on with the show."

Morty sat at the piano, and started to play; and Sammy started dancing all over the stage, getting the feel of it. As Morty picked up the tempo, so did Sammy; and he really got into it. He sang a couple of songs, and you could see the old Sammy coming back. I was sitting at one of the ringside tables as he finished. "Well, Bojangles, looks like you're doing okay to me," I said.

"Bojangles, your ass, Silber."

"Maybe so, Sam, but at least I got you out of your funk, didn't I?"

"Yeah, man, I guess you did. But, you know what really pisses me off; and that's when you're right!"

"It's not a matter of right or wrong, Sam. It's just that I know you so well. I know what it takes most of the time to get you going."

With that, we all went back to the dressing room. Sammy looked around and said, "It looks great, Murph. Keep up the good work."

"Thank you, Mr. Davis. I'll always try to do my best for you."

"Cut that 'Mr. Davis' shit, Murph. I'm Sam or Sammy to my family, and you're now part of that family. It's just Silber who calls me names, but we forgive him because he's Jewish and cute."

"Cute my ass," I retorted.

As we left the club to return to Sammy's house to get dressed for the big night, we passed George Schlatter, and the owner, Herman Hover. Herman grinned, "Great to see you back, Sammy; and as good as ever."

"Thanks, Mr. Hover. I'm trying my best."

"Don't worry, Sammy. Your worst is always better than most other performers' bests." He patted Sammy on the back and walked away.

George said, "You can't believe who has reservations for tonight."

"Anybody in particular?" Sam querried.

"Just about every big name in Hollywood and some from out of town. We're packed to the walls, and the calls keep coming in. The way it's looking, maybe we should be doing this at the Hollywood Bowl."

"Oh, God," I said, "that's all he needs to hear right now."

Sam raised his hand to protest. "Calm down, Silber. I'm cool now." With that, we left for the house.

About ten o'clock we returned to the club, which was located in the heart of the famous Sunset Strip, and discovered that we couldn't get near the place. Cars were everywhere. It seemed no one in Hollywood had any place else to go that New Year's Eve except to Ciro's. The traffic was so bad Sammy and I got out of the car and started walking, leaving Rudy Duff driving the car. Big mistake! Some of the people started recognizing Sammy, began calling his name and asking for autographs. We had to start running and finally made it to the club.

Will, Sam Sr. and Murphy were already in Sam's dressing room. It was so full of flowers it was hard to move. There were literally hundreds of telegrams from all over the world, from Walter Winchell to Eddie Cantor, from Clark Gable to Judy Garland.

"Well, guy," I said, "I guess no one has forgotten you and the Trio, and they never will."

Sammy pushed some flowers out of the way and plopped down on the couch next to Sam Sr. He asked Murphy for his dancing shoes, took his little screwdriver and started to adjust the taps on his shoes. No one talked at all; and as Sammy sat there working on his shoes, the tears streamed down his cheeks. For a few moments, everyone in that little dressing room shed a few tears. Sammy finished adjusting the last tap, jumped up and yelled, "Well, that's enough of this shit! Massey, Dad, we got a show to do. Let's go do it!"

The mood and all the air in the room changed instantly. The place became full of light and energy. Just another door to be broken down— and Sammy was now ready to smash it to hell. That he did!

All dressed and ready, Sam Sr., Will and Sammy stood in back of the curtain. Morty started the music, and the announcement was made: "Ladies and Gentlemen, Ciro's is proud to welcome back the Will Mastin Trio, starring Sammy Davis Jr."

Out they came to face every star in the business that could squeeze into the place. All Sammy's fears had disappeared. Father, Uncle and Sammy Davis Jr. had arrived on the stage like a thunderbolt, lightning and all, as if there was nothing else going on in the world. Sammy was back, and he was king! The applause and cheers went on for over three hours. At least that's what all the newspapers said. They were even on the cover of *Life Magazine*. The king was back; long live the king!

Opening night, Ciro's after the accident

Always practicing fast draw

Sammy and the Sands

After the smash engagement at Ciro's, Sammy, Will and Sam Sr. next set their sights on the Sands Hotel in Las Vegas. At that time it was the hottest hotel on the strip, the king of Las Vegas hotels. It was "home" to Frank Sinatra, Dean Martin, Danny Thomas and others of the biggest names of the day in live entertainment.

While still in Hollywood, Sammy and I talked about the big adventure about to unfold. "Well, what do you think, Silber? What are we going to be doing in Las Vegas all day every day for the next few weeks?"

"I don't know, man. I guess I'll just have to sit around and look at your ugly face. Or maybe we can go out in the desert and practice our fast draw. Then again, you being so slow and all, that won't be too much fun for me."

"Oh, I see," he snapped back. "It's the Black guy against the White guy who thinks he can outdraw the Black guy!"

"Well, was there ever any doubt?" I asked.

God, how I loved to bait him! We lounged around throwing barbs at one another for a while, then got down to more serious talk about the hotel and how much freedom Sammy would be allowed. We wondered how much he could get away with, without "the Boys" clamping down on him.

"Sam," I said, "I feel that this time you might find it different. Remember they called you and asked you to headline at the hottest hotel in town. Just handle it like you did at the Frontier."

"Yeah, Silber, I guess that makes sense to me; but you know, man, I'm still scared shitless. Ciro's was great, but Hollywood's my home, and they are my people. In Vegas, I got a different world of people to deal with."

"What in the hell are you talking about?" I retorted. "People are people, and you are still you. Or are we back to, 'I don't know if they will remember me' again? We've been down that street enough already."

"Yeah, Silber," he answered, "what you say makes sense; and if it don't go well, I can always blame you."

We had a good laugh, then Sam got serious. "Man, how are we going to get to Vegas?"

"Well, we can fly or walk; but we'll be there for four weeks, so we might want to drive. Sam, please don't think that I don't know where you're going with that question and how you might feel about driving. God, I'm sure I'd feel the same way. But remember the old saying about getting right back on the horse if you fall off. Granted, that was no horse, but you've been driving all over this town and it hasn't bothered you. Come on, buddy. Let's you and me get back on that horse together. Ride right through that bad time and get it over with once and for all. What do you say, little man? It's the last hurdle left from that bad, bad day."

Sammy just sat there looking out the window not saying a word, then turned to me with tears in his eyes. He jumped up, came over to me and plopped in my lap, put his arms around me and said, "Well, big guy, if you insist. But you will have to drive. I always wanted a White, Jewish chauffeur!"

"Good for you, Sam! That's the Sammy I know and love. It's just another door for you to push open."

We were going to be driving Sammy's new Cadillac, a gift from Sam Sr. and Will to replace the one he had lost in the accident. I drove the car to Sammy's house where Rudy and Murphy helped me pack it. Murphy was going to fly to Las Vegas ahead of us to start setting up our suite.

I knew Sammy was really going to be nervous about this drive, but he wanted to drive rather than fly, to overcome his fear and get that worrisome thing out of his mind once and for all. However, I had to plan well to make it work for him.

At that time, 1956, there were two roads leaving Los Angeles to get to Highway 15 going to Las Vegas. One way was Highway 10 to San Bernardino where it met up with Highway 15. The other was the famous Route 66, which joined Highway 15 just a few hundred feet north of where Sammy's accident had happened. It was my plan to take Route 66 rather than Highway 10, so we would not go by the rock wall that had taken his eye.

We chatted as we drove, making small talk because we were both a little uptight. After driving for about an hour, we approached the junction and the little gas station where that soldier had been standing when Sammy hit the wall. Sammy didn't notice since we had come from the other direction. We sailed right by, and Sammy never knew it.

About fifteen minutes later, when we started up the hill to Barstow, Sammy said, "Where is the place the accident happened?"

"Man, we passed that spot a long time ago," I answered.

"Why in the hell didn't you tell me?"

"Well," I said, "I thought if you didn't notice anything, why should I bring it up and put you through that kind of shit?"

"Yeah," he said, "but I needed to see what would happen."

"I understand that, but we sailed right by and you didn't know, so that's the end of that!"

"Yeah," he snapped back, "I guess you're right again—and God I hate it when you're right!"

"I love when you have to admit I'm right," I said. We had a good laugh as we rolled along, and I thought this would be the beginning of a whole new set of experiences for us. It turned out to be true. The extended years of experiences at the Sands are incorporated in the next couple of chapters.

We reached that famous sign which is still standing today: "Welcome to Las Vegas." We both saw it about the same time, and Sam grabbed my leg. "Well, big guy, here we are, safe and sound."

"I know! Would you expect any less from a White, Jewish chauffeur?"

"Kiss my ass, Silber!"

"I would, but it ain't soft or supple enough, so I'll pass for now."

As we pulled up in front of the Sands, Sammy said, "Go right to the front door, 'cause that's the only way I'm ever gonna enter a hotel again!"

"That's where I was gonna go anyway," I answered. "You didn't expect me to drive up to the back door, did you?"

A couple of bellhops came up to the car. One opened my door and the other opened Sammy's. "Welcome Mr. Davis," he said. "It's sure great to have you here."

"Well," Sammy answered, "it's sure great to be here."

They took all our bags and placed them on a golf cart, and one of the bellhops escorted us into the lobby toward the check-in clerk. A very big, tall man came over, stuck out his hand to shake ours and said, "Welcome to the Sands Hotel, Sammy. I'm Jack Entratter, general manager." He then turned to me and said, "And you must be the Arthur I've heard so much about."

"You've heard about me?" I replied.

"Oh, yeah! I hear you're the one who keeps Sammy out of trouble."

"Yeah, sure I do! At least, that's what everyone thinks. I'm also the one who's told to keep him from going to places where he's not supposed to go," I answered.

"Let me put you both straight right now," Mr. Entratter said. "There are no such restrictions in this hotel. There is no coming in and going out of back doors. However, we must have certain restraints to keep some people from getting out of line."

He told us we had already been registered, and the bellman took us in a golf cart to our suite of rooms. At that time the Sands Hotel was a series of large one-story buildings, each named after a famous race track. Our building was on the rear end of the complex, not due to racial discrimination, but because all the star suites were located in the rear building. That made it easier to keep the general public away from the stars and allow them their privacy. It also kept the stars' partying from disturbing the paying guests.

The suite had a large front room with three couches and several chairs and was full of flowers. A small bar was fully stocked with liquor and bar snacks. There were two bathrooms and a large master bedroom for Sammy with an adjoining door into another bedroom, which was to be mine. My room also had a second door that opened into the hallway, an arrangement that would later become important and very convenient to both of us.

Our luggage had been brought to the room by the bellman; and when he left, Sammy and I plopped down in the living room and just looked at each other. I spoke first. "Well, little man, we came in through the front door, and the big boss met us himself. Then they drove us to our suite—not our room, but our suite. Quite a little change since the last time we played Vegas, wouldn't you say?"

"Yeah, Silber, it damn sure is! What do think it all really means?"

"Are you serious, 'What does it mean?' It means that you are the star performer headlining at the Sands Hotel in Las Vegas!"

"Do you really think they're going to give me the run of the place?" he asked.

"Well," I answered, "I don't think you should push it too far. Just take it easy before you get me into trouble, as it seems my reputation for looking after you precedes me. What's that all about anyway? If you fuck up, I catch hell for it. I don't think I need that in my life, being responsible for you. That's not really my idea of fun."

"Yeah, you just say that, but you know ya love it!"

With that, we set about unpacking the few things we had brought with us, as Murphy had done most of the unpacking before we arrived. We just settled in. After a while, Sammy walked into my room and leaned against the door jamb. "Well, my little mother, let's go eat some dinner."

"And just where would you suggest we do that?" I asked.

"I don't know, man. It's your job to know these things."

"Damn, Sam, my job just seems to get bigger every day, but the pay stays the same."

We both had a laugh, then I picked up the phone and asked to speak to Jack Entratter. He came on the line. "Hi, Arthur, what do you need?"

"Well, Mr. Entratter...."

"Call me Jack."

"Thank you, sir. I just wanted to check with you on where we're supposed to eat or not eat, as the case may be."

"Anyone headlining in this hotel may eat any place they want to," he said.

"Thank you, Mr. Entratter...Jack. Sammy just didn't want to do anything he shouldn't do and embarrass the hotel."

"You and Sammy, or any member of the Trio and your people, should feel free to treat this hotel as you would your home, as for sure it is."

"Thank you, sir, we will." I turned to Sammy and said, "Well, Sam, the man said to treat this place as if it were our home. So let's go find a dining room to eat in."

"Sounds good to me, but what kind of food do we want tonight?"

"Man, I don't know what kind of restaurants they have in this place. Let's just go walking and see where we end up." And that turned out to be a very interesting move.

Walking through the Sands, we heard the clanking and bells of the slot machines and the calls of the craps and roulette dealers, sounds which are unique to gambling casinos throughout the world. Wending our way through the maze of machines and gaming tables looking for a restaurant, we felt the rumbles start. The majority of the casino guests were surprised, to say the least, and some were even shocked. "Look! That's Sammy Davis Jr.," and "Oh, my God, it's Sammy!" Then came the autograph seekers.

"Well, Sam," I asked, "shall we run, or are you going to stand here in the middle of the casino signing autographs?"

"I'm gonna stand here as long as the people want me to."

"Okay, then how about I go find a place to eat while you stand here?"

"No, you ain't goin' nowhere, cuz' if someone decides to take a poke at me, then you gotta be here to step in!"

"I see," I said. "You want me to stand here in harm's way to keep some fool from swinging on you."

"Well, who better? Remember, you're the one who's supposed to make sure I don't get into trouble."

"So let me get this straight! If some fool wants to stick you, I'm supposed to step in front of the knife!"

"Yeah," he laughed, "something like that."

Much to my relief, hotel/casino security was all around us, not saying or doing anything, just there. I asked one of the security guards where Sammy and I could get something to eat.

He pointed out the way to the coffee shop and said, "Most of us eat there in the Garden Room. It's one of the best coffee shops in town. You'll have your own booth with a telephone, and nobody will bother you. There is also a buffet with the best Chinese food in town, and the Copa Room serves dinner."

When Sammy had finished his impromptu autograph session, I grabbed his arm. We walked into the Garden Room, sat down to a big steak dinner in our own booth and nobody said a word. It goes without saying this became one of our favorite places to hang out.

This is where I would eat many of my meals at the Sands because I had a phone in the booth where the operators and Security could always reach me. After we ate, Sammy thought we should take a stroll around the hotel, but I thought that might not be the best idea he ever had. "No, Sam, let's not push it any more."

"Why not, Silber? The man said to treat this place as if it were our home."

"Well, I wouldn't take him too literally. Just be a little cool right now."

"Hey, man, I'm always cool," he answered with a cocky attitude.

There was no doubt Sammy was having the time of his life and wanted to take in as much as he could. He grabbed my hand. "Damn, Silber, don't you understand what's going on here? I'm walking through the best hotel and casino in Vegas, and ain't nobody stopping me. Just a few months ago, this little Black guy couldn't even **enter** the casino, or stay in the hotel just across the street. Do you know what that means?"

"Yeah, Sam, I do know what it means. It means that, thankfully, they haven't realized it yet. Come on now; you know, as sure as we're walking through this hotel that some damn fool is going to come up and say or do something stupid. We both know that's gonna happen."

"Jesus, Arthur!" (Sammy always called me Arthur when he was really serious.) "Just for a minute, can't you understand how I feel right now?"

"Of course I can, but you're letting all this good stuff go right to your head. Think, man, think! You just got on the merry-go-round, but you ain't caught the brass ring yet!"

"Yeah, Silber, I guess you're right, but maybe we can do a little gambling."

"Same answer I just gave you, Sam. Why don't we just go back to our suite and kick back, and I can practice outdrawing you like I always do."

"You couldn't outdraw me on your best day!" he retorted.

"Then you must have a lot of bad days!"

"Damn, Silber, you're beginning to piss me off!"

"Why? Just because I'm a little faster than you?"

"That tears it!" he snapped. "Let's go, and we'll see who's the fastest!"

God, how I loved to bait him. He always took the bait.

When we arrived at our suite, we both plopped onto our beds to stretch out for a while. I lay on the pillow with my hands behind my head and let all kinds of thoughts run through my mind. I wondered if the customers and the Sands Hotel would really accept Sammy, or if we would just be in for more of the same racial shit as before, but on a higher level.

We had to walk right by the pool and spa area to get to the Copa Room where Sammy was performing. As we walked to rehearsal the next day, passing by the pool was uneventful except for a few surprised looks and a few people whispering to each other. Rehearsal went great, and this was the first time the Trio had a chorus line opening the show.

Returning to the suite, we passed by the spa area again and Sammy stopped. "Come on, Silber, let's check this out."

"I don't think that would be very smart at this particular time, Sam."

"Why not? The man said to treat this place like our home."

"Well, to begin with, you don't have a spa in your home; and in the second place, I'm sick of hearing you say 'the man said to treat this place like home.' That's bullshit, Sam, and you know it! If it's so much like home, why don't you jump in the pool and swim a few laps? Never mind that you can't swim and you don't like the water. Don't let that stop you."

"What bug is up your ass, Silber?"

"The only bug up my ass is that we've only been here a day and a half, and you're trying to go everywhere and do everything all at once. And please don't forget that my ass is hanging out there as, for some reason only God knows, I've been appointed the keeper of your flame. I'm not pissed, man; I just think it would be wise to take it slower and easier. That's all."

"Okay, I'll try. But what harm is there in checking out the spa?"

"No harm at all. Let's go in and check it out."

Nothing happened in any casino in Las Vegas at that time that wasn't all over town in fifteen minutes flat. The mob owned and ran the town in those days, and it was to their benefit to know what was happening anywhere in town at all times. It's been said, no one ever got hurt or killed in Las Vegas in those days who wasn't supposed to.

It was very safe for men and women alike to walk the streets at all hours of the day and night. No one got robbed, and the big winners didn't get jumped in the parking lots. The Mob wouldn't allow it! And if something did happen—well, let's just say there is a lot of desert around Las Vegas in every direction. There are many unmarked graves out there of people who tried to get one over on the Mob and mess up the wonderful fun-loving place Las Vegas was in those days.

So into the spa we went and were greeted by Bill, the manager. He showed us around and explained this was the first spa in Las Vegas and still the largest. They had a big steam room and another large area for massages, plus another area of rooms that were curtained off for privacy. In one corner was a table and chairs. Sammy, ever the curious, asked, "What's the table for?"

"Oh," answered Bill, "that's just in case one of the bosses or one of the stars performing here wants to eat in here."

"Well," Sammy tested the waters, "maybe Arthur and I could come in for a steam sometime."

"Any time, Mr. Davis. You're both welcome."

"Well, I kind of meant is there some time it would be uncomfortable for you or the hotel to have me sitting in the steam room? What if some bigot comes in and starts something?"

"Mr. Davis…"

"Sam, please."

"Okay, Sam, if that should ever happen, I would be forced to ask the troublemaker to leave; and I would not hesitate to call Security if necessary."

I turned to Sammy and said, "See how easy it works when you don't push it?"

"Yeah, man, but I just wanted to make sure before I came in and plunked my little black ass in the steam room."

"Well, my gorgeous little white ass will be sitting in there as well, and in the steam room all men are equal. Maybe not equal, but you get the gist." We all had a laugh, and our visit to the spa area was quiet and peaceful, this time.

Opening night was the smash of the Las Vegas Strip. During the first week, everyone who was anyone came in to see the show. Sammy was brilliant on stage and smooth as glass. He was finally beginning to enjoy the performances he, Sam Sr. and Will had worked so hard to perfect. It was their time in the sun; and at that moment, all was right with the world. However, dark clouds are always looming on the horizon, and in time Sammy would get his share—more than his share!

In the remaining two weeks, business had been so good Jack Entratter offered the Trio a contract to play the Sands four weeks at a time, four times each year for the next three years, with a substantial raise in salary each year.

Sammy and I started going to the spa three or four times a week, and it became our usual place to eat our evening meal. The people we met and chatted with in the steam room could fill a book of who's who in show business on the Las Vegas Strip. Name a star and he was there. It was virtually the only place in town they could come to relax without being bothered. Can you imagine Jerry Lewis, Don Rickles, Dean Martin, Danny Thomas and countless others all sitting around in our birthday suits together leaving nothing to the imagination? I was like a naked fly on the wall, privy to the most famous and entertaining stars show business had to offer. It was like being in some kind of a time warp story and comedy zone. Some of the stories are impossible to re-create; you just had to be there. It was quite an experience for both Sammy and me, and over time some of these people became close friends.

One of the biggest Mob guns was Mo Dalitz; and when he came into the spa for his massage, things got very quiet all around him. If you were smart, you might want to get dressed and leave; but if Mo spoke to you, then it was kind of okay to speak to him. Of course, the one thing you could never do was be in the steam room with him, as that would put you directly in danger; and Mo would never want to put any innocent parties in harm's way. With him at all times were a couple of other guys with big guns to make sure that all went well. Mo Dalitz was as tough as he could be, and very high up on the ladder of crime bosses. He died only a few years ago, having lived a full life.

All things considered, our two weeks at the Sands were great; but what was lying ahead would later boggle the mind.

Sammy relaxing

Far right: comedian, Joe E. Lewis

Jerry Lewis shares a joke with me

Sands

A PLACE IN THE SUN

JACK ENTRATTER PRESENTS
SAMMY DAVIS JR.

Sam with "The Gypsies" chorus girls

Slots, Sex and Sammy at the Sands

On our next trip to that desert oasis, things were low-key until we got a call from a very dear friend from New York named Joyce Rodman. Joyce had been a very high-priced New York call girl who had quit that business to become a dancer. She just wanted to get out of that life of prostitution.

Most of the hotels in Las Vegas had two shows a night—a dinner show at eight and a cocktail show at eleven; a few still had late shows at 1 A.M. on Friday and Saturday. Joyce called Sammy to invite us to her late show at the Dunes, another one of the big casinos on the strip just down the street from the Sands. The Dunes had a big review playing there called "Minsky's Follies." Minsky had been, without a doubt, the most well-known and biggest producer of burlesque shows in the country. He had more burlesque shows running simultaneously on Broadway than any other producer, ranking up there with Ziegfield and Earl Carroll.

Minsky's shows had strippers in them, such as Sally Rand, Gypsy Rose Lee, Tempest Storm and many others. Most all of the top comics in the world at that time came from burlesque. Minsky's Follies at the Dunes featured the first nude chorus line in Vegas, women nude to the extent that they walked around the stage with large headdresses, bare boobs and thong-type G-strings; and Joyce was one of them. It was quite a sight in those days to see a bunch of girls walking all around the stage virtually naked, but being our age, we just had to grit our teeth and bear it.

Blacks were still not allowed in the casinos or showrooms, which I quickly brought to Sammy's attention. His response was, "Fuck 'em. I'm headlining at the Sands! What are they gonna do, throw me out?"

"That's is exactly what they will do!" I said. "Damn! Sam, you know who you're dealing with. Why don't you let me call Jack and see what he thinks?"

"You do that, Silber. But I'm going over there anyway!"

"Not with my ass hanging out there, you ain't!" I replied.

"All right, if it makes you feel better, call Jack!"

I called Jack and explained to him about the invitation from our friend, and asked what I needed to know and what I needed to do. He started to laugh and asked me whether I was serious.

"Yes, Jack I am very serious."

His voice dropped several tones, "Do you know what's involved with this request?"

"Yes Jack, I do. That's why I called you."

"Okay, I understand; but Sammy just can't start running all over the Strip. That is not going to happen; there's too much involved. Can't you just sit on his ass?"

"Not really," I said.

"All right, I'll see what I can do and call you back in a few minutes."

In about five minutes the phone rang and Jack said we could go to the Dunes, providing we went directly to the showroom. "Keep that little guy in line—and I mean it!"

"Thanks, Jack. I'll do my best."

"Well, Silber?" asked Sammy. "What did the man say?"

"He took care of it, but told me to keep you in line—or it's my ass. By the way, why is it always my ass out there when you're about to make one of your moves? Not only are you about to take this new step by going out to see a show in another casino, but you are going to be looking at a bunch of bare tits, and you know what that does to you."

"Yeah? And what that might be?"

"Well, first your eyes start to glaze over. Then you start to drool out of the corners of your mouth. And then you start to play with yourself."

"Fuck you, Silber! You just try and watch out for your own self!"

I called Joyce to let her know we were coming to see her show. After our show at the Sands, we jumped in a cab to go over to the Dunes. The look on the cab driver's face was kind of funny, but you should have seen the looks we got once we arrived at the Dunes!

Sammy declared, "Come on, Silber, let's make them **all** look. They damn sure better start getting used to it!"

"What in the hell do you mean?"

"I mean if I'm good enough to star at the premier hotel on the Las Vegas Strip, then they better get used to seeing Sammy Davis Jr.

walking the streets, or walking into the hotels, casinos, restaurants and showrooms!"

"Sure, Sam. You're going to walk the streets and get both you and me put into a little hole out there in the desert to spend the rest of eternity. I keep telling you, Sam; don't push so hard, and it will happen. Remember, the bigger you get on that stage, the more power you have. The Mob bosses don't want to lose a star who is bringing in all those people. Those people convert to gamblers, and gamblers mean money. At that point, they will be faced with giving you a little bit more of the leeway you want. Chop down one tree at a time; remember that's what gets you down the path."

"It's just that it's a hard thing to do, and it eats at my guts all time."

"But play their game, and you will win in the long run; and you know it. Now enough of this kind of talk. Let's see the show, and go backstage after to see Joyce."

"I guess that sounds like a better plan to me, man; and I am sorry about bringing down all that racial shit on you, but sometimes it overwhelms me."

"I know, Sam. I know."

There is a kind of unwritten rule in show business that the cast is informed whenever a big name or personality is in the audience. It just puts a little lift into their performance. After the show, we went backstage to see Joyce. Of course, everyone knew that Sammy Davis Jr. was there. When we walked through the door, we walked into a department store of gorgeous girls, and a forest full of bare boobs, all of them coming right at us. It's the kind of thing young men dream about. I mean tits—tits everywhere—and not a bite to eat.

Everyone was clamoring to talk to Sammy, and right there in the middle of it all was a familiar face bouncing our way: Joyce pushing her way through all those tits. She grabbed Sammy, planted a big kiss on him and then turned to me and did the same. I must tell you that when Joyce plants one on you, you do feel it right down to your toes. She introduced us around, and Sammy was mobbed with questions while Joyce and I chatted for a while.

Finally Sammy jumped up and invited everyone to come over to his suite at the Sands and have a party. This started the reign of Sammy Davis Jr. parties at his place, which became a tradition in the annals of Las Vegas.

One of the many girls in our lives

Soon we were back at the suite. A few minutes later, there was a knock at the door. "Silber, answer the door."

"Okay, just keep your pants on for a few more minutes."

I opened the door and lined up down the hall was Joyce, all the chicks and most of the boy dancers.

"Well, Silber, who is it?" yelled Sammy.

"Oh, it's just Santa Claus with all his little elves, and most of them forgot their long underwear."

As they filed past it struck me that here were a bunch of real lookers. I mean not your slutty kind of chicks, but damn beautiful women. I told them to make themselves comfortable and get whatever they wanted from the bar and a huge deli tray we had set up. When Sammy joined the group, the fun began. He bounced around the room like a bee in a flower garden, trying to get as much nectar as he could from each flower. Of course, I wasn't cooling my heels either.

After a while things started to calm down. It was late and many of the people in the group left to get some sleep. However, there were as always, a few hangers on. Of course, they wanted to get laid. It was only a matter of who Sammy and I wanted to be with. There was no doubt Joyce had first choice between Sammy or me, and it didn't matter much to her which one of us it was.

Joyce got up, walked over to me and said, "So, you think you can handle me?"

"Well," I answered, "I damn sure will give it my best try."

"It's not your best try I'm looking for; it's you that I want."

"Okay, lady, you've got me, but what about poor Sam? He may need some help picking someone out for himself."

"Just leave it to me, I'll get him two of the best still here."

"How come he gets two, and I only get one?"

"Honey," she winked at me, "I'm better than any two other women, and you know that!"

"Then go get the two for Sam. But you have to tell the others that the party is over because I don't want to be rude."

"You just leave it all up to me."

"Thanks, Joyce. You really are a good friend, and great in bed as well."

"You got that right, big guy!"

You could say that our suite literally became *The Valley of the Dolls*. Day after day, night after night, this endless string of girls and guys would show up at the new party headquarters in Las Vegas. Truthfully, they were great times; and Sammy and I made many good, and some even lifelong friends. Chicks! Oh, yeah! Most any time of the day or night!

I remember one time in particular when Vince Edwards, a good friend of ours, came from Hollywood to visit. He was a former Mr. America, and later became a big star with his own television show, *Ben Casey*. He came to Las Vegas for two main reasons. He wanted to gamble, which later in his life became a huge downfall for him; and he wanted to ball as many chicks as he could.

I had an idea I thought was funny, so I told Sammy. "When Vince comes to Vegas today, let's get a couple of gals to take him into my room and really screw him to death."

Sammy started laughing like hell. "God, Silber, what a great idea. Call Joyce, and let me talk to her."

"Okay, man, but tell her to really lay it on if she can."

Not only did Joyce line up a couple of real hookers, but she came with them, and brought another friend as well. There we all were in the suite, four broads and three guys. Right off the bat, two of the girls grabbed Vince and literally dragged him into my bedroom, leaving Sammy, Joyce, the other gals and me alone in the living room.

Joyce promptly jumped up, "Well guys, that leaves just us, so let's go into Sammy's bedroom and have some fun."

Sammy agreed, "Okay, why not? It sure beats the hell out of standing in front of a mirror with Silber, practicing our fast draw."

Joyce added, "You can still practice fast draw, but with your other gun."

Laughing, we went off to Sam's big bed to get down to some serious business. It was sure more fun than straight sex with one partner. We were laughing and fucking all at the same time. At one point, Sammy and I were both pumping away when Sammy tapped me on the shoulder and said, "You know, my mom would be disappointed in me for doing this. She thinks I'm in Chicago selling dope."

We were laughing so hard we had to stop what we were doing. Sex back in those days was definitely not like the sex scene is today. We had just gotten back to what we were doing previously when the door to my bedroom opened and out came Vince with his two girls. He really looked like he had been through the Second World War all by himself. The women followed him out of the room laughing and said, "He ain't all that good. With all his muscles, he just couldn't handle the pressure."

Vince spoke up and agreed they had raked him over the coals, and he just couldn't handle the two of them. We all sat around naked and had a real good laugh. I couldn't resist saying, "What's the matter, Vince? Can't Mr. America handle two all-American girls?"

Just another afternoon at Sammy's place. These kinds of activities went on for months, even years. As Sammy's popularity grew, so did the parties. They weren't all sex, but they were all good times. However, there is one time that stands out.

For quite a while, one girl in particular, who was absolutely gorgeous, used to attend all our parties. Her skin was alabaster white, her hair platinum blonde. She looked like she had come straight off a Southern plantation, the kind of girl you would picture in *Gone With the Wind*. She was always very quiet, soft spoken and demure. One night, I had gone to my bedroom early, as there was not much going on. Sammy knocked on my door, popped his head in and asked if I would mind if this girl sat in my room until the rest of the people in the suite left. I did not mind at all, and she quietly entered my room. In almost a whisper she spoke. "Hi, Arthur; my name is Shannon."

I have always slept nude and was sitting up naked in my bed. Shannon sat down in a chair not saying much. Finally I asked if there was anything I could do for her. "Yes, Arthur," she answered. "Do you happen to have a robe I can change into?"

"Sure, right in the closet. Help yourself."

"Thanks, Arthur. I think I will."

Shannon went into the bathroom to change; and when she came out, she neatly placed her clothes on a chair. Without so much as a "how do you do," she walked to one side of my bed, pulled back my covers exposing my totally nude body and grabbed my cock, then started to play with it. Being the red-blooded all-American boy that I am, my cock just stood right up. Off came her robe, and down went her head.

"Jesus, Shannon, you shouldn't be doing this. What if Sammy comes in?"

Without missing a beat, she moved her hand indicating that I should shut up. "Okay," I thought to myself, "she damn sure is in control."

Just about that time, Sammy came through the door dressed only in his shorts. "God damn, Silber! What in the fuck is going on here?"

"What the hell does it look like? This girl just had to have me so, what else could I do, being the weak person that I am?"

During this little exchange Shannon still did not miss a beat. Again with her free hand, she motioned Sammy to come over to her. Never being one to turn down that kind of an invitation, he walked over and stood next to her between my beds. Again without missing a beat, she reached up and pulled off his shorts, a little difficult because Sammy was erect by this time. Shannon began working with his cock, and at the same time I gave in to all her desires and mine.

When she finished with me, Shannon took on Sammy right there on the floor between my beds. When Sammy figured they were finished, that was not what Shannon had in mind at all! She chased and seduced him in every room of the suite. She had him on the couch, in the bathroom and everywhere in between. All this time I was following them from room to room, having the time of my life watching the show and laughing while Sammy kept yelling at me to help him. All I could say was, "I'm just a poor mortal man, Sam. I've done all I can do to help you out. What more can I do?"

"You son-of-a-bitch," he yelled. "I'll get you back for this one of these days, so help me God!"

"I can't wait, Sam. I just can't wait!"

As quickly as the sexual assault started, it stopped. Shannon went back to my room, got dressed, redid her makeup, kissed us both goodbye and left as quietly as she came.

After she left, Sammy turned to me. "What the fuck was that all about?"

"I'm damn sure I don't know," I answered. "But I will say this much for her. She is the first nymphomaniac I've ever seen."

"You got that right, Silber. She damn near killed me!"

We went to bed, exhausted but smiling.

On another trip, I got a page from the operator just as my meal was put in front of me. I often ate my dinner in the Sands coffee shop in the special reserved booth with the telephone so Sammy, or anyone else who needed to, could reach me.

The operator said, "I have Sammy for you."

Each building at the Sands was named after a different race track. When she connected me, all I heard was Sam saying, "Room 147, Churchill Downs." That was it!

Whenever I got a call like that, it meant "Trouble!" and "Come now!" I called my waitress over and asked her to keep my dinner warm until I got back and rushed immediately to Churchill Downs where I was searching for Room 147. As I approached the room, I put my ear to the door to try to hear if something was going on inside. I didn't hear a sound.

With a great deal of trepidation, I knocked on the door. No response. I started to get a little worried because I hadn't liked the sound of Sammy's voice on the phone. One more time, I knocked a little louder and decided that if there was no response this time, I would call Security.

Just then, I heard a faint voice calling, "Who's there?"

"Arthur," I replied.

The door swung very slowly open. But there was nobody standing there. My eyes focused on a long thin table that was filled with empty shot glasses and booze bottles. Strange, because Sammy didn't drink. As the door opened a little wider, I could see a king-size bed just covered with the bottom sheet and pillows. Then a little voice from behind the door said, "Come in, Arthur."

As I stepped into the room, across from me a door opened, and out popped Sammy wearing nothing but a towel. He was followed by three naked women. He struck a pose and said, "Do you believe this shit?"

"No, Sam, I don't! But you sure scared the shit right out of me."

"Oh hell, Silber; take off your clothes and jump in."

"Sam, I just left my dinner getting cold on the table because I thought you were in some kind of trouble."

"I am in trouble! I can't handle four chicks by myself. Come on, man. Get with it!"

"Okay, I'll tell you what. I'll just sit here in the chair and watch."

"Hey, man, whatever turns you on."

I grabbed the desk chair, turned it around, straddled it with my arms over the back and told the girls to go at it, which they did. I could only see little parts of Sammy here and there because they had him buried. It was quite a sight.

It was winter time in Vegas, and I had on a heavy sweater. After a little while, it started to get a bit warm so I took off the sweater. As I did one of the girls patted the bed. "Come on, Arthur, it's your turn now. As you can see, Sammy's in no trouble."

"No, I guess he's not, except he still has to dance in the second show—and when you all finish with him, he'll be lucky if he can walk."

Sammy invited, "Come on now—just stick something in her pussy."

What could I do but try to help out this person who was in such great need? I pulled off the rest of my clothes and piled into the fray. Finally they let poor Sammy go, and he headed for the dressing room, leaving me there alone to perish in a sea of nude bodies.

While I was doing my best to help out, the phone rang. One chick answered the phone. Of course, I could only hear one side of the conversation. "What the hell do you want?" she yelled into the phone. "No, I don't want to see you. What airport? Fuck you!" and she slammed the phone down.

I lifted my head up, "Who was that?"

"My old man," she said.

"What airport was he at?"

"Here, but just fuck him!"

"You mean to tell me that your old man is here in this town at the airport, and I am lying here fucking with his lady?"

"You bet, but you've got nothing to worry about. He won't come here."

At that point, what had been hard was hard no longer. I jumped up and dressed while running down the hall. When I reached the dressing room, there sat Sammy in his white robe with his feet up on a chair with a big grin on his face. Also sitting there was Jack Entratter, and they both burst out laughing at me. Jack spoke first. "Having fun, Arthur; are we?"

"I was having a ball until one of the chick's husbands called from the Las Vegas Airport. I got my ass out of there quick!"

"Tell him, Jack," said Sammy.

"Well, Arthur, you have just been screwed by a bunch of star fuckers."

"Star fuckers? What the hell does that mean?"

"These chicks, and others like them, come up here and all they want is to fuck every male star on the Strip."

"Thanks, Sam, for getting me into this shit."

He really started to laugh. "Remember, Silber, a couple of years ago when I told you I would get you back about that chick Shannon? Well, now we're even."

Funny thing though, after the show that night, a couple of the chicks from earlier that evening were sitting in the lounge, including the one who answered the phone. Sammy said, "Why don't you go over and invite the chicks to our place where we can continue the party?"

"You must be some kind of crazy motherfucker if you think that I'm going anywhere with them!"

"Go ahead, Silber. The worst thing they can say is 'No.'"

"Okay, man, but if that one says so much as anything wrong to me I'm going to come and bust you in the nuts."

I approached their table, "Good evening. Sammy wants to know if you all would like to come back to his suite and continue the party."

The chick who had been on the telephone looked at me like I was crazy saying, "I beg your pardon?"

I repeated myself, and she said, "Sammy who?"

"Sammy Davis."

"I don't know any Sammy Davis," she retorted, "and no thanks."

I could not believe my ears. We had spent hours rolling around the bed with these chicks, and they didn't know Sammy Davis Jr.! And that, ladies and gentlemen, was my introduction to what is known in the entertainment business as "the star fuckers."

Center stage—the Sands

Above: Sammy having a ball—I am smiling (far left); looking over my shoulder, Charlie Head (hand on table)

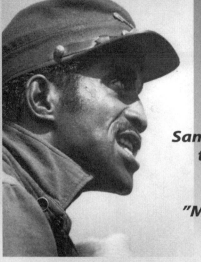

Sammy starred in the first Negro western on television— "Mission," Zane Grey Theater

Living at the Sands

Many noteworthy things changed during the numerous years that we lived and worked at the Sands in Las Vegas. I will start with the big guy himself, Jack Entratter. Before coming to Las Vegas, Jack, a large man who stood well over six-foot-three, was just a bouncer at the Copacabana in New York. He was such a personable guy when dealing with the stars who played there that when the Sands was built, the Mob sent Jack out to manage the place. Jack had a special way of dealing with the big names, and was a savvy businessman. Soon he had most of the major stars signed up with the Sands on long-term contracts. Big names, like Frank Sinatra, Danny Thomas, Martin & Lewis, Sammy and many, many others. Jack was able to pull the stars away from other major hotels and that's why and how the Sands became the hottest hotel on the Las Vegas Strip.

On a personal note, Jack treated me like a son—Sammy, too. He gave Sammy so much leeway that Sammy was able to open many doors for people of color. Jack backed Sammy as much as he could, and that was a lot—so many ways it's difficult to count.

For example, it was one of Dean Martin's favorite pastimes to go into the casino and deal blackjack to the customers. Of course, no one ever lost when Dean was dealing the cards. The players just loved it. What better publicity could a casino have? However, when Sammy wanted to do the same thing it became a very big deal. It didn't seem the time was right to see a Black man dealing blackjack in a major hotel-casino, and certainly no Black man ever had. The Mob would not be happy about this at all.

But Sammy, being Sammy, still felt he was pulling in the people to see his show and to gamble. Therefore, why should he not have the same rights as Dean or any of the other personalities who might be dealing cards, or craps, or spinning the wheel on roulette where all the players won? Sammy wanted to do that in the worst way but would not approach Jack himself. Guess who he asked to send the message out? Yeah, me!

"Silber, I need you to talk to Jack about letting me deal some black-jack."

"You want me to talk to Jack about that?"

"Yeah. You and he are on such good terms."

"No, Sam. You don't seem to remember my orders from Jack to keep you out of trouble. I'm not supposed to get my ass in a sling by asking Jack to let you into the forbidden land and to let you become a dealer. Just how do you think the pit bosses are going to take it? Never mind all the Texans and other bigots and Black haters who come here to gamble. You might be king of the showroom, but you sure ain't king of the casino."

"Ah, come on, Silber. Give Jack a call."

"Damn it, Sammy, why do you always drag me into this kind of shit? I know you just want to find me a little hole out there in the desert where I can spend eternity. That's your master plan, isn't it?"

"Come on, Silber, just this one last time. Please!"

Of course, for Sammy, one last time came about once a week.

I picked up the phone. "Hi, Jack. How's it going?"

"Well, Arthur, it was going just fine until I got this call, which I know must be something new from the little guy that he doesn't want to talk to me about himself. Right?"

"Gee, Jack, how much you have learned about the man. His new thing is that he wants to deal blackjack in the casino once in a while."

"Damn it, Arthur. You know better than that, and so should he."

"Yeah," I answered, "but you know him when he gets on one of his kicks. To be honest, if Dean and some of the other guys can do it, it's really not fair that Sammy can't."

"Maybe it's not fair, but you know better than anyone what he's running up against. I'll give it some thought and talk to Carl Cohen and some of the casino managers. Why in the hell does he keep want-ing to do these things?"

"That's simple, Jack. The man just wants to be free to do what all the others do. You know Sammy is going to push hard until he gets equal treatment. What do you think the big boys are going to do Jack? Fire one of their biggest draws?"

"No, Arthur, that may be true, but on the other hand...."

"I know. On the other hand is a shovel to dig holes in the desert for one pushy little Black guy and his Jewish friend, who is supposed to keep him in line. How in the hell did I ever get that job in the first place?"

"Because you're so pretty. Okay, Arthur, let me see what I can do. But I wouldn't hold out too much hope, if I were you. I'll get back to you."

"Thanks, Jack."

"Well, Silber, what can the man say besides 'No'?"

"That just about covers it, but Sammy said call, Jack, so I did."

"Okay, Silber, I got the message."

Sammy seemed a little sullen that evening before the first show. After the second show, he and I were just walking along by the side of the pool when Sammy grabbed my arm. "Come on, Silber. I've made up my mind."

"About what?"

"Never mind, just come with me."

"This doesn't sound good to me, Sam. What's in that mind of yours?"

He pulled me into the casino door, walked up to the first blackjack table he saw and said to the dealer, "I'm gonna deal a few hands if you don't mind. These people don't seem too happy."

The dealer was taken by complete surprise. The players were yelling and screaming with delight. Can you imagine Sammy Davis Jr. dealing blackjack to them? The dealer looked over at the pit boss, who just gave him a smirk and nodded his head in permission. What else could they do? Here stood the star of their show wanting to have some fun with some of their gambling patrons. You can't buy that kind of publicity. In stepped Sammy, behind the table, against even my wishes. It was my ass on the line, but there was nothing I could do. When Sammy got his mind set on something like this, only God or guns could stop him.

Thank God all went well—more than well. The customers were going crazy putting down all kinds of money. If the house won the hand, Sammy would pay the losses anyway. That's what made it so much fun.

Sammy dealt for about fifteen minutes when I saw Jack's head bouncing above all the other heads, coming our way; and I could see the anger in his face. I informed Sammy that Jack was coming. He wisely gave the deck back to the dealer.

Grasping my arm, he announced, "Come on, Silber. I think it's time to go."

"No you don't!" I said. "This time it's all on your ass."

Jack asked us to follow him to his office. Once in his office, Jack motioned us to sit down. "Okay guys, what in the hell was that all about? Every pit boss and floor manager has been calling me asking if I okayed your little stunt. I mean, they didn't know what to do. Now Arthur, I told you I would get back to you."

"I know, Jack, but before you jump on me…."

Sammy jumped up. "Jack, Arthur had nothing to do with this. I will take full responsibility."

"Then why, Sammy? Why?"

"Simple, Jack. If I had waited until you got an answer from Chicago, or wherever the answers come from, it would have been 'No!' That would not have been fair to me. I bring as many people into the Sands as the other acts, and a lot more than some. I feel in my heart that I should have equal rights and freedom with the other main room acts.

"Damn it, Jack! What the hell's the matter? Do you think that some of the black's going to come off on the cards and some White guy is going to catch that horrible disease called 'Black?' No, man. That ain't gonna happen. And I don't have any other diseases either. I just want equal treatment, that's all; equal treatment!"

"Sammy, I know how you feel…."

"No you don't, Jack! And you never will, 'cause you ain't a Black man working in Vegas."

"Okay, okay. What I am trying to get across is that I can only go so far here. My hands are tied. I've got the owners of this place to deal with. You've come a long way in this town Sammy, and many other towns as well; but you just have to take time and move slowly. We all have to be sure that the customers are okay with this kind of thing."

"Why don't you go out to the casino and ask them, Jack? All those people yelling and screaming around that blackjack table didn't seem to mind at all. Times have got to change, Jack. All the big money guys from Texas are going to have to learn, too. I ain't no Dorothy Dandridge, nor am I going to stick my foot in the pool and have some Texas asshole make you drain the pool because of it. Like I said, the black don't come off—even from Dorothy Dandridge."

"Sammy, I like to think that we have come a little further down the track since then."

"Oh yeah? When was the last time you saw Black people swimming in your pool?"

"Okay, enough of this shit. Like I said, I'll see what the pit bosses and managers have to say, as well as the big guys. Then I'll get back to you like I promised. Until then, no more taking over any blackjack tables. No dealing of any kind. Now, are we in agreement?"

"All right, Jack. I'll go along with you, and take you at your word."

"Okay!" Jack turned to me, "Arthur, you make sure of that."

"Hey, don't put me back on the table for this one. Sammy is his own man, Jack; and he doesn't need me to play watchdog over him. He's my best and dearest friend in the world. I can only give him my thoughts. Whether he acts on them or not is up to him."

"Damn! You guys are really giving me a run tonight."

"No," said Sammy, "we're not. It's just a little truth bubbling to the top of the pot. Do you think that I really want to stand out there and deal blackjack for the fun of it? Monopoly is my game, not blackjack. But looking at it from my viewpoint, if I, a Black man, can deal blackjack in a major casino, that might open the door for Black people to come in and gamble their good money in the casino. That's the reason behind all this, Jack; that's the real reason behind all the things I do. It isn't for me alone, it's for all Black people in the world."

"Okay, okay. I understand. But now we must all agree to understand what I have said—we'll wait and see. Now you guys get out of my office and go get some chicks or something."

When we got outside of Jack's office, Sammy jumped up and hugged me. "We did it! We did it!"

"No, Sam, you did it; just like you always do. The good news is, one day maybe some people will understand why you keep putting yourself, and me too, on the line to prove you can get equal rights and respect like all people should have. You'll have it, if you just continue to go after it."

That, too, came to pass when the word came down from on high that it would be all right for Sammy to deal blackjack once in a while.

It seemed the gamblers loved it, and gambling is what Las Vegas is all about. That's what makes Vegas breathe.

Speaking of breathing, that was never an easy thing to do in the Sands steam room and spa. It was the original type of steam room: flat rocks, cold water and steam. It's a little known fact that in all of Las Vegas in those days, of all the Strip hotels, the Sands was the only one with a steam room and spa.

What banter and huge laughs went on when the biggest men in show business were sitting around nude telling stories and jokes. God, it was wonderful just to sit there and be part of this experience. In this room I was accepted, not because I was just another White guy, but because I was Sammy's best friend. But boy, did I take a lot of ribbing. It was a fun time.

However, it would get a little scary when the Mob guys came in. Everyone else was given the unspoken word to leave; and it was understood by all.

One of the things the Sands was noted for was its chorus line. Jack Entratter came up with an idea to put together a chorus line for the Sands main showroom, the Copa Room, made up of girls from Texas. Patterned after the Copa Girls in New York City, the "Texas Copa Girls" was a brilliant promotion created to bring in the big Texas money, those famous high rollers from the Lone Star State. There was much publicity in Texas about choosing and picking the best looking girls from all around Texas to train and become the Texas Copa Girls. It was a great success, quite a little coup for Jack and the Sands. It was a great treat to be opening at the Sands when all these gorgeous gals, the best Texas had to offer, started to rehearse for their opening. Of course, Sammy and I just had to go and check out the rehearsals, which were closed to everyone. But Sammy and I had connections in high places. What a candy store for our eyes. And the band played on.

What more is there to say about the Sands? It was the hottest, hippest hotel on the Strip. It was the place to work, the place to play. It was the meeting place for most of the gamblers to play on the Strip. It was the Sands!

**Singer,
Nat King Cole**

**Dancer,
Juliet Prowse**

**Sam with
comedian,
Jack Benny**

Me and dancer, Patsy Rees

Patsy

"**M**an, get a look at all those gorgeous gams!" Rehearsals for the Texas Copa Girls had begun. They struck their first pose, and we were just like any other guys, wondering if we might get a chance at one or two of them. As the rehearsal progressed, my eyes locked on one particular girl. She had legs that went on forever—long, slim and muscular. Her waist was so small it appeared as though you could touch your fingers together if you put your hands around it. From the waist up, she got even better, one of those figures that every man dreams about but seldom finds. I could not keep my eyes off her. I leaned over to Sammy. "Man, check out that long-legged beauty on stage left, the one with the eyes and lips to die for."

"My God, Silber, you ain't gonna get ga ga on me are you? Geez, man. There are still plenty to choose from. Take your time and look over the field."

"Nah, Sam, this one is the pick of the litter. She's really special. She's got it all."

Sammy turned to me with that smug look he could get sometimes. "What the hell is going on with you? It sure ain't your lack of companionship."

"I know, but this one...I don't know...she just kind of hits me right. Look at her. As a matter of fact, look at all of them. They're all gorgeous chicks. They're all young women who have won beauty contests and are now training to be dancers. They aren't yet spoiled or jaded by the show biz thing."

"I don't know, man. I think you've gone off the deep end."

"That may be true Sammy. But there is something very special about this one. Just you wait and see."

"Will I have to constantly be going through this thing with you and this chick?"

"First of all, let's not call her a chick, Sam. She doesn't fit that bill. She's a gal, a girl. She's young, fresh and vibrant."

"Oh, my God! You've been hit with a bat, and your nose has been busted wide open."

"I guess so. It sure feels different."

"Okay, man, but let's just be cool and see what happens."

About this time my eyes and the girl's met. An electric shock went through my body. My heart began to pound and a warm feeling came over me. At that moment she and I were the only two people in the world. A magic key for a special lock that only existed between the two of us had just clicked, a rare lifetime event.

Sammy gave me another hard nudge. "Come on, Silber. Snap out of it! You're distracting her, and she's not following the routine."

"I can't help it, Sam. I just want to go up and snatch her off that stage and keep going."

Just then, the choreographer stopped the music and asked her if something was wrong. That was the only thing that could have broken the lock our eyes had on each other. She turned red and said she had just forgotten the steps for a moment.

Sammy grabbed me saying, "Come on, man. I've gotta get you out of here before your heart starts bleeding all over the place."

"No, Sam, I can't leave now. I don't even know her name."

"Well, I'm sure you'll make a point of finding it out very soon."

"But, Sam...."

"What in the hell has come over you, Silber? You're beginning to piss me off."

"Okay, okay. But I know she doesn't want me to leave."

"Oh, God! Move your ass!"

As we left, I looked back; and she was still gazing at me with those eyes. I fantasized to myself that they were telling me: "Don't leave." Was it just wishful thinking? "Don't worry, baby," I thought, "I ain't gonna leave you either."

Outside, Sammy kicked my butt. "What got into you, man? Have you gone girl crazy or something? Ain't there enough pussy for you around here?"

"This ain't about pussy, Sam. It's really different."

"Different, my ass!"

"Just wait 'til it happens to you. Then you'll understand."

"I guess I'll just have to grit my teeth 'til something happens," he said.

"While you wait, bite on this."

I couldn't wait to go to the show that night, hoping that she would be backstage. It was not to be though, at least not on that night. In fact, none of the new girls were there. The choreographer had asked Sammy not to come to the next two rehearsals since these were the last ones before the Texas Copa Girls' opening show. Sam's presence made the girls a little self-conscious. Sammy understood and had no problem with it, but that was not the case for me. I needed to find out about this girl who had completely taken over my mind. I didn't even know her name! I asked Sammy to try and find out for me, but he told me to cool it for two more days. I agreed, but it was tough.

A couple of nights later Sammy and I were in his dressing room while he was getting ready for his show. Opening night for the new chorus line was finally here and there was a lot of activity backstage. I was anxious to finally come face to face with her. But no, not yet. Then a cute little brunette stuck her head in the door. "Excuse me, Mr. Davis. Could I just pop in for a minute?"

"Of course you can—any time you want. My door is always open to the other performers."

"Thank you, sir."

"Not 'sir,' never 'sir.' I'm 'Sammy' to all of you."

"Thank you, Sammy. I just had to pop in and take a good look at him." She looked straight at me. "Yeah, I just had to see for myself if you're everything Patsy said you are."

"I don't understand," I said.

"Well, I'm sure of one thing you will understand real soon. I think that you're in real trouble. It's really simple. I'm Patsy's roommate; and for the past three days, you are all she can talk or think about. I had to see you for myself. Your name's Arthur, right?"

"Yes. So…her name is Patsy?"

"That's right, lover boy," Sammy chimed in. "'Lover boy?' What's going on here?"

"I don't know, Mr. Davis…Sammy. I've never seen anything like it before. Here's two people who have never met. But for me it's like living with someone who's been struck by lightening. He's all she can talk about."

I had to jump into this conversation. "Look you two…." I turned to our visitor, "First of all, what's your name?"

"Virginia," she answered.

"Okay, Virginia. I'll admit I am going through the same thing."

Sammy exploded, "That's for damn sure! I don't know what the hell's going on with him, but I'm getting the same kind of stuff from him. Maybe we should keep these two apart and not let them ever come face to face. Maybe the world will explode or something."

"You're right, Sammy. But we can't stop it. It will be something to see, that's for sure. Sorry guys, gotta go now, or I'll miss my own opening number. Arthur, hang in there. You've got hold of a comet. She's really a great gal. Bye for now."

"Damn, Sam! Did you hear that?"

"Oh yeah, I heard. Now what do I have to do to keep you in your pants?"

"Man, I can't wait to see what happens next."

It didn't take long to find out. The first show came and went without a hitch, and I was hanging around waiting for something to happen. Nothing did, so I went to dinner by myself, as I did some of the time. When I got back to the dressing room, Sammy was sitting there reading. It was very quiet. "Well, Silber, found your true love yet?"

"No, I haven't—and fuck you. You know, I think you're loving all of this agony I'm in."

"You're right. It's like some damn soap opera, watching for the next scene. As far as you're concerned—I've seen you in love before. But this time you're falling into a big black pit."

Just as he finished saying that, a beautiful face with blonde hair and a little cowboy hat came peeking around the door, pointed her finger at me and said the first words. "You, here, take this note please. Read it and don't laugh; just read it."

I jumped up and took the note. Somehow I was able to babble out, "You're Patsy, aren't you? Do you think we could get a drink after the show or something?"

"Yeah, that's for sure," was her answer. "Just read the note, and it will explain everything."

As I took the note from her hand, she patted my cheek, winked at me and blew me a kiss. "See you later, Arthur."

She turned and walked away in her little costume with those long legs and that incredible body. Then my mind started racing.

"Jesus!" exclaimed Sammy. "I'm getting sick of this already. Now the chick is chasing him. I don't think I can take too much more of this."

"Dammit, Sammy, can you back off a little and let me read my note?"

"God forbid I should stand in the way of true love. Please, read your damn note!"

The note read: "Dear Arthur, It's very hard for me to know what to say. Since the other day when my eyes met yours, funny things have happened to me. I have never experienced anything like this before in my life. Please don't think me foolish, but I would love to sit down for a while and just talk to you. Could you meet me in the lounge after the last show? As you may know, we girls have been asked to mingle with some of the patrons after the show. We're just supposed to mingle and nothing else. If that's okay with you, then I will stick my head in the door as we go on to do our last number; just nod your head. All this can't really be happening, can it?"

"Damn, Sam; she wants me to meet her in the lounge at twelve-thirty. You got any plans for tonight that I should know about?"

"Yeah, Silber, as a matter of fact, I do. I plan on being in the lounge at twelve-thirty, watching you come apart. I wouldn't miss this for the world."

"Be kind, Sam. I am a man floating in a sea of mush."

Sammy kept me really busy after his show until about twelve-fifteen when he grabbed me by the shoulder and very quietly said, "Come on, man. I'll walk you right up to her and drop you off. I wish the gods of love will smile you on this night and every night if that's what you want."

This was the private side of Sammy that only a few close friends ever got to know. When he knew something was very important to me, Sammy would act as a brother—no jokes, no bull, tender and from the heart, sharing the special love we had for one another. Yes, this was going to be a very special evening, indeed. It was in the air.

Sammy and I quietly walked into the lounge and approached the table where Patsy sat with three of the other chorus girls. Sammy stepped out in front of me, walked up to her, dropped down on one knee, took Patsy's hand, kissed it and said, "Your majesty, I have brought forth Sir Arthur, the king of all knights, as per your bidding."

Patsy's face began to get red. Of course, I knew what this was all about. Sammy had gone back a few years to the Fairmont Hotel days when we were doing our Sir Lancelot thing. Her friends at the table were looking around the lounge, slightly embarrassed. By now everyone there was wondering what he was doing. As he rose from bended knee, Sammy pulled Patsy to her feet.

There she stood, gorgeous as she could look, dressed to the nines and bang! Our eyes met once again. She spoke to Sammy, "Thank you, sir, for bringing this royal knight to me."

"My pleasure, your majesty," he answered, playing the part to the end.

Sammy took Patsy's arm and placed it in mine saying, "Begone from this place. Go out yonder into the darkness," and he pointed to the door.

"Thank you, sir knight," I said.

"My pleasure, my liege," Sammy said as he drew a fist and arm across his chest and bowed.

"Damn, you really had to do this, didn't you, Sam?"

He bowed and bid us goodbye.

Patsy and I walked to the door. Neither of us spoke a word, but she sure had a grip on my arm. We walked a short distance, and I couldn't stand the silence any longer. "Patsy," I said; and without a moment's hesitation, she put her fingers to my lips to silence me.

"No, Arthur, not a word. Just kiss me before I jump right out of my skin."

And that I did. Talk about sparks rushing between our lips, bells going off, thunder and lightening. It was all that. But when our mouths touched it was a cotton candy kiss, soft and tender, light, fluffy and damn sure sweet. It was very long and lingering, and underneath it all was a great sense of passion that could not be denied or stopped.

I had been in love a few times during my life, and certainly in plenty of sexual situations, but never anything to equal this. We hadn't had a real conversation yet. My God! What was still to come? The kiss lasted such a long time I knew the people sitting around the pool area must have wondered what was going on. When our lips parted, Patsy spoke first.

"I am so sorry, Arthur. I don't know what's come over me in the past three days. All I know is that if I hadn't kissed you now, my mind would have just exploded. I can't explain it. Nor do I understand it. I've never had anything like this ever happen to me before."

"Well, dear lady, you have just taken the words right out of my mouth. It's like I'm some kind of a kid running through a candy store and don't know which candy I want. I can only say one thing. I don't know where we're going, but I can't wait to take the ride."

"Then may I join you on the trip?" she asked.

"Damn sure can."

Then came another one of those kisses. After this one, Patsy asked, "What now, Sir Arthur?"

"I haven't a clue. Do I take you right here and now, or do we just walk hand in hand all around the hotel?"

"Well, what about both? Let's walk for a while. And when you think the time is right, take me. 'Cause I'm damn sure I want to be taken by you. Please don't think badly of me because I'm not easy, cheap or some kind of a sex fiend. Whatever is going on between us is really scary, but I have to go along with my heart. Please, Arthur, be kind and gentle with me as I have never been down this kind of road in my life."

She was looking into my eyes, inches away from my face with tears in her eyes. "Don't worry, Patsy, you're in good hands as I am walking down the same road as you."

We pulled away from each other and started walking again, our hands reaching for one another's, our fingers laced together. A funny thing about that, every time we held hands after that, it never changed. That grip was so strong and tight two trucks couldn't have pulled us apart. The electricity would not stop either.

We walked and talked for quite some time. "Well, dear lady, what do you think?"

"I think it's time you take me to that castle of yours."

"Yeah, I think you're right."

We entered my bedroom through the hallway door, not through the suite. "Please don't turn on the light yet," Patsy said. "I'm a little bit nervous. Please point me to the bathroom. And you, kind sir knight, get into bed."

"As you say, my princess."

I lay there in the dark, my mind going like crazy. You'd think I'd never had a girl in my room before. What, when and how should I go about this? I sure didn't want to mess this one up. Then the bathroom door opened and out came this goddess, this gorgeous creature with a towel wrapped around her body. The light from the bathroom dimly lit the bedroom.

Patsy climbed on the bed and sat astride me. "Here I am, sweetheart. Make it tender. Make it last all night. And don't take your hands off me, not for one moment." She fell forward, our lips touched and the wondering of the last three days began to unfold and continued until the sun started showing through the curtain. All the questions had been answered. All the doubts were gone. We lay there, bodies entwined as sleep overcame us both. This thing between us was indeed scary, but it was surely a good thing—a damn good thing!

About noon there was a loud knock on the door between Sammy's bedroom and mine, and a voice rang out, "Sir knight! What is going on in there? This door blocks my passage to the bungalow of love."

"Blocking your passage, sir black knight? Damn sure there is a lock of love barring you from entry."

"Nothing should ever block the entry of the black knight!"

Patsy chimed in, "What's going on with all this medieval talk? Do you guys do this all the time?"

"Yeah," I answered. "We used to do it for days on end, but we really haven't for a long time until he took me into the lounge last night."

"Well, I think it's pretty funny...and different," she said.

"Okay, black knight, I shall remove the lock of love so you may behold the beauty which lies beyond the door."

I told Patsy to run to the bathroom and put on some clothes. However, she pulled the sheet up around her and said, "He might as well see it now 'cause he'll be seeing a lot of it in the future."

"You mean we might do this again sometime?"

"Yes, that's exactly what I mean—and real soon, too."

To Sammy I yelled, "Yes, my liege, I will unbolt the door that blocks your passage into the den of love!"

Patsy was getting a kick out of all this, so I jumped up, unlocked the door and yelled, "I bid you enter, sir!"

Sammy came through the door wrapped in a bed sheet made into a toga. "My God, man! There is a naked damsel in your bed!" he pointed to Patsy. "Can you explain, Sir Arthur, the meaning of all this folderol?"

"Yes, my liege, I can. You see this broad came walking down the hall nude and wanted to get laid, and here I was. So she laid me."

"My God, man! You mean she really wanted to get laid?"

Patsy was now in hysterics and joined in. "Damn sure right, black knight—and I intend to do it again."

"Have you no shame, woman?" he asked.

"Not when it comes to this guy, I don't," she answered.

"Well, bang on my shield and flub my dub. I can't stand the sight of all these goings on, so I must withdraw to another part of the castle 'til you both are to be seen in a more traditional manner. I will await your arrival at the round table." And with that, Sammy left the room, closing the door behind him.

By that time, Patsy was in stitches. "Does he do this all the time?"

"No, not at all any more."

"But, why now?"

"Well," I answered, "if I'm right—and I know I am—he has just welcomed you into the inner circle. You are now about to become part of the Sammy Davis Jr. family. I gotta tell you, this hasn't happened in a very long while. Trust me when I say you've just jumped onto the top of the family pile."

"But, why?" she asked. "What have I done to get myself there?"

"It's really simple. Over the past few days, he has seen it in my face and actions—and seen you as well. You'll learn when it comes to Sammy and me, we are both very sensitive and intuitive about each other. He knows me like I know him—inside out. He knows you are very special to me, so he wants to welcome you into our family."

"I can't believe all this. A few days ago, I would never in my wildest dreams have thought I would go ga ga over someone I hadn't even met, or spoken to. My life has changed so damn fast, what am I supposed to do?"

"Well, you can start by putting on some clothes. Then call your roommates and tell them where you are, just in case they may be wondering."

"Okay, I'll put on some clothes. Do you have a shirt I can wear? As far as my roommates are concerned, they knew not to expect me back last night. At least I thought I might not come home. But I will call and let them know I'm okay and with you and Sammy—which, in fact, might make them wonder what happened."

"Then find whatever you need in my closet to be presented to his serene highness, the black knight."

"You guys are really nuts!"

She picked out one of my long-sleeved dress shirts to wear and did her makeup thing as I got dressed. But before we went in to see the man, I sat her on the bed. I just couldn't help myself. I had to know. "Patsy was it special for us last night, or what? Was it just me or did you feel the same thing?"

"Sweetheart, it was the most incredible night of my life."

"Then I guess I'll take that as a 'Yes.'"

"You sure can!"

"You might want to think about moving in while we're here," I said.

"Do you really mean that?"

"I sure do."

"Then, baby, move your toothbrush over 'cause Patsy's coming. Oh, geez, I forgot. None of the girls are supposed to fraternize with the help. As a matter of fact, I could be in big trouble right now. Oh, God, this can't be happening to me!"

"Well, first of all Sammy ain't the help, and neither am I—but not to worry. I have friends in high places. I'll take care of it."

"Oh, please, Arthur. I couldn't bear not having you around. That would just kill me."

"I said not to worry. You just think about what you'll need to bring over here."

With a quick kiss, we went to take on the black knight and could see him as we approached the front room of the suite. There he sat on the couch, toga and all.

"Forsooth, what people through yonder doorway cometh?"

"It's just Patsy and me, you shithead."

"Shithead you sayeth. What doth that mean?"

"I mean you're a shithead"

"Okay, Silber, I guess I've pressed it long enough. Come on in, you two and tell old Sam all about it. No, never mind; I can see it in your faces."

About three months later, Patsy and I became engaged. Each time we played the Sands, or I would visit Las Vegas, she would move in with me.

The enchanted couple, their fingers entwined

Kim Novak

Sammy and Kim Novak

After finishing Sam's engagement at the Sands in 1956, we returned to Los Angeles where Sammy was to record a new album. One evening, Sammy went to a small party at Tony Curtis and Janet Leigh's house, but I stayed home. The next morning I picked up the paper and saw an item in the gossip column saying the studio heads at Columbia were concerned about Sammy and Kim Novak. I wondered what that was all about, since I knew nothing about it. I never knew he had ever met the lady.

I popped over to his house and found him playing some new cuts for his upcoming album. "Well?" I said.

"Well, what?" he asked.

"Well, Kim Novak; that's what!"

"Oh, that," he said. "How do you know about that? I just met her last night at Tony and Janet's."

"I'm not the only one who knows about it," I answered. "It's in the morning papers."

"In the papers?"

"Come on, Sam. It's not like you to hold out on me about someone like Kim Novak."

"Okay, so I met the lady, and things happened."

"Things happened? What things?"

"We didn't do anything but talk for a while. But as long as you know now, you should be aware of the fact that she has invited me to her house for dinner."

"Invited you to her home? Don't you think that might be a little dangerous, things being what they are in the press right now? Don't you think someone might be paying close attention to her?"

"Yeah," he replied. "That's possible. But I only met her last night. How much can anyone make of that?"

"Plenty, if they catch you guys together again tonight."

"Okay," he said. "Then this it what's going to happen. I need you to go home, put on Levis and a leather jacket, pick me up and drive me to her house, 'cause I sure can't drive my car there."

"No you can't." I went on, sarcastically, "So you want me to dress up like some kind of a tough guy and drop you off. I'm sure that if anyone is watching, they'll never think that's suspicious! Come on, Sam, start using your head and stop thinking from between your legs!"

"Jesus, Silber, give me a break! I'm just going to dinner."

"Sure you are. And I'm driving the getaway car."

Sam then proceeded to lay down his plans. "This is what we need to do. We'll synchronize our watches. Then I'll get out of the car about half a block from her house."

"Yeah," I answered. "I'm sure no one will notice you at all— Sammy Davis Jr. walking down the street to Kim Novak's house. Great plan, Sam—foolproof!"

"At exactly ten o'clock you'll pull up in front of the house, and I'll run out and jump in."

"Okay, let me get this straight. You'll get out of my car about half a block away from Kim's house and walk up the street, unobserved, and go in. Then at precisely ten o'clock, you'll come running out the door, jump into my waiting car, and we'll speed away. Right?"

"Right!"

"Well, that sounds like a foolproof plan to me," I scoffed, "especially if you want to keep a low profile. Ten it will be."

I dropped him off. Then, at ten on the dot, I pulled up in front of Kim Novak's house. Sammy ran out, jumped in the car as planned, and we made a clean getaway. God, the intrigue—better than a B movie!

We were moving into our suite at the Sands Hotel in Las Vegas for our next engagement. Some guys were there installing a telephone in the front room of Sammy's suite. Originally I thought they were working on the hotel phones, until I noticed they were actually installing a new phone. Sammy was getting a private line, one that would not go through the hotel switchboard. After everybody left, we unpacked. I asked him what was up with the telephone.

He confessed. "You and Patsy are the only ones who are going to be involved in this, so you have to know. This is a private line only to be used between Kim and me. When she calls the hotel, or when I call her, we'll use this phone. I don't want anyone in the hotel to know what's going on."

So I asked him the big question, "What **is** going on?"

I knew Sammy had met Kim Novak casually a few times, but I didn't know anything beyond friendship had come of the meetings. I had never met her, or even heard him say much about her.

Sammy answered, "We're very much in love."

I was flabbergasted. "Jesus, how could you hide that from me? I didn't pick up on it at all."

Sammy said that if she called and asked for "Gummy Bear," that would be him. A short time later the phone rang, and it was Kim. I left the room discreetly so they could talk in private, but Sammy called me back in. He said, "Arthur, I'm going to introduce you to Kim on the phone. And Kim, I'm going to introduce you to Arthur. He's everything I told you he is, and you can trust him. You can say anything you want to him, openly." He passed the phone to me.

"Good evening, Miss Novak," I said.

Without any question at all, I heard the sexiest, most come-hither voice I have ever heard in my entire life say back to me, "Don't call me 'Miss Novak.' Call me 'Kim.'"

First hearing a voice like this leads you to believe it's put on, like someone trying to impress you. Later I learned that, in Kim's case, this wonderful voice was absolutely real. That is exactly the way she talked, and her nature was as sweet as her voice. Over the next couple of weeks, she and I had many conversations when she called and Sammy wasn't there. We became quite friendly over the telephone.

After a week in Las Vegas, Sammy couldn't stand it any longer. He just had to see Kim. It was pouring rain in both Las Vegas and Los Angeles this day, and Sammy told me we were going to Los Angeles after the show. I informed him there were no planes we could catch after the show, and asked him when and how he planned on coming back if we did go. He said he'd be back the next afternoon and told me to hire a private plane to take us to Los Angeles. Sammy had flown all his life, but he was still very nervous about flying, He never wanted to fly unless he absolutely had to.

After calling around, I found a private plane and a pilot. Flying out of Las Vegas toward Los Angeles is always bumpy because of the high mountains around Las Vegas. It's even bumpy when the weather is good. But this night it was most certainly not good. The plane I had rented was a little four-seater Piper Cub. Sammy had gotten Kim an adorable tiny black cocker spaniel puppy. He had this puppy stuck inside his coat with its little head peeking out. Sammy had hold of my leg almost the entire way to Los Angeles, squeezing it because the plane was jumping around and shaking.

When we landed, I asked him what he was going to do now, and how he was going to get back to Las Vegas. He said Kim was going to be outside the airport waiting for him, and he would take a regular scheduled flight back. I asked how she would know he was there. He replied she knew what time we were supposed to arrive and she would just keep circling the airport until he came running out. We landed and taxied up to the main gate of Western Airlines, a major airline at that time. The pilot had somehow gotten permission for us to do this. When we opened the door, it was pouring rain. Sammy stepped onto the wing, jumped off with the little puppy inside his coat and ran into the terminal building.

Kim was driving a station wagon and happened to be sitting at the curb when Sammy ran out. He jumped into the car, onto the floor in the back and rolled himself up into a rug so no one could see him. The pilot and I flew back to Las Vegas, and he let me fly more than half of the way since I was working on my private pilot's license at that time.

Later, Sammy told me he returned to the airport the same way he left—rolled up in the rug on the floor of Kim's station wagon, behind her seat. It's amazing what lengths people will go to just to be together. For a man and woman like Sammy and Kim to go to the extreme of rolling themselves up in rugs and jumping out in obscure places, like parking lots, so they wouldn't be seen—well, this was some romance.

Sammy had returned to Las Vegas the next afternoon. He told me what a wonderful time he had with Kim, how much he loved her, and how they felt that everything they were going through to be together was worth it. The romance between Sammy Davis Jr. and Kim Novak wasn't just a quick sexual thing—not at all. It was a very deep meaningful relationship. What made it more difficult was the time in which it took place, and the fact that both of these people were such highly visible personalities. Their relationship at that time would have been difficult enough, but because they were both instantly recognizable, they found it extremely hard to spend any time together.

They managed to find some clever ways to be together and had some rituals special to both of them. For one, they had a blanket, blue plaid such as anyone might carry in a car, but special to them because wherever they went the blanket went with them. They made love on it, wrapped themselves up in it; and it was extremely meaningful to them. On this blanket was a little silver dove pin that signified love and peace, which later became Sammy's closing statement after each and every show he did. Being together was so valuable to them, that they would not pass up any opportunity. However, they were not able to see each other very often, in spite of their best efforts.

It was approaching Christmas and Kim was supposed to visit her family at their home in Illinois—a farm about sixty miles outside of Chicago. One day, as it got closer to the holiday, I could hear Sammy yelling at Jack Entratter over the phone that he must have a couple of days off. I heard them arguing a number of times back and forth, but I didn't know why Sammy was so hell bent on getting that time free. I couldn't imagine why he wanted the day off as there was nothing wrong with his throat or his feet. I asked him, "What in the hell is the matter, Sam?"

He was pacing back and forth across the room, swearing like a truck driver. "Those sons of bitches won't let me have a couple of days off!"

"Let you off for what?" I asked.

"To go back and meet with Kim's family."

"What the hell are you talking about?"

"I've been invited back to have a holiday dinner with Kim's family."

I could not believe he said that. "You're going to have a holiday dinner with Kim's family! Are they aware of your romance?"

"No. No, absolutely not! They're not supposed to know," he answered.

"And how do you think you're going to hide the fact that Sammy Davis Jr. pops up in some farmhouse in the middle of nowhere at Christmas time for dinner?"

"Well, Kim's already explained that I might be coming back and that I'm a good friend of hers."

"Sam, you may buy all that bullshit; but I don't!"

"No…no. It's been all worked out. But the hotel won't let me have the night off."

"Of course not!" I said. Who's going to substitute for you?"

But there was no stopping him. "Oh, I'll get Dean Martin or Buddy Hackett or the Mills Brothers. Somebody will come in for the night."

I told him he just could not do this, that he was asking for major trouble if he even tried it. "You know," I said, "this is all really getting out of hand. You can only keep these things under cover for so long before they start to get out."

At this time in American history, interracial relationships—especially between Blacks and Whites—were absolutely taboo. They definitely were not casual and wide-spread as they are today. Interracial relationships did happen in those days, but not with major stars like Sammy Davis Jr. and Kim Novak, who had just finished filming *Vertigo*. Then, those kinds of relationships were career killers, and could even be very dangerous physically—perhaps even life-threatening, for those involved.

The arguing went on and on between Sammy and Jack Entratter. Then Frank Sinatra got involved. Frank had an interest in the Sands Hotel and had great control over what happened there. Sammy called Frank. He begged. He pleaded. He cajoled. He cried like a baby. He did everything he could to convince Frank to let him have this time off. Sammy was like a kid begging for candy—whining and pleading to God. It was absolutely unbelievable! I had never seen Sammy in this kind of a state before and simply could not believe he was literally in tears and begging like this.

But Frank responded, "Absolutely not! No way on Earth are you going to get out of your engagement here to go back East and be with Kim and her family!"

This went on for two days. Finally Sammy called me in and said, "Art, old buddy, you got to do me a big favor. You've gotta go back to Chicago and tell Kim that I love her."

I looked at him like he was nuts, exclaiming, "What?"

"You've gotta get on a plane, go back to Chicago and tell her I love her."

"Yeah? And then what am I supposed to do?"

"Well, then you come back."

"You want me to get on a plane, fly to Chicago, meet this woman—who I've only talked to on the phone—say 'Sammy loves you,' then get on another airplane and come home?"

"Yeah!"

"No way!" I told him. "There's not a chance in your life that I would ever do something that stupid."

Sammy jumped off the couch, got down on his knees in front of where I was standing, took hold of my belt and begged me to do this.

Nothing much surprised me with Sammy because I had been everywhere with him and done everything you could think of with him. But I had never been so shocked at him in my life. It was beyond my conception that he was this hung up and this adamant about something this childish, foolish, outlandish and outrageous. "Why don't you just get on the phone and tell her that you love her?"

"I can't do that because they only have one phone in the house, and we can't say what we want because of the family being around. I haven't been able to talk to her the way I want for almost a week now. I just can't take it any more."

"Well, if it means that much to you, then you know I'll do whatever you want me to—no matter how dumb I think it is. We all know that when you're really in love, nothing makes much sense except to the two of you. So, Sam, I'm your man. But I still think it's dumb."

At that time, there was a TWA flight from New York City that stopped in Las Vegas at three o'clock in the morning before going on to Los Angeles. I made arrangements to take that flight into Los Angeles after the second show. Peewee, Sammy's stepmother, met me at the Los Angeles Airport. She took me to Sammy's house where she and Sam Sr. fed me breakfast. We discussed how his relationship with Kim was not only foolish, but also very dangerous. They drove me back to the airport so I could catch an early flight to Chicago. Needless to say, I had not slept and was dead dog tired.

I got off the plane, headed down the steps—there were no ramps into the terminal in those days—and saw our good friend, Donjo Medlivine of the Chez Paree in Chicago. Donjo was still affiliated with the Mob. He greeted me with "Arthur, what in the fuck is this little son-of-a-bitch trying to do? Is he trying to get himself killed?"

I answered that I had no clue what Sammy was doing except being in love. Donjo asked me what I was supposed to do in Chicago, and

I told him I was supposed to wait there for Kim's brother. It had been arranged that when he arrived at the airport he would page me. I was to be driven by her brother to their family farm, fifty or sixty miles out of town. There I would see Kim and say "Sammy loves you." Then I would find my way back to this airport, get on a plane and fly back to Las Vegas.

"This is madness," said Donjo, "sheer madness!"

I heard my name paged. It was Peewee in Los Angeles calling me to say Sammy was on the next flight to Chicago, and he would be there in about a half an hour. I asked her how he got away from the shows at the hotel, and she said he finally convinced Frank to let him go.

We agreed that it was crazy. Donjo and I met Sammy's plane, and Sam was really happy to be there. Almost simultaneously my name was paged by Kim's brother.

Sammy and I rode to Kim's hometown of Aurora, Illinois, with Kim's brother. There was snow everywhere. We checked into a funky hotel—the kind of place you'd picture in an old western movie, a rinky dink little place. We had a tiny room with an old iron bed over in the corner—not a wrought iron bed, just iron. The heater was a radiator heater, the kind that hot water runs through. The telephone didn't even have a dial on it. You just picked it up and got the operator.

So here we were, two guys from Hollywood, dressed to the hilt, no farmers for sure. And one of us was a little Black man. No one knew who he was. We were to wait at this hotel until Kim's brother came to pick us up for dinner. As the car drove up to the farmhouse, Kim came out the door, shook hands with Sammy and gave him a quick hug and kiss on the cheek. Then she came over to me—remember, we had never met—and said, "Oh, Arthur, how lovely to see you again," and gave me a big kiss on the cheek. She played the scene for all it was worth.

We went in to meet her parents, who were absolutely delightful. They told Sammy how thrilled they were to have him at their home for dinner.

Kim suggested that she show us around the farm. Mind you, the snow was about two or three feet deep everywhere, and we were wearing mohair slacks, car coats and three hundred dollar shoes. But we're going to go walking around the farm.

It was my assigned duty to walk with Kim's little sister. I was supposed to try to walk a little in front of Kim and Sammy, so they could talk privately for a few minutes. I spotted a barn in front of us and began walking a little faster. As we got to the barn, I took the little sister; and we turned the corner around the barn, which left Sammy and Kim alone for a few precious seconds, during which they were able to share a quick embrace.

We had a lovely time at the home of Kim's family, staying late into the evening. When we went back to the hotel, we were too tired to sleep—as if we both even could on that one iron bed.

Sammy told me to get us back to Las Vegas on the first plane out in the morning. I called the airlines to get tickets. But what are we talking about here? We're talking about going to Las Vegas during the Christmas holidays! Of course, they'll have plenty of seats this time of the year, and we'll have no trouble at all. Yeah, right!

There was no possible way I could even get one seat, on any airline, let alone two. And the name "Sammy Davis Jr." didn't do squat! There were no seats! There were two choices left to me that I thought would work.

I called Donjo in Chicago, feeling the Mob was so well connected, it wouldn't be a problem for him to get us seats. I told him not to worry about getting me back, just to get Sammy back, as he had a show to do. Donjo said he would see what he could do. But he was still cursing about the fact that Sammy came in the first place, endangering himself.

Hollywood was already a-buzz about Sammy and Kim. But no one had yet been able to catch them together, to see them together. Everyone was waiting for someone to make a mistake—especially Harry Cohn, the head of Columbia Pictures, also rumored to be very heavily connected with the Mob.

Donjo called back about twenty minutes later. He explained that there was absolutely no way he could get even Sammy Davis Jr. on a plane to Las Vegas.

Next, Sammy told me to hire a private plane to take us from Chicago to Las Vegas. When this didn't seem to be possible either, Sammy started to panic.

I had one more thing I could try. I told Sammy I would have to call Jack Entratter at the hotel.

"You can't do that!" Sammy exploded. "Jack will kill us! We've got to find another way."

I told him there was no other way. So, I called Jack and told him of our plight. He went ballistic! When he started to yell and scream, I told him that wouldn't help—we really had a problem, and he had to get Sammy on a plane; but I would find my own way back.

In about five minutes, Jack called back and told me we were both on a flight. As I said before, Sammy didn't like to fly and only flew because he had to. When he did fly, however, he always went first class, never coach. In this case, I just wanted to get on a plane, wherever they had a seat. On this flight, we were definitely in coach—in the last two seats on the plane, right up against the bathroom. This was before the speed of jet airplanes. The flight was jam-packed with people and kids, who were in and out of the bathroom the whole flight—a total nightmare.

That holiday season, the weather across the United States, all the way to Los Angeles, was really lousy. It was so bad that we literally flew across the country at about twenty-five hundred feet of altitude wherever we could. We were so low that we could see the cars and people. Whenever we came to mountains, the plane would climb to clear them, then go back to a lower altitude again. It continued that way until we were very near Las Vegas. Then we finally rose to a more normal altitude. This flight made both of us, especially Sammy, extremely nervous.

We finally landed in Las Vegas that night. At the airport, a limo was waiting to pick us up. The car sped us toward the Sands, pulling up, at last, to the backstage entrance. Sammy ran up the steps. Just inside the door were Will Mastin and Sam Sr. with Sammy's dancing shoes on the floor in front of him. Throwing off the shoes he was wearing, Sam put on his dancing shoes. His entrance music had already started, so he walked straight onto the stage. That's how close the call was.

When Kim came home from Chicago, she didn't fly. She took the train. It was up to me to make arrangements for Kim to take a compartment on the train. I was to take the adjoining compartment with Patsy. Sammy was to have a roomette on another car. The reason was that this train stopped in Las Vegas about two or two-thirty in the morning, on its way to Los Angeles.

The plan was for Patsy and me to go directly to the train station when the show was over—which we did. Patsy didn't have a chance to remove her stage makeup. She was a pretty blonde loaded with false eyelashes, mascara, shadow, high-gloss lipstick and wearing a tight black skirt with a bright yellow bolero jacket trimmed in black.

It was my job to get on the train and, as it pulled out, check on Kim to see if she was also on the train in the correct compartment, next to mine. In the meantime, Sammy donned a pair of tennis shoes, Levis, and a leather jacket, instead of his usual natty dress. He had gone to the train station alone, and was standing between two boxcars in the dark. I knew that he planned to get on the train without being noticed, but I did not know how he was planning to pull it off. As the train started to pull out, he ran and jumped onto the train, then went to his roomette.

Once on the train, Sammy called for the porter. When the porter came into the room, Sammy said, "Hold out your hand." The porter held out his hand, and Sammy put three one hundred dollar bills in his hand saying, "You don't know who I am. You have never seen me and I'm not here. Now you can leave."

I waited about ten minutes, until we got out of town. Then I knocked on Kim's door. She called out, "Who is it?"

I answered, "It's Gummy Bear."

She said to come in. I walked into the compartment, which was bathed in a dark blue light. Kim was lying on the bed nude. She had their blue plaid blanket between her legs and clutched at her breasts. All vital parts were covered, but underneath that blue light with the makeup perfect and every hair in the right place was Kim Novak. It was a sight to behold that any red-blooded man would have died to see. It was hard just to breathe.

She asked if Sammy was there. I told her my first job was to make sure she was there. Now that I knew she was, I'd go locate Sammy.

I found his roomette. He was all excited. I gave him her compartment number and left, telling him to wait five minutes, then go over.

Meanwhile, there were rumors—rumors everywhere and not an ounce of proof to be found. Irving Kupcinet, from the *Chicago Sun-Times*, was looking for a supposed marriage license application which never existed. Walter Winchell told his radio audience Kim Novak was involved in an interracial romance. We also received word from friends that, while they were dining at the Brown Derby in Hollywood, unbeknownst to them Louella Parsons was sitting in the next booth. At that time and for many years after, Louella Parsons was the biggest female gossip columnist in the world, along with Hedda Hopper. Louella Parsons overheard part of the conversation between our friends, and she calculated that Sammy and Kim would be on this train from Chicago. Louella had photographers ready to get an exclusive on this story.

But Hedda Hopper had also gotten hold of the same information, and was on the trail as well. To top it off, James Bacon of the Associated Press had someone chasing after Sammy in Las Vegas, tracking his every move. They were all sure Kim and Sammy were on this particular train, and that Sammy would get off the train in Riverside, California. That was the last stop this train made before Los Angeles.

However, we had anticipated problems. So when the train pulled into San Bernardino, Sammy, Patsy and I got off in the parking lot where no one could see us. It was hysterical. Here was a little Black man hunkered down trying to look anonymous, a blonde showgirl, and me. As we got off the train and started to walk away, every cook and porter in the dining car stuck their heads out and waved, yelling, "Hey, Sam, how are you?"

Sammy just wanted to die because he didn't want anyone to know he was on the train, but everyone who worked on the train knew he was there. Unfortunately, the porter Sammy had called into his roomette didn't have a clue who Sammy was until Sammy gave him the three hundred dollars to keep his mouth shut. Then, of course he told everyone.

We caught a cab to Hertz Rent A Car. There Sammy and Patsy stood outside while I went in to rent a vehicle. Imagine this 1956 scene in the sleepy little town of San Bernardino: a little, short Black man in a leather jacket, tennis shoes and Levis, standing with a tall, very blonde showgirl in a tight black skirt and bright yellow jacket with full stage makeup smeared all over her face. They looked like a two-dollar hooker and her pimp. I drove us back to Las Vegas while Sammy and Patsy slept.

**Left to right, above:
Julie and Harry Belafonte,
Gordon and Sheila MacRae**

**Harry Belafonte looks on
as Sands manager,
Jack Entratter, signs
the marriage license**

Mama and Peewee

The Wedding

We returned to Las Vegas and I crashed for about twenty-four hours. Once again, I had been without sleep for two days. Being with Sammy meant that, at times, one didn't get much sleep.

When the train pulled into Los Angeles, every reporter in Hollywood was at the station to see Sammy and Kim get off the train. But they saw only Kim. They asked her tons of questions, but she played it dumb; and of course, Sammy wasn't on the train.

A day or two later I was sitting at the end of my bed polishing my shoes, facing directly into the doorway of Sammy's room in our suite at the Sands Hotel. He sat at the end of his bed where he was going through his address book with his finger, obviously looking for an address. Finally I asked him what he was looking for. He said he was just looking for "somebody."

I reminded him I had more addresses than he did, and asked who was he looking for. My address book, which I still have, was like a who's who of Hollywood. After I asked him a couple of more times who he was looking for, he finally answered. "I'm looking for someone to marry."

Never thinking for a minute he was serious, I said, "Okay, I didn't know it was something that unimportant," and I just blew it off.

He kept looking, so I finally got up. Going into his room, I asked him what in the hell he was doing.

"I told you!" he said. "I'm looking for someone to marry."

"What are you talking about?"

"Well, since you're kind of caught up in this too, I guess I have to tell you. They put a hit out on me."

"What?...Who?"

"Harry Cohn, the head of Columbia Pictures."

"How do you know that? I asked"

"Mickey Cohen told my dad. When Dad couldn't find me he told Will and Will found me. He said Harry Cohn is going to send some guys to break both my knees and put out my other eye if I don't find a Black girl to marry within forty-eight hours."

"Oh, shit! I can't believe this is happening!"

"Neither can I," he said. "I'm so sorry Arthur. This puts you in danger too because you're with me all the time and, all joking aside, these people really do think you help keep me in line. We could both end up in a hole in the desert for real!"

"Don't worry about me. Do you want me to call security?"

"No," he answered. "I already have Donjo working on it. I just talked to him about forty-five minutes ago."

"What are you going to do?" I asked.

"I'm gonna marry somebody Black, and quick, to take the heat off!" This was big time trouble, we both agreed. He kept going through the book and finally said, "Yeah! Here's one!" He pointed to the name of Loray White. "She's a good looking chick. She's working over at the Silver Slipper. Call her and ask her if she'll come over here."

Sammy had dated her a couple of times in the past, nothing serious on his part. But Loray had a big crush on Sammy, as did a lot of women. She was beautiful, very nice and a pretty good singer. I called the Silver Slipper, which was down the street from the Sands. Over the phone, I introduced myself to her. I asked her to please come over to Sammy's room at the Sands, saying that he wanted to talk to her. She was thrilled and said, of course, she'd come over.

"Now look," Sammy said, "when she gets here, I want you to be in the room with me. I'm going to make her a business proposition, and I want you to witness it."

Loray came over, all happy, not having a clue what Sammy wanted. We sat in Sammy's bedroom. He opened by saying, "Loray, I have something very important to talk to you about. I want you to marry me."

Loray's mouth dropped to the floor. "Oh, my God, Sammy!" she exclaimed. "Yes! Yes!"

"No, you don't understand. This is a business proposition."

"What do you mean?" she asked.

"This is a business proposition. Let me finish talking. Then we can take it from there. I will give you ten thousand dollars to marry me and stay married to me for one year. I will give you a house to live in. You will go to all functions with me as my wife, and you will get the benefits, whatever they might be, from being Mrs. Sammy Davis Jr., but that's as far as it goes. We will have no intimate relationship. This is strictly a business proposition." Loray started to cry, but Sammy went on, "I'm sorry, I didn't mean to upset you, but that's the deal."

"Sammy…Sammy," said Loray, "don't you know I've loved you for so long? You don't have to make a business deal with me. I know we could make this work."

"I'm sorry, Loray. No! I'm deeply in love with someone else and this is strictly a business deal. Take it or leave it."

Loray answered, "If that's the only way I can get you, I'll take it."

That night between shows we went to the Silver Slipper where Loray was performing. This was one of the first times I had seen Sammy drink. He began to get drunk. Loray introduced him. He got up on the stage and announced they were engaged to be married.

Naturally, the Las Vegas Press picked **that** up fast, which was the point. It had to get onto the wire services quickly so it would get back to Hollywood and stop him from being maimed for life, or killed.

There were other forces at work to stop this hit. The call to Donjo Medlivine brought in forces of Sam Giancana, head of the Chicago Mob, and Mo Dalitz of the Las Vegas Mob. They said they could protect him in Chicago or Las Vegas, but not Hollywood, and only to a certain point because of the strength of some other factions of the Mob. These important people were brought into play to keep anything bad from happening to Sammy, and to put a lid on his romance with Kim. So the danger would pass, and no one would get hurt. This would make everyone happy, except for the two people involved.

Loray, and Sammy filling out the marriage license— I am behind them—Jess Rand is far right

Best man, Harry Belafonte, applauds the wedding kiss

Moulin Rouge, site of the wedding reception

left to right:
Will Mastin, Peewee, Loray, Sammy, and Loray's relatives

The marriage to Loray was scheduled to happen a couple of days later. Sammy, Loray, Jess Rand and I went to the courthouse to get the marriage license. Sammy couldn't write; he had never gone to school, but had taught himself to read. He was a voracious reader, but could not write much more than "Best Wishes," and his name. Jess told Sammy, letter by letter, what to write and how to fill out the marriage license.

This was a very sad moment for all of us, knowing what was behind it was terrible. We never knew when we walked out the door if we were going to get jumped on, shot, or what. It was a very scary time.

Prior to the wedding ceremony, as we walked out of Sammy's room, we were met by Sam Sr., Peewee and Will. Peewee had a big box in her hand wrapped in silver paper with a big white bow on top. She had instructions to give this to Sammy before he got married. Sammy wasn't in a very good mood about this wedding, anyway. Opening that box started the downfall of the evening to come. Inside was the blue plaid blanket with the silver dove pin in the middle and a card that simply said "K." When he saw that box and its contents, Sammy came unglued.

Sammy had asked Frank Sinatra to be his best man, but Frank was too concerned about trying to keep people off Sammy. Harry Belafonte stood in for Frank as Sammy's best man. The wedding was in the Emerald Room of the Sands Hotel. The reception took place at the Moulin Rouge, which had just opened. It was a big fancy Vegas Strip-type hotel on the Black side of town.

**Loray White,
the new bride**

Sammy was not a drinking person, but that night he started drinking out of his league. He proceeded to get so drunk he was pouring Jack Daniels into the ice buckets on the table and drinking from them.

He began to get belligerent, crying and screaming things like "Why can't they let me live my life like a human being? Why must I always have to fight, fight, fight for everything I do, everything I want? I'm sick and tired of rolling up in a smelly old rug, on the floor in the back of a car, breathing in all of the dirt and crud.

Big John, Sammy's bodyguard

What is it that they want me to do? Are they telling me that I'm not good enough to be seen with a White woman? Do they want me to get my skin bleached white? What is it? I'm a human being. Why can't I be with the woman I love?"

This was causing quite a scene, and of course Loray was completely distraught and crying. This was one hell of a wedding party. It finally got so bad that I had Big John Hopkins, Sammy's bodyguard, come over to help me get Sammy out of there.

The Sands had given Sammy the bridal suite for the occasion. The suite was not in the building our regular rooms were in. Big John literally picked Sammy up and took him kicking and screaming, out of his head, to the car. We finally got Loray into the car, hysterical as well; and I drove the three of us back to the Sands Hotel.

By this time, the sun was coming up. It was very short, but one of the worst drives of my life. When we got there, Loray jumped out of the car and ran into the room. I pulled Sammy out of the car and picked him up like one would pick up a child and held him in my arms.

He was screaming at the top of his voice, the same rhetoric. "Why me?" He grabbed the shoulder of my right jacket sleeve and ripped it right off. I took him into the bedroom and threw him onto the bed.

Loray was crying hysterically in the front room, so I went in to calm her down. Something just told me to go back into the bedroom.

As I hit the door, Sammy was putting a gun to his head. I jumped on top of him, put my knees on his shoulders and pinned his arms down to the bed. I wrestled the gun out of his hand, trying to keep him from pulling the trigger. It was loaded. I twisted his arm and the gun fell to the floor. Then I slapped him across the face very hard, cursing at him, "You stupid son-of-a-bitch. What are you trying to do? There's no reason for this. It'll all work out; don't worry."

Sammy was groggy, so I stayed there on top of him until he passed out. I picked up the gun and went back to quiet Loray down. I gave her a wet towel, asked her to please calm down, and told her I just couldn't keep dealing with this. She kept crying about how much she loved him, but finally calmed down. I got her to go back to our regular room to sleep. I stayed on the couch for a long time to make sure Sammy was really passed out, which he was, dead to the world.

Then I searched the room for more firearms, but didn't find any. It was not unusual for Sammy to have guns around him. He had a permit to carry a gun. Also, we both practiced quick draw, and he used it in his show. Sammy must have had about four Colt .45s—short barrel, long barrel—boxes full of full-load blanks, and all sorts of live .45 cartridges, as did I. We used to go out in the desert and target practice. He also had two .38s. One was a silver semiautomatic and the other was a snub-nose, the one that I had taken out of his hand.

After Sammy had completely passed out and Loray was back in his other room, I went through every piece of luggage, every drawer, everything in that entire suite. I collected every gun that was there—his and mine—as well as all the ammunition, including the blanks. I removed them from the rooms and put them someplace so no one knew where they were, except me and the hotel security person who told me where to put them.

Sammy's marriage made news all over the world, which we hoped would take the pressure off. However, he was still going through the pain of receiving the blanket. Although probably unintentional, I think it was the worst move Kim could have made. This was like putting a dagger into Sammy's stomach and twisting it four or five times. Kim loved him dearly and would never have meant to cause him such pain It was just too much for him to handle. Being under the threat of having his other eye put out and both his knees busted so he could never dance again was bad enough. Add to that not being able to be with the woman he truly loved, and being forced by these dire circumstances to marry someone he did not love. The blanket was the kicker.

I insisted Peewee take the blanket back to Los Angeles when she left; it just needed to be kept away from Sammy. Patsy and I would be the only ones there with Sammy when everyone else left, so I had to keep things together. This was major, major stress!

The next day things began to calm down. We got word the Columbia people had backed off their threats. The message was: "Tell the little Black bastard to keep away from Kim Novak, and there won't be any more trouble. But, if he makes another move on her, he's a dead man."

In my personal opinion, I truly believe it was a matter of money, rather than a relationship, that was behind all the threats and pressures put upon them. Kim was the hottest property Columbia Pictures had; and nobody in Hollywood would put love before money.

Sammy and Loray now shared the suite with me, and there were some very pitiful goings on. I witnessed things that were very unpleasant, to say the least. Unpleasant because here was a woman who was very much in love with a man who could care less that she even existed—he was so much in love with someone else.

Once, in the living room, Loray dropped to her knees and started to take Sammy's pants down right in front of me. She didn't care who was there; she just wanted to make love to him. He stood there like an icicle. She was crying and screaming how much she loved him and had to have him. I excused myself and said I couldn't stay there and watch; I had to get out of there.

Loray cried, "I don't care, Arthur. I don't care if you're here or not. It makes no difference to me. I want him. I've got to have him."

I told her it was not going to happen, and finally got her to go with me into my room where I sat her down and talked to her. She was not drunk. She had made up her mind she was going to make a go of this marriage. Sammy was equally insistent that nothing at all was going to happen between them, other than the show they put on when they went out in public.

Things calmed down a bit after a while. Loray started to play the part. Sammy played his part, but the phone kept ringing—**the** phone, and the conversations never stopped.

Upon our return to Los Angeles, Sammy rented a house in Malibu where he and Kim could meet in relative seclusion. I was the one who used to drive him there. But this arrangement only lasted for a few months. The pressure on Kim from the studio and Harry Cohn was so heavy, plus the pressure on Sammy's life and safety, that this romance didn't have a chance in hell. It was a shame, because they loved each other deeply; but it was the wrong time for these two people. Finally, tragically, it had to come to a stop—one of the saddest things I have ever witnessed. I'd seen Sammy go through a lot of hell in his life, but I never saw anything more painful to him than the ending of his romance with Kim.

She wasn't really a Hollywood person. Though she had a home in Beverly Hills, she lived a good deal of her life up the California coast in Big Sur. When the relationship between Kim and Sammy finally ended, they never spoke. They never saw one another again, except years later at an important Hollywood function which they both attended. She and Sammy danced one dance together. And that was it. When it was over, it was over. Any more seeing one another was just too hurtful, and I don't think Sammy ever took anything harder in his life than breakup with Kim Novak.

Sammy bought Loray a beautiful home up the hill from where he lived. He did not live in that home with her. He did not spend any time with her as a husband, though she accompanied him on all social occasions. She tried, every way she could, to be a good wife, to really be his wife, and to really land him, but it never happened.

That relationship lasted a lot longer than a year because Loray's love for Sammy eventually turned into an extreme dislike, perhaps even a hate. While she was with Sammy, she took him for a lot more than that original ten thousand dollars she was offered to marry him. She got houses, money, furs, and jewelry; and she played it to the hilt. I can't honestly say that I blamed her. It was a difficult time for us all.

AUGUST 20 – SEPTEMBER 21

SAMMY DAVIS JR. SHOW

SAMMY'S 100th ANNIVERSARY WEEK!

Sands

LAS VEGAS, NEVADA

The Mob Rules

Carl Cohen had just died of a heart attack. Carl was the casino manager of the Sands, the "real big boss." Casinos ruled Las Vegas hotels, but Carl Cohen was so important to the Sands that on the day of his death—for the first and only time in the history of the hotel—the Sands closed the casino.

Later that day, when Patsy and I had dinner, she asked, "Honey, what's all this stuff I hear about the Mob guys?"

"You mean you haven't learned anything in the length of time you've been here?"

"Well, a little," she said. "It's kind of like not knowing at first about the thing with Sammy and Kim. I've heard some things, but I think there's a lot more I don't know."

"Okay, I'll try to explain what I've learned, as I've dealt with it for years everywhere."

"I'm all ears."

I chuckled, "There's a lot more to you than ears...but that's where I'll start. The Mob is like a giant octopus. Each of its many tentacles is a Mafia family unto itself headed by its own boss, called 'The Don,' like Al Capone or Sam Giancana. Each family is like an army that has its own lieutenants, sergeants and soldiers. Each of those arms reaches out into every part of casino life, though most people aren't aware of it.

"Take this table we're sitting at, for instance. The table linens, silverware—even the glass of wine you're drinking—are all controlled by the Mob, as well as the bed linens and towels in all the hotel rooms. The Mob controls the laundries that clean the linens. They control the slaughter houses that provide the steak you're eating. They own the bakeries, pasta companies, canning plants and produce companies, as well as all the imported Italian olive oil."

"Are you telling me that everything I eat in Las Vegas, the beds I sleep in and the towels I dry off with in the hotel, are all owned by the Mob?" she asked.

"Yes, if not owned, most certainly controlled," I answered. "It's all true, and that's just the tip of the iceberg. Remember hearing about the days of Prohibition? The Mob controlled all the bootlegging operations, and still controls the liquor that goes into the major nightclubs, bars and hotels in this country, as well as all the casinos. They are the liquor distributors. And all the distilleries are still owned or controlled by them, as well as the pinball machines and vending machine companies from which you get your soft drinks, candy and such. They also control most of the trucking companies that haul all these things across the country. The Mob has its hands in every aspect of show business, such as nightclub acts, movie studios, talent agencies and record companies."

"Stop!" said Patsy. "This is a lot to take in. It's really hard to believe they have so much control."

"Well, you asked. But, you ain't heard nothing' yet!"

"How much more can there be?"

"The Mob is into prostitution—which is legal in some parts of Nevada—drugs and loan sharking. Damn, Patsy; I know you're a young gal from San Antonio, but you must know about some of this stuff."

"I give up. It's just hard for me to take all this in."

"I can understand you not wanting to hear all the details. Most people don't know, or care for that matter. But it's all true. On the lighter side, when we get back into the casino, take a good look around and try to find a clock. In fact, there are no visible clocks in any casino."

"Why?" she asked. "That doesn't make any sense to me."

"Because they don't want anyone to know what time it is, if it's late at night or early in the morning. The casino managers don't want anyone to have any distractions from gambling, and they don't want anyone to leave and go to bed. For the same reason, there are no windows where people can look out and see the sun coming up or going down.

"Look at how the gambling tables are laid out. Blackjack, craps and roulette are in 'pits' surrounded by slot machines; but baccarat, the big money game, is in a room of its own, away from the noise. No one can go into the baccarat rooms except the players, bosses and security. There are no chairs or couches around the other table games, only at the tables themselves, and some of the slots. So, if you sit, you have to be gambling. No table games are near any outside doors."

"But, I don't understand. What's the reason behind all these rules?"

"It's all psychological, honey," I said. "It's all about the money. Most of the casino ceilings are low, and the carpets and walls are mostly red nowadays. The red is supposed to make people feel comfortable, cozy, and safe, while at the same time making them feel reckless enough to take chances with their money.

"Many casino pits are at a lower level than the rest of the casino floor, and you have to step down into them. This is another way to make the people feel they're 'inside' and don't want to leave. The Mob wants as much control over each person as they can get."

"Why do they call it the pit?" she asked.

"It could be because the table games are a couple of steps lower than the main floor. But I like to believe the story told to me by an old pit boss who said the oldest gambling game known to modern man is craps, or dice, which originated in the days of the Roman Empire. He told me that in those days it was played by throwing the dice into an elongated box, or against the side of a wall which they called the dice pit, and that the name has stuck. I don't know how true that story is, but it sounds okay to me."

"Now that's an interesting story and makes a lot more sense to me than all the other stuff you've been telling me."

"Well then, I have just one more story to tell you. It's not a pretty story but shows you just how far the mob can go, and the power they really have. In Hollywood, there is a club called Earl Carroll's. Earl Carroll was second only to Flo Ziegfeld, and to be an Earl Carroll Girl was like being a Ziegfeld Girl. Earl had a huge, impressive nightclub, on the corner of Sunset and Vine, with a huge archway. Above that archway was a gigantic picture of a woman's face that said, 'The most beautiful girls in the world pass through these portals.' The stage was enormous, and they had a revue that always featured big name stars.

"Sammy had lost his eye in the accident, and during his impersonations he used to do *Dr. Jekyll and Mr. Hyde*, without any props. He would make believe he was drinking a chemical of some sort, then duck behind a table on stage. When he came up from behind the table, he would have taken his glass eye and turned it around so you could only see the white. It was truly frightening. His hair was long at the time, and with all the goop he wore on it, he could make it stand straight out and straight up in the air. He would come up with this look on his face so horrible that the audience would actually scream.

"Earl Carroll's had a very high stage and had tremendous curtains that circled the front of the stage. Sammy would run, grab hold of the curtains, jump eight or nine feet in the air and swing out over the audience.

"George Rhodes was with us then as our piano player. There was a very large area backstage with dressing rooms and a telephone on the wall across from Sammy's dressing room. One night, Sammy was in his dressing room with Sam Sr., Will and Donjo Medlivine, who was visiting from Chicago. The phone rang and I was walking by, so I answered it. The call was for George Rhodes. Soon we heard George scream, 'What? What? I'll kill that son-of-a-bitch! That motherfucker! I'm on the next plane out of here.'

"We came running to see what was happening. Now, George was a big, muscular man physically, yet a very quiet man. Nothing seemed to ever bother George. He always talked softly and was as mellow as they come, acting nothing like he appeared to be in size. George was always in control; but that night, he lost it.

"George's daughter was married to a young man in the Marine Corps. The two of them had gotten into an argument over the best way to cook macaroni and cheese—on top of the stove or in the oven. That's how stupid it was. That's the God's truth. The argument had become so violent, the young Marine picked up a Coca-Cola bottle— one of the original ones that you could bash in the top of a car with— and actually broke this Coca-Cola bottle over George's daughter's head. When the bottle broke, it put her eye out and left a big gash down the side of her face. She was in the hospital. Now George was going to go and kill the Marine. He was enraged!

"Donjo came out, grabbed George, and took him into the dressing room, trying to calm him down. George told Sammy he was out of there. Donjo told George, 'There's a better way to take care of this. Don't worry. I can pick up the phone and have this guy's arms and legs broken within ten minutes, but what's that going to do? His arms and legs will get better. Do you really want to get back at this kid? I'll take care of it. We'll make sure that when he goes on trial he spends the rest of his life in jail, with no chance of parole.'

George Rhodes

"That's exactly what happened. And if he's not dead by now, the guy is probably still in jail. Sammy paid for George's daughter to have plastic surgery and a glass eye. It was so successful that unless you knew she had an artificial eye, you couldn't tell by looking. Her face healed almost completely, and she was just as pretty as before she was hurt. This was part of the diamond-in-the-rough side of Donjo. 'No, we won't kill him. We'll just put him away for life so he'll remember every day for the rest of his life what he did.'"

"My God!" she said. "What a price to pay for macaroni and cheese!"

After dinner, we headed back toward the stage entrance to get ready for the first show and detoured through the casino because Patsy wanted to see for herself if some of the things I told her were true.

She said, "You know, Arthur, I really didn't believe all that stuff about no clocks, no chairs and no windows; but you're absolutely right. I would never have noticed any of that if you hadn't told me."

"That's what I was trying to explain to you. It's so subtle that nobody else notices it either."

We arrived backstage and passed by Sammy's dressing room. He yelled out, "Well, princess, did you finally bring your prince back to work. Or must I get in line to speak to sir knight?"

"Well, Sammy, I've given him a short time off so he could spend some time with you." She popped inside the dressing room, gave Sammy a quick kiss and tweaked his nose. "See ya later, sir star."

Patsy had really picked up on all that "sir knight" stuff and played around with it whenever it suited her fancy.

As I walked into the dressing room, Sammy said, "Damn, Silber, can't you get enough of that girl?"

"Not so far. As you can see, she's quite a package to handle."

"Oh, Christ, Silber, let's not go down that road again. I'm getting nauseous already. Sit your butt down 'cause there are some things I need to go over with you. After the second show, you and I need to go back to the suite alone. Patsy mustn't come back right away or if she does, she has to go into your bedroom immediately and shut the door between your bedroom and mine. No big deal, but there is something we have to do privately; and you and I are the only ones who can know about it."

"For God's sake, Sam! Are we planning some kind of undercover job or something?"

"No, not quite; but it's a little bit undercover."

"What in the hell are you up to now?" I asked.

"Don't worry, you ain't gonna get in any kind of trouble. And neither am I. Just be cool, and you'll find out later."

That was typical Sammy Davis Jr. stuff: making a movie production out of everything. "Okay, my liege," I said. "Later."

After the second show Sammy wanted to return to the suite right away, by far not his usual routine. As we walked out of the dressing room, Sammy reached into the closet and pulled out one of those little shoulder bags the airlines used to give out. It was blue, with "Pan American Airlines" on it, and was obviously full. Sammy was adamant that I not say anything about this to anyone; not Patsy, not Massey and not his father—no one!

"Damn it, Sammy, what do you have in that bag? It's either someone's head or all the gold from the Lost Dutchman Mine."

"Not quite," he said, "but close."

We entered Sammy's bedroom. He immediately closed the drapes, and locked the door. Then he motioned me to sit on the bed with him. Without another word, he unzipped the bag and dumped the contents on the bed between us. It was bundles of money.

"My God, Sam! Where in hell did you get all of this? There must be thousands here!"

"Yeah, that's right! Thirty thousand to be exact."

"You've got thirty thousand dollars sitting on this bed when anyone could have followed us here, come in to kill us both, steal the money and be gone? Did some of the Mob guys give you this for some stupid reason, or what? And why am I supposed to know about it?"

"Cause you and I are the only ones who know I've got it, and are the only ones who can touch it."

"Nah, man, I don't want any part of this one. I don't want some Mob guy gunning after me."

"Wait a minute, Silber. That ain't gonna happen 'cause the money didn't come from the Mob."

"Then, where did it come from?"

"While you were out having dinner with the princess, I was meeting with an Australian promoter who wanted to pay me some up front money to play a gig for him in Australia."

"Come on, man. You mean he's paying you under the table money for the gig?"

"Well, kind of."

"What do you mean, 'kind of?' We're sittin' on this bed with thirty thousand dollars, and nobody but you and I are supposed to know about it? And all you can say is 'kind of?' You're full of shit with this thing. It's dumb—dangerous; and you're a stupid motherfucker for doing it. Then I took a deep breath. "All right, given all that, what are we going to do with all the money?"

"I'm gonna put it in my briefcase, the one with the combination lock on it that only you and I have the combination to. Then, whenever I need a little extra spending money, here it is."

"What in the hell are you thinking?" I asked. "You plan to keep this kind of money in the room so you can get to it when you need it. Just where do you intend to put the briefcase?"

"Right there, against the wall with the rest of the luggage."

"And, you think there's no way that some maid or someone else won't ever think to take an alligator briefcase from here and get away with it? No, Sam, this money's going into a safe deposit box in the hotel. I can go get one right now."

"No, you can't! You know Vegas. If something different or out of the ordinary happens, everybody knows about it within five minutes. If the hotel knows we've gotten some kind of a safety deposit box, they'll know something's up. Then in come the big guys asking lots of questions. This has got to be like when I had the private phone line installed in here so the phone calls between Kim and me would not be listened in on—and you know they do that."

"Sammy, look me straight in the eye and tell me this is not the most stupid idea you've ever come up with."

"Okay, what do you think I should do with all the money then?"

"How about let's give it back to the guy who gave it to you?"

"I can't do that, man," he answered. "Besides he's left by now."

"All right, Sam. I can see you're not gonna change your mind, but understand one thing. You're my best friend and my blood brother; but if anything happens to this money, don't even look my way! It's a bad idea; but if that's what you want, then I'll do what you ask."

"Remember, no one knows," he reminded me again, "not even the princess."

"Not to worry. She's the last person I'd tell, because I don't ever want to put her in that kind of a position."

We locked the money up in the briefcase and tossed it in the corner with the rest of the luggage. I sat back on the bed and grabbed Sammy's hand.

"Sammy, we both know the trouble you're already in with the Internal Revenue Service. How in good common sense can you even think of keeping all that money for yourself?"

"To hell with the IRS! Chicago is sending out one of their bookkeepers to take care of all my IRS shit."

"You know what will happen to you if the Mob guys get mixed up with your finances. For Christ's sake, Sam, they'll find a way to lock you up to them; and that's the one thing you said you never wanted to have happen to you."

"Don't worry! The guys just want to help me out by sending their bookkeeper who knows a lot more than my old guy."

"Damn sure they know a lot more, Sam. They'll own your dick if you give them the chance. And I'm not too sure they don't own your balls already because of Kim. It's your life, man. But remember, your life is my life, too. I just see a black cloud coming your way; and you know that when they've got ya, they've got ya for life."

"That ain't gonna happen to me, Silber. They like me too much; I make them too much money in their clubs."

"Okay, my brother. I've spoken my piece."

"Silber, I've heard everything you've said, and I appreciate your opinions; but it's all going to be cool. I promise."

"Cool, maybe, but not safe."

I went to my bedroom and the minute I got there Patsy asked me what the meeting was about. I told her Sammy had just made two of the stupidest moves of his life and that I couldn't tell her much, but I could say Sammy had some Mob bookkeepers coming out from Chicago to help him with his IRS problems.

"And," I told her, "that's a bad thing."

"What do you mean 'a bad thing?'"

"Once those guys get involved with your money, they've got you by the short hairs. And they'll get you so tight that you'll never get away again. They'll have control of your financial life forever."

"But I don't understand how that can happen," she shrugged.

"Haven't you heard anything I've told you tonight? It's like everything else I said. You either can't see it, or you just don't want to. We know Sammy doesn't care about money or making any plans for future investments. Money to Sammy is just a way to buy the things he wants. He doesn't care about all the legal stuff. All he wants to know is when and where do I play my next gig, and how much are they going to pay me? But if the Mob takes over his financial business, Sammy won't really know what's going on behind the scenes."

She tried again, "I don't mean to be that stupid, but how can they do that without him knowing about it?"

"Okay, this is the last thing I'm going to explain to you about the Mob tonight. Let's say a promoter wants Sammy to play his nightclub or theater. The promoter starts by dealing with Sammy's representative, and his representative says it will cost the promoter sixty thousand dollars. The promoter agrees to the deal. Then Sammy's representative goes to him and says he just locked up a deal for fifty thousand dollars. Sammy trusts his people to do right by him, so he doesn't question the deal. The Mob ends up ten thousand dollars richer, and Sammy still has to pay commissions to his representative. Everybody makes money, but Sammy still loses ten thousand dollars; and that, sweet princess, is called skimming.

"Another game the Mob plays is that when a performer who gambles heavily plays his clubs, they allow that performer to draw gambling money against his paychecks. If these performers are big losers and lose more than their salaries, it can keep them indebted to the hotel for years. They have to keep coming back to perform at the hotel until they've repaid their losses. It's a vicious circle."

"Oh, my God! Poor Sammy! Doesn't he know about all that?"

"Yes, Sammy knows about skimming. But he thinks that these guys love him so much and have taken such good care of him in the past that they would never do anything like that to him. Of course, that's pure bullshit! That is exactly what these Mob guys wait for. They don't love Sammy. They use him, then call him 'Nigger' and much worse behind his back. Remember, it's all about the money."

"Can't you do anything to help him out?" she asked.

"No! All I can do is give him my thoughts and feelings, which I have done; but it's his decision."

"God, I'm so sorry for Sammy. I wish there was something I could do to help him."

"I know; me too."

A week or two later, during the Thanksgiving holiday, I flew into Los Angeles for one night to have dinner with my mother. While I was gone, one of our women friends, a small-time lounge singer named Ruth, asked Sammy if she could borrow five hundred dollars. Sam, being Sam, never gave it a second thought, and got the money out of the briefcase.

I flew back to Las Vegas the next day and went straight to the dressing room from the airport. A jeweler friend of ours from New York was visiting, so I bid all a hello and left to put my travel bag in our suite. A few minutes later the phone rang and Sammy asked me to bring him a couple of thousand dollars from the briefcase. He was buying some expensive jewelry as gifts for the Maitre d' and the other guys who worked the door in the Copa Room.

I looked and looked, but couldn't find the briefcase anywhere. Sometimes Sammy didn't put it back in the same place he took it from. So I called the dressing room asking, "Where in the hell did you put the briefcase this time?"

"What the hell do you mean?"

"I can't find it, and I've looked all over these rooms."

With noticeable panic in his voice, Sammy responded, "Look harder! It's got to be in there. I went into it just this afternoon to loan Ruth five hundred."

"Okay, I'll look again."

I looked everywhere, but no briefcase. I went through every piece of luggage, searched his room, my room, the living room. I even looked through the bathrooms. Still no briefcase. I picked up the phone again. "Sammy, it just ain't here; and I've looked everywhere."

"Oh shit! You better call Security and have a guy come help you look one more time."

"Call Security? I thought we weren't supposed to let anyone in on this. Security should be the last ones we call. What do I tell them is in the case?"

"Just tell them there are very important papers, contracts and such."

I called Security and they sent a guy to the suite within a few minutes. I explained to him that Sammy's black alligator briefcase was missing and Sammy wanted him to help me look for it one more time. We looked everywhere, but just couldn't find it. The Security man took out his little book and asked me to give a full report. I knew Sammy didn't want to file a formal report, so I told him Sammy and I would deal with it from here.

"Are you sure?" he asked.

I nodded my head, and he left.

I called Sammy again announcing, "It's gone, and gone for good!"

"God damn it," he swore. "Who in the hell could have taken it?"

"When you were getting the money for Ruth, did you close the door to your bedroom? Do you realize that from certain parts of the living room, one can look straight into your bedroom?"

"No, I guess I didn't close the door. But Ruth would never steal from me."

"Thank God I was in L.A. with my mom. I hate to say 'I told you so,' but I told you so!"

"Shut the fuck up, Silber. I don't need to hear all this shit right now."

"I'm sorry, Sam; but you know how I felt about keeping all this money in the room. Now what do you want me to do?"

"Nothing we can do except keep a sharp eye on Ruth and see if she starts coming up with a lot of new stuff. Damn it, you were right again; and you know how that pisses me off. I could kick my ass big time…but oh, well…it's only money."

"Yeah…it's only money!"

We kept a real close eye on Ruth, but nothing. However, one member of Sammy's entourage did show up a few weeks later with a brand new car. Who can say for sure? The funniest thing of all is that Sammy never did play that gig in Australia and had to pay the promoter back the thirty thousand dollars. A hard lesson learned.

Samart Enterprises, Inc.
1584 A CROSS ROADS OF THE WORLD
HOLLYWOOD 28, CALIF.

HOLLYWOOD 7-6114

Applying for our business license—thinking we'll make millions in our new venture

Once Upon an Idea

For several weeks, I had been thinking about the Mob people moving in on Sammy's finances, and it really bothered me. This concerned me so much that I had been trying to think of ideas for a business he and I could run together that would not be of interest to the Mob. My idea was to use the power of Sammy's name to draw people in and maybe get endorsements. It was hard to think of something viable because, in those days, the only things that Black people were able to endorse were products that just people of color used, like hair products.

Then it hit me! We could open a business helping people develop new products or produce movies and television shows. By this time, Sammy had made his share of movies and TV shows, which gave us some connections. However, it would be necessary for me to come off the road from time to time and stay in Los Angeles until we got the business going, something Sammy couldn't and wouldn't do; he was never able to sit still in one place for very long.

Even I could hardly imagine staying in one place for a while; no more nightly parties and hanging out with stars all the time. It wasn't that I would be completely locked down—Sammy wouldn't go for that at all.

One night as Sammy and I were sitting at his house, having one of those long talks we used to have, I threw out the idea. Much to my surprise, Sammy flipped over it. He got so excited that his mind began to run at full speed. "Silber," he said, "just think! We could make our own movies and TV shows, and develop all kinds of things."

"Yeah, that's kind of what I had in mind," I nodded.

If the truth were to be known, as much as Sammy loved being on stage and performing before all those live audiences, in his real gut and heart he wanted to be a movie star. This is something he never said to a living soul, except me. He had done television drama and received Emmy nominations for "Memory in White," and "Auf

Wiedersehen," both *General Electric Theater* productions. Still that wasn't enough; his greatest dream was to be a movie star.

"Well," Sammy started, "We'll have to open an office, and give the business a name…get publicity out. God! I'm getting so up on this I might just pee myself."

"I don't think you need to go quite that far. But I do have a name for the business, if you agree. What do you think of 'Samart Enterprises,' combining your name and mine?"

"That's great! I love it. So, as of this night, we have a new business called Samart Enterprises. Fucking great!"

"Damn! Sam, I haven't seen you so excited since you got laid four or five times in one day."

"Okay, Silber, cut the bullshit. You really came up with a good one this time."

"I am only here to serve you, my liege."

"Tomorrow you gotta start looking for an office to rent, maybe even in the same place where your dad had his office."

"That sounds good to me. Cross Roads of the World is a pretty prestigious place to have an office, especially since it's on Sunset Boulevard; and it ain't cheap either,"

"Well, neither am I! Do you think maybe they'll have some empty office space we can rent?"

"I've known the manager, Bill Andrews, since I was a kid. I'll go see him tomorrow. You know, my dad had his office there from the time I was born until he died. Bill just loved Dad; if there's an empty office, I'm sure we can get it. I feel like we're coming full circle."

When I walked into Bill's office his mouth almost dropped to the floor. He shook my hand and gave me a big hug. Then he asked what I was up to. I told him Sammy and I had formed a business and asked if he had any vacant office space. His response was immediate and to the point. "If I didn't have any, I'd throw someone out. However, it so happens that I have a swell office open. It has one very large room, a slightly smaller room, and space for a waiting room and secretary. For the sake of my long relationship with your dad, and you—and because Sammy's involved—I'll give you a good rental price on a year-to-year basis."

"That sounds great, Bill. I'll run it past my partner, Sammy, and let you know tomorrow."

When I told Sammy he was thrilled, especially when I told him this office happened to be right across from my dad's old office.

"So, Silber, what do we do next?"

"How about you coming over with me and checking it out?"

"Let's go!"

Sammy became excited when Bill took us through the suite of offices. It was carpeted with a black and white zebra-like pattern that looked very expensive. Sammy loved the big office which, of course, would be his. The other office would be mine.

Now all we needed was a business license, checking account, stationery, business cards, office furniture, typewriter, file cabinets, and we were good to go. I had one desk at home from my father's office and would use that myself. But that was just about it. I had sold everything else in my dad's office after he died. What were we to do next? You guessed it! We had to go shopping! And how convenient was it that there was a large office furniture and supply store right across the street from the Cross Roads? We told Bill to draw up the papers and we'd come back later to sign them.

Sammy just couldn't wait to get into that store; and he spent big bucks in there. I had to hold him back because he was really caught up in the whole idea of Samart Enterprises. He could see himself sitting behind the big desk, feet up, leaning back and talking big business. It was that Sammy thing again—making a movie production out of everything.

I spent the next week getting all the necessary papers for the business license, opening bank accounts, ordering business cards, and telephones. After everything was set up, we sat in Sammy's big business office with nothing to do. I said, "Sam, here we are, all dressed up with nowhere to go. Don't you think we need to call the press and let them know what we're doing?"

"Yeah," he answered. "As a matter of fact, I thought we should run an ad or get someone to do a little story on us."

"Like who?"

"How about calling *Ebony* and *Jet* magazines to ask them if they'd be interested in doing an article? I'll call *Variety* and the *Hollywood Reporter*."

They **all** wanted to do a story about us; Sammy's name always drew attention. *Ebony* and *Jet* wanted to send out reporters and photographers. Sammy and I set up appointments with them to come to the office for the interviews, because the office was genuinely impressive. Sammy wanted them to know this was no joke—we were sincere about our business endeavors.

In fact, all the media we contacted came, and articles resulted. Someone had to be in the office to answer the phones when the articles broke. That someone was naturally me.

Phones started ringing nonstop. Everyone wanted to talk to Sammy, of course. It got to be too much, too fast. I told Sammy I couldn't be running around all over the country with him and sit in the Hollywood office at the same time.

"You're right, Silber. Run an ad for someone who can answer the phone, take dictation and type—and make sure she's attractive. Get a Black girl who has all the attributes, and who can sit here all day just taking messages until we get this thing going."

"Yeah," I answered, "and maybe we should get a small television as it's damn sure better than looking at the walls all day."

"Okay," he said. "That's no problem. Just take care of it all. But when it comes down to the final choice, set up interviews with me so I can choose between them myself."

"Of course, what else would I do?"

We hired a girl named Jean Fleming.

The entrepeneur and businessman, in his office

Starting this business caused a real problem for me. I had to deal with Patsy, and our relationship. We had been engaged for months now. The Sands had put together another chorus line to replace the Texas Copa Girls because their contract was up. I made the decision to try and set a wedding date with the princess. We had talked about this many times, but I hoped the Samart thing would now bring our relationship to fulfillment and marriage.

I called Patsy at her home in San Antonio and asked her when and where she wanted to get married. Much to my surprise, she was hesitant, saying, "I'm not sure."

"What do you mean, you're not sure?"

"Well," she hesitated, "I got an offer to do a USO tour...and I really want to do it."

"What the hell are you talking about, 'USO tour?' What are you supposed to be doing with the USO?"

"They're going to have a little chorus line made up of a few of us from the Sands."

"No, Patsy!" I exclaimed. "That ain't gonna work for me at all!"

"But I really want to do this. We'll be all over the world, going to places I've never been to before, and might never see again."

"Are you telling me that you'd rather put our marriage off to go romping around the world—after all we've planned? Why this now? And more to the point, why at all? Do you have some kind of doubts about me, or our love?"

"No, Sweetheart, never," she answered. "It's just that I'm scared to make this kind of commitment right now."

"Are you saying that if you go running off with the USO for several months, when you come back, you won't be scared any more? That's all bullshit, Patsy, and you know it!"

By this time she was hysterical, and wasn't making any sense at all, "You're going to have to give me more than that or it's over."

"I can't believe all this! You've just taken my heart and jumped on it. And you've kicked my guts out—all without any warning."

"Oh, God, Arthur, I am so sorry. And I do love you so much—more than anyone or anything in the world."

"Except the USO!" I said.

"Can't you understand? I'm just scared."

"Yeah, I can understand scared—but not running away from all this professed love. What are your plans?"

"We have to go to New York for a few of days of rehearsals, then off we go on the tour."

"And just when were you going to tell me all this?"

"I've been trying to tell you for a week now, but I was scared."

"So you were going to take off without telling me at all?"

"No, Honey," she said, "I never would have done that. Never! You are the love of my life, but this is just something I have to do."

"Well, here is what I must do. If you go, you'll be walking out of my life, and there won't be any coming back! I can't and won't live with all this hurt, pain and uncertainty. That's the way it is Princess."

I hung up the phone and started crying, until I got mad—real mad!

Sam Sr. had a custom Jaguar in New York that he wanted driven to Hollywood, but wouldn't trust just anyone to drive it. After hearing about my dilemma, he said, "Son, go back to New York and talk to your gal, then you can drive my car back home."

When I told Sammy, he just couldn't believe it. "What in the hell are you talking about? The princess don't want to get married?"

"No, not exactly that. She says she's scared."

"Scared of what? Seems to me that I could never get you two apart. Do you want me to talk to her?"

"No, Sam. It isn't gonna do any good. She's made up her mind to do this USO thing, and it hurts, man, it really hurts."

"God, it seems neither one of us has had a good time of it with our lady loves lately. You know I'll do anything you ask of me to help you through this, just as you did for me. Are you sure there's nothing you want me to do?"

"Nah, man, you've already done it, just being my friend."

Sammy let me know that anything he could do, he would do and asked if I needed money to go to Texas to talk to Patsy, or to fly to New York. But no one can mend a broken heart that easily or take away the pain. No one knew better than him; no matter, Sammy had to try. It also just so happened Massey's man, Nathan, was driving back to New York and offered to take me with him. He said if I would share the driving, we'd go non-stop; and that we did.

Much to her surprise, I met Patsy at the hotel where she was staying. We talked and talked, cried and cried, but nothing changed.

I gave it my best shot, but she was just too scared to commit. Walking out that door, I closed a chapter of my life.

I returned to California; and it was time to change the pace a bit, because the Samart saga had begun. During the years we had our Hollywood office open, many people came through the door and many potential projects came our way.

One day a guy walked into my office, introduced himself. Then he threw onto my desk a little piece of plastic shaped like a bent 'V,' with a little hook on the back. He said, "Twenty-five hundred, and you own fifty-one percent."

"That's fine with me," I answered, "but just what is this thing?"

He showed me how it worked. I got excited and had a gut feeling the thing would take off. I thought it was so important I called Sammy in New York and told him I would need twenty-five hundred dollars so we could jump on this thing.

"Okay, Silber," he said, "I know you're all turned on by this thing, so explain it to me very slowly."

That I did, but he just couldn't picture it being worth anything. "Sam, I just have a gut feeling about this thing, and I'm sure it's worth trying it out."

"Nah, man," he said, "I can't see it. Just forget about it."

At this point I had to turn the man down, knowing Sammy could spend more than twenty-five hundred just going out to dinner. It was really a bummer for me. Had we invested twenty-five hundred that day, Sam, Arthur and our families would have been set for life and Sammy would not have died owing the IRS a couple of million dollars. Today, I don't think you can go anywhere in the developed world without seeing clip-on ties. That little crooked plastic thing was the thing used to hold the tie onto the shirt. We didn't make a dime, but I still have that crooked little piece of plastic.

Then, there was the little red tablet. This time a guy we knew came into my office and asked me for a glass of water. I told him the water cooler was in the outer office and to help himself. He returned with two glasses of water, put them down on my desk and said, "Okay, Arthur, I have something I think you guys might want to invest in. You can probably get in for about five grand."

He dropped a red tablet into each glass. They made little fizzy noises and started to bubble up. Once the bubbles settled, he asked me to drink mine. "I think not, my friend. You might want to drink yours first."

He drank his, and then I tried mine. Much to my surprise, it tasted like a cherry soda. "Damn, man," I said, "that's really good."

"Yeah, I know. It's a bitch, ain't it?"

Once again, I called Sammy and went into a whole explanation, and he wasn't too excited about it. Again I tried to tell him I had a gut feeling about it. But he said, "Silber, I'm getting tired of you telling me about your belly."

"Well, that's my job, isn't it, to find these things and tell you about them?"

Shit! Not again! It turned out the little red pill became a popular drink for many years called "Fizzies," and they made lots and lots of money.

However, when we were approached by a sport shirt maker to do a line of sport shirts, Sammy jumped at that. He even did a whole picture shoot wearing each of the shirts. That endeavor fell flat on its face and went nowhere.

I could go on for days about all the stupid things we invested in that went belly up, and all the things we didn't invest in that became huge success stories. We never knew if we were doing something wrong, or just had extremely bad luck. On the other hand, my personal luck turned good.

Peppi Borza was a friend of ours, who hung out with us when we were in Vegas. He and his sister, Nita, were the top acrobatic dance act in the world; they headlined everywhere they appeared. They were the fifth generation of a noted circus family.

When we went back to Las Vegas, Sammy decided we should make "the great American western" film and call it *Captured*. He wanted us to go out on location early in the morning and just shoot it. Of course, we needed props. So we went backstage and got a gold-flecked wooden pick axe and shovel that they used in the show. Nita was enlisted as script girl, although we had no script either. All we had was empty desert—where the Mirage Hotel and Casino stands today.

Nita came out with us, even though she had been up all night—she and Peppi had barely finished performing three shows—and she pitched in willingly. We even used her purse, which looked like a pony express bag, to hide the gold in our story.

Since we didn't have a camera, we enlisted the help of Joe Moll, lighting director for the Sands Hotel. He brought his 16mm Bolex and shot the film. Today I have the only, original of this film.

Peppi Borza

Peppi, me and Sammy

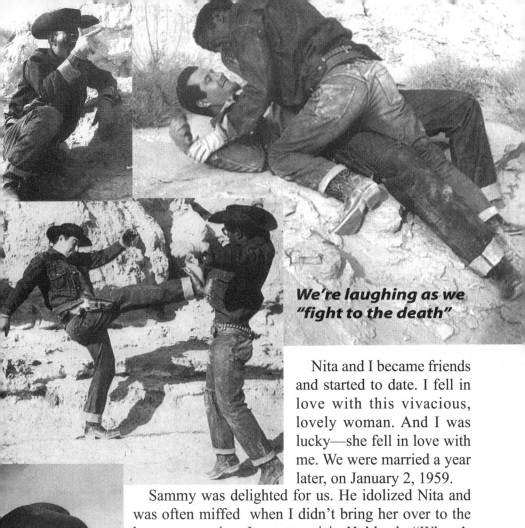

We're laughing as we "fight to the death"

Nita and I became friends and started to date. I fell in love with this vivacious, lovely woman. And I was lucky—she fell in love with me. We were married a year later, on January 2, 1959.

Sammy was delighted for us. He idolized Nita and was often miffed when I didn't bring her over to the house every time I went to visit. He'd ask, "Where's Nita? Damn it, I want to see her face around here more often!" Sammy understood how much I'd been hurt when Patsy left me, but he also understood that this time around, I'd found gold.

Sammy was booked into the Sands again and insisted I be there, so off I went to join him. While in Las Vegas, we met an Englishman named Al Burnett, who wanted to book Sammy in the United Kingdom. We both really wanted to go. Just the thought of going to the land where the Knights of the Round Table reigned really made our hearts jump, since we had been playing that game for years. I wasted no time in making all the arrangements.

Nita

Mr. & Mrs. Arthur H. Silber Jr.
[In the Sarasota Tribune]

Movie star, May Britt [May is pronounced "my"]

My, my, May—When the Queen of England Calls, You Go

While preparing for our first trip to the Mother Country, Sammy and I hung around the movie studios, as we often did. One fateful day we went to Twentieth Century Fox to visit one of our dearest friends, Barbara Luna, and have lunch with her at the commissary. We were sitting and talking with Barbara when I looked up and spotted a tall blonde girl walking toward our table.

"Geez, Sam, don't turn around yet, but wait till you see what just walked in, and is moving this way!"

She was astonishingly beautiful with her long hair just trimmed around her face. As she passed our table, Sammy whispered, "Oh, shit! Who in the hell is that?"

"That's May Britt," Barbara answered. "She is the star of *The Blue Angels*, the picture I'm working on."

"Yeah, now I remember," said Sammy. "I saw her in that Brando picture, *The Young Lions*. She looked good—but, my God! In person, she is unbelievable! I can't take my eyes off her!"

"Hold it, old friend," I said. "We've been down this road before, and I'm not ready for another trip like that again…at least not this soon."

May had gotten her lunch, and she was sitting at a table by herself a short distance from us. She kept glancing our way.

I joked, "I know she's looking at me—I'm the best looking one at the table—except for Barbara. In fact, I don't know if I should be seen with someone who looks that good. I'll try and be as aloof as I can."

"Shit, Silber!" Sammy couldn't stand it. "You must be losing your mind! I've got to meet her!"

"Hold on there, guys," Barbara interrupted. "You can just stop right now. She is straight as they come."

"What do you mean 'straight?'" asked Sammy.

"She's all business. Every day she comes to work, knows her lines and is damn sure not part of the Hollywood scene. She has no group of guys hanging around—nothing like that, all business—but she is as nice and sweet as can be."

Sammy exploded, "Come on, Barbara. Help out your old friend. Introduce me!"

"Well, I'll do the best I can. But remember what Arthur said about your last experience."

"Oh, he's full of shit—I've really got to meet this lady."

"Wait a second, man," I said. "I'm the one she really wants...and that means she'll just be trying to get to me by way of you."

"Silber, shut the fuck up, please!"

We were laughing. But once again, Sammy was hooked. I just wasn't ready for Sammy to go through another Kim thing. As fate would have it, a couple of days later Sammy and I were driving down the Sunset Strip and stopped for a red light. Who should walk across the street right in front of us with another lady? May Britt! Sammy was transfixed. When the signal changed, his foot was glued to the brake pedal, while his eyes followed her. Finally, a cop tapped on the roof of the car and told us to move on.

I chided him, "Shit, Sam! Get this lady out of your mind or you're going to get us both run over."

We drove around a bit, then back to Sam's house to start our nightly movies. The usual gang showed up, including Barbara. Of course, Sammy had to ask if she had gotten May's phone number for him, yet.

Barbara seemed to be surprised by the question. "You mean you really want me to give you her number?"

"Damn, Barbara, didn't I ask you?"

Barbara Luna as she appeared to us, and millions of Star Trek viewers

Right: Me and Sam on the way to London

Another friend overheard the conversation and jumped in. "May? May who? You don't mean May Britt, do you? If so, you can just forget her, my friend. You ain't got a chance in hell. She's straight as an arrow."

"What in the hell is this thing 'straight as an arrow?' Every time I mention her name, that's all I hear. I've been around and had my share of chicks. A gal can't look like her and be as you say, 'straight!' It just don't smell right."

"Smell right or not," said our friend, "just forget it."

"I just want to meet the girl…that's all."

"'Just meet the girl,'" I parroted. "Sure, Sam, who in hell do you think you're kidding?"

Despite our warnings, Sammy did manage to call May, and the rest is history. When we arrived in New York a short time later, the buzz about them had already started.

While flying from New York to London, Sammy started to tell me how concerned he was about going on this trip. It was our first trip out of the United States, except for visiting Canada. Sammy was worried how he would be received. At the same time, we were excited about going to England because to us it was like stepping into an old swashbuckling movie, with all of the sirs and madams, and whatever—exciting for two young men.

Sam and I are met by Al Burnett

Traveling with us were: Sammy's conductor, Morty Stevens; his valet, Murphy Bennett; and his drummer, Michael Silva. We flew through the night wondering what was before us.

In London, we were met at the airport by Al Burnett. He was owner of the Club Pigalle where Sammy would be performing for a month. But first there would be the Royal Command Performance at the Victoria Palace Theater—for Her Royal Highness, Queen Elizabeth II, of England.

Also there to greet us was Al Hunt, Sammy's public relations person for this tour. We cleared Customs and went into the airport. Hundreds of people were there waiting—wanting to see Sammy. Stars and performers of all kinds were standing outside, reaching to shake his hand. One lady in particular was quite pushy. She came up and introduced herself as Lady Carolyn Townsend, who later became our close friend.

Al Hunt asked Sammy if he would be kind enough to do a press conference. It had been set up at the airport's VIP lounge. Sammy said he would be happy to do so. Al Burnett explained, "Your arrival here in London has created a great deal of excitement among the press. They are very eager to meet you."

Sammy replied, "I'll bet they are!"

Al smiled, "I gather you've heard about our press over here, and our relationship with American performers."

Sammy confessed that American performers who heard about his trip to London had called to tip him off. They told him to forget about going—that the press in London would kill him. "I was told they're very tricky and very dangerous. I was warned to stay away from certain members of the press...told they'll just twist things around—I was not to face them all at once, because it would be a fight."

Al Hunt offered that if Sammy would rather not meet the Press at this time, he would take care of it. Sammy said he was not looking forward to it, but he didn't mind doing interviews. He turned to me saying, "Stay close...stay close."

We walked into the VIP room. Sammy nudged me, "Are all these people reporters? There must be a hundred of them in here!"

They cleared an aisle, and he walked right through them to a little platform in the front. Al Burnett introduced Sammy, then stepped back. The questions started coming in, really hot and heavy. Sammy wanted to get control of the situation fast. He put up his hands and said, "Hold it, everyone. I just jumped off an airplane. You've got the days mixed up—tomorrow's the lynching! Today we have a press conference."

They laughed. Then Sammy looked around and picked out one gentleman. He said, "Now, sir, what were you saying?"

The reporter asked, "Is there anything between you and May Britt?"

"I sincerely hope so!" Sammy replied, and that got a laugh.

They asked if there were plans for Sammy and May to marry—and they asked about his other affairs with beautiful women. Sammy answered all their questions directly, even the tough ones. Some of the questions he answered with humor. His frankness and humor endeared him to the English Press.

"Do you intend to marry her?" came the next question.

Sammy was jousting with them verbally. He replied, "Wouldn't you want to marry May Britt? Imagine some guy saying 'No, I don't want to marry one of the most beautiful girls in the world.' Now whether or not she wants to marry me is something else."

When a reporter made a disparaging remark about Sammy's looks, Sammy took it in stride. He answered by putting the reporter on the defensive, making the other reporters laugh.

"Mr. Davis, we here in England have read of your amorous affairs with some of the most glamorous women of the world. What do you have that makes you so desirable to these fabulous creatures? If I may say, without intending to be insulting, you know you're not the most attractive man in the world."

My mouth fell, and I wondered how Sammy would answer.

His response was very simple. "Are you married, Sir?"

The reporter replied, "Yes, I am."

"Is your wife pretty—I mean, is she beautiful? Attractive?"

The reporter uneasily replied, "Yes...I think she's most attractive."

Sammy said, "Well, if I may turn the phrase around ever so slightly, you know you ain't exactly Clark Gable. What attracted your wife to you?" Everyone laughed.

"Mr. Davis, if my information is correct, you are appearing here for twenty-six nights at a flat twenty thousand pounds. In American dollars that would be approximately fifty thousand." Sammy agreed that was correct. Then the reporter said, "Are you aware that this is an extraordinary sum of money for a performer to earn here?"

Sammy replied, "I am told that. And I am most flattered by it."

The reporter went on, "Do you suppose that people would pay a cover charge of thirty dollars per couple merely to get inside Club Pigalle to watch you...plus an additional charge for every drink they want to order?"

Sammy answered, "I have to rely on Mr. Burnett's judgment in establishing his own prices."

"Is it true that you earn close to a million dollars a year?" another reporter inquired.

"Yes."

"Do you believe that you're worth being paid that much money?"

"I am to the people who pay it," Sammy answered.

"How good a performer would you say you are?" came a query.

"I am a very good performer."

There were a lot of questions about the amount of debt Sammy was in, and an insatiable curiosity about his overall earnings. Sammy was candid and funny, and with each question he answered he won another fan in the English Press.

"Mr. Davis, earning as much money as you do, how is it possible that you're in debt, or is that not true?"

"No, it is true," said Sammy.

"I suppose it's due to the fact of high taxes," said the reporter.

"No," said Sammy, "it's due to the fact that I was an idiot."

"Oh," the reporter went on, "might I inquire—are you still an idiot?"

Sammy was quick to reply, "I sincerely hope not."

From another reporter, "You dress very well. Are you influenced by our styles?"

"No, I'm influenced by good taste."

"Do you always wear a waist coat, or did you wear one just for us?"

"I often wear them at home. I love vests, as we call them. I like them because I wear watches like this one." He took out an antique gold pocket watch.

"Is that a family heirloom?" asked the reporter.

"Yes, but not my family."

"I see you wear high-topped shoes. Are those also lifts?"

"No, they're shoes that dancers wear, like Jose Greco and a few other dancers. I started wearing them because I am a great fan of President Lincoln's. He used to wear Congress Gaiters, which were a similarly high-topped shoe. I like them because they go well with my pants which are tapered."

Sammy was asked why he wore so much grease in his hair. He explained, "Because I have long hair, and I need something to hold it down. I also use it in my act when I do impersonations and I move my hair around. I have to be able to fix it fast, and the Pomade makes it stay the way I need it."

The reporters were relentless. They not only asked him about his love life, they asked about his finances, how much he was making, what he thought he was worth. Sammy just kept giving them straight answers, all the time building a wonderful rapport with them. The reporters tried their best to embarrass Sammy about the money he was making during this engagement, which was a lot of money in those days. Come to think of it, it is still a lot of money.

This kind of questioning went on for a long time, but somehow, you got the feeling there was a bond building between the British Press and Sammy. Later that proved to be quite true. They liked Sam because he was honest with them. Not only that, he was direct and polite; answering every one of their questions.

We left the press conference and went directly to the May Fair, a small hotel on a short street. Driving up, one would have no idea this was a very high-class hotel in a very posh part of London.

The doors were opened for us, as we got out of the car. A gentlemen greeted us in very proper English attire. "Good afternoon, sirs."

Joe Gromley, concierge of May Fair Inter-Continental Hotel, London

We started to walk up to the desk to register, but were escorted directly to Sammy's suite. A man named Joe Gromley entered wearing a morning suit (black striped pants and tails), carrying with him a portable writing desk on which we registered with what appeared to be a quill pen—an interesting experience. Mr. Gromley was extremely polite. As of this writing, he is still there, and now the concierge.

After the registering was finished, we were assigned our rooms; and Al Hunt showed us through the suite. The bathroom was very luxurious, and had a bidet. Neither Sammy nor I had ever seen a bidet before. We had no clue what it was called, or what it was used for. Sammy asked Al what it was.

Al Hunt, who had a great sense of humor, said with a straight face, "Well, that's for washing your feet."

Sammy said, "You're kidding!"

Al replied, "No, no, I'll show you. Take off your shoes and put your foot here. Then turn on the water and be careful not to turn it on too high. That's how you wash your feet."

Sammy turned to me and said, "What a great thing! They have a tub just for washing your feet."

Al started to laugh. Then he explained to us what a bidet was actually used for. These two young men on their first trip to Europe were really getting an education, and feeling quite stupid.

We were in the sitting room of the suite when the doorbell rang. In came a tiny little man dressed in a morning suit, carrying a top hat, accompanied by two other people. He introduced himself and said he was sent from the Palace to make sure everyone involved in the Royal Command Performance was dressed properly for the event. They had to measure Sammy for his morning suit.

The gentleman explained that at the end of the show, everybody would be singing "God Save the Queen." Everyone on the show would be given the lyrics and an opportunity to rehearse. Because this would be the first time a Royal Command Performance was televised, the men would be in morning suits and the women formally attired in gowns. The gentleman said rehearsal would be the next day at noon. He also told Sammy that he would have eight minutes in which to perform.

Sammy was dumbfounded; his mouth almost dropped to the floor. He turned to me, "I can't even introduce my dad and uncle in eight minutes. What can I possibly do in eight minutes?"

I soothed, "Sam, just take it easy. You and Morty and I will sit down later and work it out."

The gentleman went on, "That is your allotted time, sir. When you finish your performance, bow to the Queen, then bow to the audience, then leave the stage. This show has no encores—you do not come back on the stage after you leave. We expect to see you tomorrow afternoon at rehearsal." He was funny and polite, quite a charming little man.

Next a little old man with a big red nose arrived, whom Al Hunt introduced as Arthur. He was to be our driver the whole time we were in London.

Later that evening, Sammy was fitted for his morning suit. Al Burnett took us to dinner at one of the best restaurants in London, Les Ambassadeurs. This was a card club where one had to be a member to be admitted. The casino in Les Ambassadeurs was where the opening scene of the first *James Bond* picture was shot. The club had a suite in which many of big movie stars, such as Elizabeth Taylor and Judy Garland, stayed because of the elegance and privacy. Les Ambassadeurs and The White Elephant later became our two favorite restaurants in all of London.

Waiting for our dinner to arrive, Sammy asked Al how the reservations were going for his shows at the club. Al said, "Absolutely splendid!" I thought to myself that the English really have a wonderful way with words. "Danny Kaye, Bob Hope, and virtually every American performer who has been here, has insisted that you're positively one of the world's greatest performers. Frank Sinatra, for one, was asked who he thought was the best entertainer in America and, without hesitation, replied, 'Sammy Davis Jr.'" Sammy smiled, and couldn't have been happier.

The next day we went to the Victoria Palace Theater, where Sammy would perform. Morty went on stage to rehearse the orchestra. Sammy and I went to the back and sat down because Nat King Cole was on the stage rehearsing his part of the show. This was his second Royal Command Performance. The press was also there, the same people Sammy had met the previous day at the airport. They waved at Sammy and he waved back, calling out, "Thank you!" because they had written some very nice things in the papers about him.

Watching rehearsal, we got the feeling we were at the biggest international show of its kind. It was, in fact, just that. Performers from all over the world come, by invitation only. There were so many big stars there, one could not help looking around.

Giving his all in rehearsal

A man walked up to us and introduced himself as a producer of the show. He told Sammy they had to put him next to the closing—a key spot in the show—and that he had nine minutes to perform. Sammy exclaimed, "Are you kidding? You put me next to closing?"

The gentleman smiled and said, "Liberace will follow you and close the show with a simple song on the piano."

As the producer walked away, Sammy shook his head, "Well, they gave me nine minutes—one more minute than I was originally given. I don't know what I'm going to do with one more minute, any more than I knew what I was going to do with eight minutes."

We sat back and watched more of the rehearsal. Bruce Forsythe was the MC for the show. Bruce Forsythe was to England what Bob Hope was to the United States. He was a very funny man, a delightful person and absolutely brilliant at what he did. Sammy and I were impressed watching these wonderful entertainers.

Sammy turned to me saying, "Well, what do you think?"

I nodded, "We ain't out of town, old buddy. We ain't out of town yet."

A voice called out, "Mr. Davis, you're on next for rehearsal, please."

Sammy walked down the aisle, jumped up onto the stage, and looked around. Everybody in the theater was sitting there watching—backstage, on the stage, the press, the performers, the stagehands—everybody!

Sammy approached the microphone. Everyone began applauding. He was completely dumbfounded, as was I. One of the greatest things that a performer can have happen to him is the courtesy and recognition of his peers.

Sammy, Morty and I had worked out a routine the night before, In nine minutes Sam was going to attempt to get in all of the singing, dancing and impressions—and still perform well. When the orchestra started to play Sam's music, the theater began to rock. It appeared they had never heard this kind of music played with a forty-odd piece orchestra before. Everybody went nuts, tapping their feet and moving with the music.

Sammy actually held back at the rehearsal. He walked through his material, with a quick song and a little dance, because later everyone had to rehearse "God Save the Queen." Even so, when his rehearsal was finished, the people in the theater were going crazy. They came up around him, patting him on the back, shaking his hand and saying how wonderful he was going to be, and so on. Then Nat Cole came up to Sammy and wished him a lot of luck. It just so happened Nat and Sammy would be sharing a dressing room that evening.

We returned to the hotel and Murphy ordered dinner. Sammy couldn't touch a thing, he was so nervous. I told him he had to eat some food, but he replied, "I got the hots and the colds," known in the trade as "flop sweat." Sammy was scared to death. He kept walking up and down the room, and I kept telling him to relax, that he was going to be great, not to worry, that he was going to kill them. We all were excited and nervous for him.

After dinner, being the camera buff that I am, I grabbed my camera off the dresser, but left behind an extra roll of film. This was going to become very important to me later on.

We arrived at the theater early and were talking to Nat when the little gentleman from the hotel came in with the formal clothes for which Sammy had been fitted the day before. He told Sammy that after the show, the performers were to wait backstage. Each would be told whether they were to be in a receiving line for the Queen. She always had a receiving line, but this was to be the first time she would come backstage to greet the entertainers. He also told Sammy that they never know who the Queen will wish to see until after the show is over; they would come and tell him if he was wanted there.

Then the little gentleman reminded Sammy that there would be absolutely no encores. He reminded Sammy to bow to the Queen at the end of his act, then bow to the audience, and leave the stage immediately.

Sammy and Nat tried on their clothes. Everything was fine until Sammy put on his top hat. The hat fell right down over his ears, almost hitting him on the shoulders! He traded hats with Nat, thinking he had gotten the wrong one. Nat's hat was also too big for Sammy, but slightly better than the other one. Sammy got the idea to put a bunch of the toilet paper sheets around the inside of his hat brim. He thought that would hold the hat on his head until the end of the number they were to sing for Queen Elizabeth. This was a job, since the toilet paper was all individual squares.

Nat looked at Sammy, who appeared nervous. He told him, "Take it easy. I go on before you, so I'll warm them up for you."

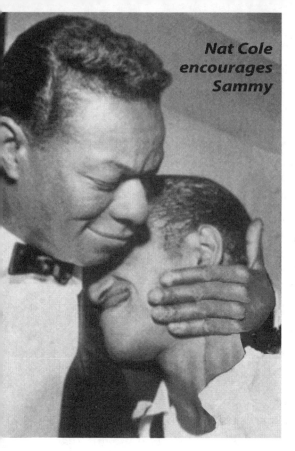

Nat Cole encourages Sammy

Nat's music began, and he took the stage. There were speakers in the dressing rooms so we could hear his performance. Nat began to sing and was doing beautifully when, all of a sudden his voice cracked! Now that might not seem like much to anyone else, but Nat Cole's voice never cracked. He never hit sour notes!

Sammy turned to me, shaking his head, "Oh, my God! Nat Cole has never cracked in his life!" I too, knew that Nat had perfect control at all times, under every circumstance. Even when his throat was bad, he knew how to play it.

Nat came off the stage, shaking his head miserably and said, "I don't never want to do dat no mo'! Not ever!" He slumped into a chair, took off his jacket, opened his shirt and told his valet to get him something to drink. "Man, they're out there tonight." Nat looked at Sammy and said, "Get yourself some kind of drink and sit down here. Everybody else, get out!"

Murphy and I were the only ones allowed to stay. When they were nervous, Sammy and Nat would do what is called "talkin' Colored" to ease the tension. Nat lapsed into the familiar vernacular. We closed the dressing room door.

Nat turned to Sammy and said, "Listen good. When you get out on da stage, go for it; don't hold back nothin', 'cause they's ready. There ain't nothin' happened down there yet. You is it! They's waitin' fo' you. When you come on," he said, "take your bow slow and easy. Don't let nothin' rush you.

"You remember what da cat told us befo'—about don't look at the Queen? Forget it! You give her a little sneaky peek out your good eye. Otherwise you'll be lookin' for her, when you should be worrying about your song. And at the end of your act…they're gonna try and rush you off da stage. Don't let 'em! Just tear 'em apart! If you don't kill 'em, I'm gonna take my fist and beat you to death."

The second part of the show started, and Sammy went to the wings to watch Charlie Drake perform. Charlie did a lot of slapstick and Keystone Kops type comedy and was an extremely popular performer in England.

Finally, Bruce Forsythe walked up to Sammy and whispered, "You're next." Bruce told him to go on stage and stand behind the closed curtain in back of Charlie while he finished.

When Charlie left the stage, he turned to Sammy, waved his hand and said, "Good luck!"

Bruce was on stage ready to introduce Sammy. The audience started making an impatient, rumbling noise with their feet. It was audible throughout the theater. I walked up the aisle and stood next to the wall just across from the Queen, so I could see her in her box as well as the stage. The audience was anxiously waiting for Sammy, who was standing behind the curtain. Bruce Forsythe stepped forward and said, "Ladies and Gentlemen, Mr. Al Burnett."

That was certainly a big surprise to me. I didn't know what was going on. Nobody had told us Al was going to speak. He walked out and announced, "Ladies and Gentlemen, I have been a performer, and a nightclub owner for the better part of my life; and as a nightclub owner, I have contracted the finest entertainers available. Three years ago, I saw a young man perform in America. I wanted the pleasure of this moment, and thanks to all concerned, and to all of the people here at this Royal Command Performance, the pleasure is mine. Ladies and Gentlemen, the greatest entertainer in the world, Sammy Davis Junior."

The curtain opened and Sammy took his bow while looking around with his one good eye. He gave the Queen that "sneaky peek," and then he went to work. He gave the greatest performance I had ever seen him give up to that time—and he did it within nine minutes. When Sammy finished his act, there was dead silence in the theater. Then he began to bow.

The next thing we saw was the Queen's white gloves coming out of the box starting to applaud. Then the audience went crazy. People dressed in frock coats, long gowns and priceless jewelry absolutely exploded with applause. Sammy took his bows and left the stage.

Bruce Forsythe thanked them, but they would not stop applauding. They began stamping their feet in unison. Bruce had no alternative but to call Sammy back on stage. Even the Queen was still applauding. I had never heard such a noise. Eventually, Sammy took six bows, before they would let him off the stage. This had never occurred before. Finally Sam left the stage. I ran back upstairs to the dressing room. Sammy was thrilled. Nat and Sammy were both crying. We all were crying. It was quite a moment.

Now we waited to see if Sammy would be in the receiving line. A few minutes passed. Liberace finished his piano number. Soon the Queen's gentleman returned. Sammy had been chosen to meet the Queen; he was fit to be tied.

"What do I say?" he asked. "What do I do? How do you talk to the Queen of England? Here I am, a little Black man from the United States meeting the Queen of England for the first time—and I don't know what to do. How do I address her?"

The gentleman responded, "The first thing you do is bow. If she decides to speak to you, you may call her 'Your Majesty' or you may call her 'Mum.' She may just walk by you, nod her head and shake your hand, or she may stop and talk to you."

It was time for the last number of the show. All the performers were to stand on the risers and sing "God Save the Queen." On stage, the performers lined up for the big moment. This was the first time a Royal Command Performance had ever been televised.

Meanwhile, Sammy was really having a problem with his overly large hat, that just barely perched on top of his ears. At the end of the song, the gentlemen were to take off their hats, bow to the Queen and as we say in show business, it was, "Roll credits!"

The song ended. I stood in the wings watching as the men took off their hats and bowed. When Sammy removed his hat, all the little squares of toilet paper came flying out. It looked like big snowflakes floating all over the stage. Watching the television monitor, all you could see was these toilet tissues flying everywhere. Sammy was horrified! The minute the curtain closed he wanted to leave the building. He was so humiliated, he didn't want to be around anyone. He had never been so embarrassed. The only reason Sammy stayed was because he was going to meet the Queen.

Behind the curtain, everyone chosen lined up and a red carpet was rolled out. Only one photographer is allowed at these receptions, a pool photographer. However, I was standing backstage, off to the side by myself. No one seemed to notice me, or the camera I had with me. Next, rose petals were sprinkled all over the red carpet. Then Queen Elizabeth, herself, came down the receiving line.

Performers were lined up according to their order in the show, so the last two people in line were Sam and Liberace. The Queen, carrying a large bouquet of roses, glided along the line, passing by some people, and stopping to speak to others.

The women curtseyed. The men bowed. She smiled at everyone, putting out her hand to some. Following close behind was Prince Phillip, Duke of Edinburgh—her husband. Behind him were other members of her royal party.

Actress, Diana Dors and Sammy, wearing an over-sized top hat with toilet paper sticking out

Queen Elizabeth II greets pianist, Liberace, and Sammy

As the Queen came down the aisle I took two pictures of her. No one said anything, so I quietly walked back off to the side. Then the Queen stopped in front of Sammy. I could see over her right shoulder, that she was talking to him. I snapped a picture of her talking to Sammy, which made three pictures in all that I snapped of the Queen.

I stood watching the Queen talking to Sammy, thinking to myself, "He has to be the happiest man in the world. Here he is standing in front of the Queen of England." This was the manifestation of those old games we used to play back in the parking lot at the Sunset Colonial Hotel. This was really it!

When the Queen was through talking to Sammy and Liberace, she started walking toward her car. As she went in that direction she was approaching me. I was standing by myself next to the door, no more than ten feet away from her. She looked at me, smiled and said, "Good evening."

I raised my camera, clicked it, the flash went off—but I was out of film! The greatest moment of my pictorial life, and I had no film in the camera. I had left that other roll back in the hotel on the dresser. So I didn't get a picture of the Queen addressing me; but as it turned out, I was the only person in all of England who got a picture of Sammy with Queen Elizabeth. The newspapers flocked to me after I told Al Hunt I had gotten that picture. They developed the film and used my picture. They offered to pay me for it, but I declined the money.

Following the Royal Command Performance, Sammy had a pre-opening show at Club Pigalle. This club was built below ground, and it had a very low ceiling. When you entered off the street, you walked downstairs.

Al Burnett had invited a lot of people from the Command Performance, the press, and numerous celebrities from all over England. The place was packed. It probably held about six or seven hundred people normally, and that night it was full to the rafters. Gregory Peck was there, along with Anthony Quinn, Robert Mitchum, Anthony Newley, Joan Collins, and many other celebrities who happened to be in, or around London.

Sammy did a two-and-a-half hour show. At the end, people applauded and stamped their feet so hard Al Burnett had to come on stage and ask them to please stop. He was concerned that the ceiling was going to cave in from the vibrations. The applause was absolutely ear-shattering.

Sammy, Murphy, Morty, Michael and I returned to the hotel. I slapped Sam on the back, "Man, you have just done it! You've taken this country by storm. They won't ever forget this night."

Next morning, the *Daily Sketch*, one of the leading papers in London, said, "Royal Command Performance," and a huge question mark ran down the entire front page. Then, "Let's call it the 'Sammy Davis Jr. Show!'" There was a picture of Sammy, with a summary, "For, in eight electrifying minutes, this…entertainer made the word 'star' seem inadequate…."

Two other papers, *The Record* and the *Show Mirror*, wrote, "…Those lucky enough to see him in person at the Pigalle, indeed saw the greatest entertainer in the world…."

And that was just our first two days in London.

Royal Performance in the presence of Her Majesty The Queen on the Evening of Monday May 16th 1960 at The Victoria Palace, London.

Sam performs "Old Man River" for Paul Robeson

A young opera star, Paul Robeson, photo from Rutgers University

Sam mugs for the camera

May and her Father Come to London

On the first day of our show at Club Pigalle, we rehearsed in the afternoon. Murphy and I went backstage to check out the dressing room facilities. Then Murphy set up Sam's dressing room. Morty passed out music to the band. Sammy hung out with the gang before rehearsal. We were meeting the girls in the chorus for the first time.

The star dressing room was located at the other end of the dressing room for the chorus girls, which meant walking through their dressing room to get to Sammy's. Unusual—and pleasant from time to time. We did a full band rehearsal, along with the chorus girls and their numbers, a typical rehearsal day. But we were still riding high on the euphoria of the previous day.

Sammy and I decided to go walking around London, just to check out some of the streets and sights. We were surprised to find the shops we visited quite different from those in the United States. In some shops, patrons were waited on exclusively by one salesperson who really attended only to them. The salespersons are extremely knowledgeable and helpful. We were constantly surprised and impressed by the English people.

Sam and I returned to the hotel. He phoned May and asked when she would arrive from Sweden. She had gone there to see her father, then accompany him to London to meet Sammy. Sam was going to formally ask for her hand in marriage. May told him she and her father, Ernst Hugo Wilkens, would be arriving in a couple of days.

Our chauffeur, Arthur, was waiting for us with a Rolls Royce for the trip from the hotel to the club. Club Pigalle had two entrances, both at street level, but the back entrance was further down the street. This was the emergency exit, and the delivery entrance into the back. Arriving at the club, we couldn't believe the throng of people waiting to enter. Some were just waiting for Sammy to show up.

Sammy got out of the car and was mobbed by a crush of fans. I struggled to clear a path through the enthusiastic crowd just so he could get to the entrance. After this experience, we started using the rear entrance as much as possible.

The first night, the club was packed to the gills and Sammy was still pretty nervous. This was his first real show in London in front of the general public. However, Sammy was very happy about the way the press had greeted him, and the wonderful things they had said about him the previous two days. Sam did two shows and tore the place up. Yes, indeed, London was happy to see him; and they let him know it. Once again the press gave him rave reviews, continuing their love affair with Sammy Davis Jr.

The next day Sammy and I went shopping at Saville Row, Harrod's and every other posh place we could get to. We even went to look at Rolls Royces and Jaguars. The London dealership was right on the corner of the street where our hotel was located. That's one place we ended up visiting almost every day. Every place we went, Sammy was immediately recognized and surrounded by people. Funny thing about the British, they are polite when approaching a celebrity, respectful of their privacy. They do not overwhelm celebrities and follow them around as people do in the United States. When they do stop someone, it is with an, "Excuse me."

Many of the shops in London have antiques. We were amidst ancient armor and every item of heraldry one could imagine; weapons and accessories of Medieval times. These items are, not surprisingly, very expensive.

Sammy was determined to buy a bowler hat and cane. It is easy to fall into the English way of things when you are there—the accent, the style of dress. The British are a bit more formal, yet charming. Sammy found a bowler hat, and we went on to purchase a cane for him. He actually bought two canes; one was a walking stick. Both were unique and extremely costly. Sammy used the walking stick most of the time, for many years after that. It had a gold top and gold-plated tip and looked quite ordinary. However, when you picked it up and gave it a strong flick, out of the end came about a sharp nine-inch dagger. It was like a long needle, but very heavy duty. You could definitely do serious harm with it. When you pressed two little sides, the dagger would fold back up into the handle. It didn't give any indication that it was anything other than a walking stick. The second cane was just a simple one, but with a twist of the handle, it became a sword. We also bought two new foils for our fencing.

All Sammy could talk about, as we went from store to store, was May's father and his impending arrival in London. He kept asking me, "What should I do?" and, "How should I act?"

I kept telling him to talk to Mr. Wilkens the way he talked to the press—straight out. I told him that's the best way to talk to anybody; Of course, he agreed. Still, he was nervous, and didn't know how he could make a good impression. "Just be yourself, man," I told him. "You always make a good impression with people. Just be yourself. Be Sammy; that's who you are, and that's who May's marrying."

Back at the suite Sammy and I were chatting when the doorbell rang. I opened the door and looked straight into a man's chest. Given that I am six feet tall, this was a pretty big man—Black and large, not fat at all—just big! With him was a petite Black woman, in a plain little dress and a small flat hat encircled by flowers. The man's voice boomed, "Is Mr. Davis in, please?"

"Yes," I answered. "May I ask who's calling, please?"

"Mr. and Mrs. Paul Robeson." To say I was embarrassed would be an understatement. At the time, Paul Robeson was a world famous opera star—the most magnificent Othello that opera had ever seen, and one of the original stars of the musical, *Showboat*.

His big hit, "Old Man River," had made him a huge star before he went into opera. I had heard of him, but never seen him.

The Robesons sat with Sammy and talked. I could see Paul Robeson was a man of quiet intensity. When he talked it seemed as though the mountains roared. Paul told Sammy he had come to ask questions, and perhaps enlighten Sam about European customs.

Delighted, Sammy said that he would appreciate any help Paul could give. The first question Paul asked was if Sam intended to marry May Britt.

Sam answered "Yes. As a matter of fact, her father is due here tomorrow, and I intend to ask him for May's hand in marriage."

Opera great, Paul Robeson

Paul and his wife wished Sammy "all the happiness in the world." He wanted to tell Sammy about life in Europe—how it was easy for a man of color, and his wife, to live there.

Sammy wanted to discuss this, "Why did you move to Europe? A lot of people assume you have turned to Communism."

Paul answered, "I'll be happy to explain it all to you. It's really very simple. Over here, I am truly a free man. I don't have to ride on the back of the bus. I don't have to go to a special drinking fountain to drink water. I am not denigrated, and always worried that something will happen to me and my family. Even though I own three plantations back home, I very seldom go there.

"Here I am respected for what I am, an opera singer. My wife and I are treated with great respect wherever we go. Here a performer is put on a pedestal and treated differently than a performer is in the United States. Performers in Europe are looked up to. They are given the best seats in restaurants. They never have to stand in line unnecessarily. And they are all treated like stars, even the chorus girls and boys. In Europe performers are special, and everything is done with a great deal of courtesy."

He said, "Sammy, you might want to consider living in Europe, like I do, to get away from the prejudices that you are facing in the United States, and always will face. That's the main reason I came here, and that's the main reason why I remain here. No matter how much money I have, what I own, and how much acclaim I achieve, in the United States I will always have the prejudice and never have the respect that I receive here as an artist."

Sammy shook his head, "Man, I don't know if I could move over here or not. The United States is my home."

Paul responded, "The United States is also my home, but I wanted to come by and talk to you, to let you know the differences— how much better you would be received here than in the United States."

Sammy then asked Paul directly, "Are you telling me this because you embrace Communism?"

"No! I am not a Communist! I just like my freedom, and a lot of people have gotten that confused. Because I have been so outspoken about my freedom in the past, people have branded me a Communist."

Murphy brought tea and sandwiches while the conversation continued. Sammy invited Paul and his wife to his show at Club Pigalle that evening. Paul said his wife would be unable to attend, but he would be more than happy to come.

Again, the club was jam packed. In this club, off to stage right, there was one large booth right on the stage for dignitaries or very special guests. It was unusual to see a table on stage. The rest of the tables ran straight out from the stage, all the way to the back of the club. They were put together end-to-end, giving the appearance that each section was one long table. There were aisles between so that people could go in and out.

Just prior to showtime, I was out in the club, as I usually was when the show started. As the house lights were dimming for the show, you could hear the buzz of the crowd—Paul Robeson had entered. Beyond being physically large, he had a huge presence. He sat down at the far end of a long table at center stage, and the show began.

As usual, Sammy gave a wonderful show and the crowd was delighted. At the end—and as only Sammy Davis Jr. could do—he made an absolutely magnificent introduction of Paul Robeson. With all the humility he could muster, Sammy said he would like to dedicate his next song to Mr. Robeson. He put the microphone down on a stool he always had on stage. Then he dared to sing "Old Man River" without a microphone. Paul Robeson possibly could have held the last note longer, but I don't think he could have sung it any better than Sammy did that night.

When Sammy finished the song, a strange thing happened. The same thing had happened at the Royal Command Performance—there was dead silence in the room. Everyone turned around to look at Paul Robeson. This was his song; how dare anyone sing this song to him?

Paul Robeson stood up straight. When he uncoiled his big body, his head nearly touched the ceiling. His form blocked out Sammy's spotlight, so he appeared as a silhouette to people sitting in front of him. Then Paul Robeson began to applaud. Tears started rolling down Sammy's face. The audience went wild! Paul then came up on the stage and made a wonderful speech about Sammy.

This night, as every other night, Al Burnett had to come out and ask the audience to stop stomping their feet. The upstairs store owners were seriously concerned about the ceiling of the club coming down with such constant pounding. It was to be this way every show. The audience just could not contain their pleasure when they saw Sammy perform.

Sammy performs at Club Pigalle

In on-stage celebrity booth, Club Pigalle: Sophia Loren (center) and I (far left) watch Sammy in drum "competition" with Michael Silva

One night, right after she had just been robbed of all her jewelry, Sophia Loren came to see the show. I took a picture of her holding up her bare hands to the camera. Later at dinner, I had the privilege of sitting across from her and truly, to this day, she is one of the most stunning and breathtakingly beautiful women I've ever seen. To look into her green eyes is to look into the eyes of a tiger.

May arrived the next day. Sammy and I went to the airport to meet her. Although May's father was also flying in, as is the custom with many politicians, celebrities and families, she and her father did not travel on the same plane. Mr. Wilkens was due to arrive later in the day.

Sammy, May and I went back to the hotel to drop her baggage, then went sightseeing. May asked if the media had learned she was arriving in town. I told her there were a lot of rumors flying around about her arrival, but that I didn't think anyone knew her father was coming as well. Walking around the shops, people recognized Sammy and May, who was at the height of her movie career. Londoners politely asked for autographs, at times, and were very nice.

Sammy asked May how and when he should meet her father. She told him to meet Mr. Wilkens as soon as he arrived. Sammy wasn't too sure about that and proposed that perhaps May and her father should come and see the show first. Sammy promised to do the best show of his life for her father and thought Mr. Wilkens should see him in his element, performing, before they officially met.

May told Sammy that was ridiculous and totally unnecessary. She really wanted Sammy to meet both her parents. However, it didn't make too much difference to her if her family liked him or not. She said her love for him was not going to change. Sammy was still petrified about that initial meeting.

While the discussion continued, we returned to the hotel because we had an appointment with English television producers. They wanted to do a show with Sam called "Sammy Meets the British." Meanwhile, May had to go to the airport and meet her father. Sammy spent all kinds of time preparing himself, dressing, and trying to look great so he could make a good impression on the producers from the television show, as well as Mr. Wilkens. Finally we were late, and he was in a mad rush. We dashed to the elevator. When the doors opened into the lobby, Sammy jumped out. Now we were running through the lobby. He was trying to hurry me along, "Come on! Come on, man; we're late."

Just then Sam bumped hard into an approaching man, knocking his hat to the floor. Sammy and the man both bent over at once to pick up the hat. Their heads bumped into each other. They both grabbed the hat at the same time. In trying to return the hat, Sammy yanked it out of the man's hand. Then the hat fell on the floor again. Sammy made a dive for the tumbling hat, and grabbed it. As he picked it up, he was apologizing profusely, and trying to smooth out the now battered hat.

When Sam looked up, he froze dead in his spot. To be honest with you, I was cracking up as it was a hilarious scene. Of course, I was standing back a little further, and saw that with this gentleman was May!

"Sammy, I'd like you to meet my father," she indicated the man.

Crumpled hat in hand, Sammy said, "Damn! What is it with these damned hats that I'm having trouble with over here? All of a sudden I've got a thing for hats!"

Mr. Wilkens laughed and greeted Sammy warmly. Sammy made arrangements to meet with May and Mr. Wilkens later. As May and Mr. Wilkens left, Sam turned to me, "Do you believe my luck? With all the elevators in this hotel, I had to pick that one; and I had to run into Mr. Wilkens and crush his hat."

Sammy and I went into the lounge to greet the producers of the television show. One of the men introduced us to a famous English choreographer, a young man named Lionel Blair. He was to do the choreography for this show.

Sammy was not used to being choreographed by others. He always did his own choreography. But the show turned out very well. Much of it was performed outside, and one of the numbers was done with children. The show was a hit, and Lionel became one of our dearest friends. In fact, he was Sammy's friend for life.

Choreographer, Lionel Blair, Sam and singer-dancer, Joyce Blair (Lionel's sister)

Scenes during production of "Sammy Meets the British" at Battersea Park, London
top right: Sam performs for the children

Morty goes English

Sam asked me to join him, and May, and her father for dinner. I protested, "Absolutely not!" I felt I shouldn't be there.

But he insisted, "Man, I need somebody friendly there with me."

"Sammy, you couldn't have a better friend than your fiancée. This is no place for me to be."After bickering back and forth over the issue for a few more minutes, I relented. But I let him know I did not feel comfortable, and did not feel he needed me with him. Sammy kept insisting he needed someone on his side there.

Dinner progressed; the conversation was light and cheery. Nothing serious was mentioned with respect to why Mr. Wilkens had come to London. Finally, we were eating dessert and May's father was drinking coffee. He looked directly at Sammy and said he and May's mother knew all there was to know about Sammy from their daughter—they still called her by her given name, "Maybritt." She had communicated to them through many letters and phone calls. "As far as we are concerned," he went on, "we will be proud to have you for a son."

Sammy and I looked at one another. Sam released his anxieties. He looked at May, and they gave each other a hug. I must admit I was kind of dumbfounded, as I'm sure Sammy was, that right out of the blue, with no prompting or previous entry into this serious matter, Mr. Wilkens was just simple and to the point. Sammy asked, "Then it's okay? It's all right with you?"

Mr. Wilkens replied he had wanted to meet Sammy, but he hadn't come all the way from Sweden just to see him. "I came to see my daughter with you." He spoke very slowly, as would a man speaking from his heart. Then he said, "I will now speak to you most seriously, because you will be my son. If Maybritt wishes to marry you, we have no objection. Of course, marrying Maybritt and living in America could create hardship; but if your love for each other is strong enough, then that's all that's important. All other problems can be solved. The color of your skin is not important to us; it is what is in your heart that is important to us. In Maybritt's letters and phone calls to us, she has expressed that she loves you so very much. We have never seen her like this before. You make us all very happy."

Mr. Wilkens was finished, and I could see Sammy starting to tear up. He excused himself from the table and went into the hallway, where May followed him.

When they returned Sammy walked up to Mr. Wilkens, put out his hands and said, "Thank you, sir, thank you very much. You've made me a very happy man."

"God bless you, Sammy," said Mr. Wilkens. "God bless you both."

The next day it started—little items in the paper: "Are Sammy Davis Jr. and May Britt going to wed?" Sammy told May it was time they made an announcement, or be raked over the coals and have all the crap in the world coming down on them. May didn't particularly want to do that, but Sammy insisted. He called Al Hunt and told him to set up a press conference to announce their engagement. Al warned Sammy to be ready for some heavy questions, then he set it up.

Sammy stood up at the press conference and read a statement Al had prepared for him. It went: "Ladies and Gentlemen, Miss May Britt and I have been subject lately to newspaper items questioning whether or not we are seeing each other, and if we intend to be married. You asked me that yourselves when I arrived here. At that time I could not properly say 'yes' because I hadn't yet met, and received the approval of, May Britt's father. However, I am now at liberty to tell you that I have his approval, and we are engaged to be married.

"I hope to impress upon you that I would not call you all here to make this announcement as if I believed it were to be earth-shattering news. You have been overwhelmingly generous to me, and I wouldn't have the audacity to impose upon you for publicity's own sake. We hope you will publish it for the one reason that we are anxious to avoid any of the unnecessary and sometimes vicious public speculation. We want it to be a matter of record so that we can end all of that."

At that point, the reporters offered congratulations and asked questions about how and where Sammy and May met. Sammy answered all their questions graciously. However, one American reporter was there representing a wire service. He was particularly vicious and began a verbal assault immediately. He asked how Sammy thought this would be received back home. He asked if Sammy ever thought he'd be able to work in the States again, and if this would mark the end of his career. This man was relentless and began to annoy many of the English reporters. He continued taunting Sammy with questions like, "Are you announcing your engagement here because you're afraid to do it at home?" and, "Are you afraid that you can't go home?"

Sammy looked at me, fit to be tied. He gave me a look that said, "Get this man out of here!" The English press was clearly on Sammy's side. They pushed their way around the obnoxious American reporter, but even they couldn't stop this ruthless man or his stupid questions.

When he asked about Black men marrying White women movie stars, I could see Sammy was really getting angry; so was the English press. One of the British journalists spoke up and said it was obvious Sammy had answered all of the questions this man had asked. Yet that still did not shut him up.

Again, he asked Sammy about the people in America being tough on mixed marriages and what were the chances of the marriage being successful? Sammy replied, "Wait a minute! I don't know what America you're talking about. But I do know something about mixed marriages. Most of them work out, because no one would go out of their way to take the abuse heaped upon them unless their love for each other was strong." He continued to say he and May were prepared to take whatever would come their way.

This reporter still would not be stopped. Then came the bombshell question: "What about your children?"

An English reporter snapped back, "He's already answered that question. He wants what we all want, healthy and happy babies. If you missed the exact wording, I'll be delighted to give it to you. This isn't a trial, you know!"

The idiot kept hammering on that Sammy had not answered his questions about the kids. So Sammy shot back, "Well, what do you want to know about them? What exactly are you asking me?"

"What do you figure they'll look like?" The British reporters were obviously disgusted. But Sammy responded that he and May expected their offspring to look like babies and children.

"You know what I mean." the reporter needled. "Do you have some kind of preference about color?"

"Mister, I've known what you mean since you started. Now, as far as the children are concerned, it would be no matter to us, in terms of our love for our children, if they were White, Black, brown or polka dot. We don't think in terms of color. We care about if God gives us healthy, beautiful children. And we will love them with all the love we have. But I am sure that, somewhere along the line, when these children run into bigots like you, it won't be that easy. However, we will teach our children, and they will be able to handle it."

With that remark the questioning ended. The British press applauded Sammy. The American journalist went off shaking his head.

Sammy turned to Al and me, "Wouldn't you know it! Of everybody here, it would be an American who starts in on me right away."

The next day during lunch, while we were reading congratulations in telegrams and newspapers, the phone rang. The operator said Sammy had a long distance call from Hollywood. It was Sammy's public relations agent from the United States. Sammy came to the phone in his typical British manner saying, "Tally ho!" There was a long pause, then he yelled, "What? What are you talking about? Read it to me! That's it? That's all it said?" He pulled the phone away from his ear and said, "You will not believe what papers are saying in the U.S.!"

The direct quote was: "Sammy Davis Jr., Negro entertainer, announced today he will be marrying Swedish blonde actress, May Britt. Asked about children, Davis said, 'I don't care if they're polka dot.'"

Sammy told his press agent to wait a minute while I handed him the English papers. Sammy read the original statement to his press agent, just as he had said it. Sammy told him the damn American reporter had taken the whole thing out of context and changed its meaning into the most sickening, God-forsaken, gut-wrenching statement he could have made. He told his press agent to handle the matter in the best way he could. Then he turned to me and said, "What the fuck is going on with this reporter and papers back in my own country?"

He had me read aloud to him all the English articles. The quote was there exactly as it was originally given. Sammy said, "That son-of-a-bitch! If I could just get my hands on him right now, I'd wring his damn neck, or find some way to get him fired! But that won't change the minds of the millions of people who have already heard and seen this shit."

The phone rang again. It was Frank Sinatra calling from the States to wish Sammy and May all the best luck in the world. He expressed how happy he was that they had finally made the announcement, and said he was behind them one hundred percent. Frank also told Sammy that if he had any problems to let him know. Sammy turned to tell May what Frank had said and tears were running down his face. May started to cry and we all hugged one another. It seemed Frank had helped lift a great weight off everyone's shoulders.

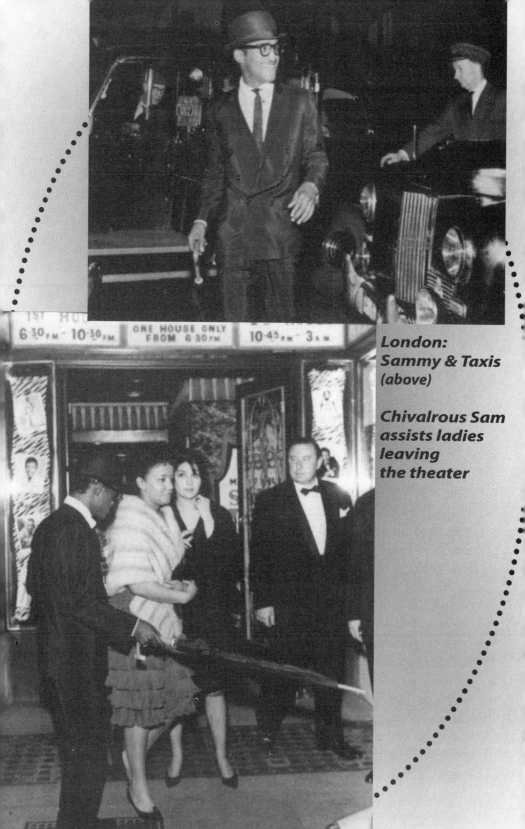

**London:
Sammy & Taxis
(above)**

**Chivalrous Sam
assists ladies
leaving
the theater**

We Meet the Nazis

After the engagement announcement, the phone rang off the hook for days. It was calls from the States. Everyone wanted to know what was going on.

A couple of days later, Sammy, May, Murphy and I were walking down a London street. I must have been looking at Sammy strangely because he asked, "What are you looking at?"

"Well," I said, "you won't believe this. Do you know, you look different?"

"What do you mean, I look 'different'?"

"Maybe you don't realize it, but usually your teeth are clenched a lot of the time. And when you clench your teeth your jawbone protrudes by the sides of your ears. You clench your teeth when you get uptight, and a little muscle pops out of both sides of your mouth. But, today your face isn't the face of the man I came here with; it's more relaxed. You look like a different person. You've changed. You're looking kind of handsome. The stress seems to be gone out of your face, even amidst all this shit coming down around us."

"What in the hell are you babbling on about?" he asked.

"Well, I don't know. You've...become handsome."

Then Murphy chimed in, "Yeah, I've noticed it, too. I've noticed it in your demeanor. You've become more relaxed."

It turned out to be true. Spending time in England, it was easy to pick up their mannerisms, customs, and even their accent. The English way was very contagious.

That evening, Sammy, Morty and I were on our way to the club in the Rolls. As we approached our destination, a van cut in front of us. On top, a loudspeaker exuded all kinds of racial epithets—things like: "Nigger Monkey, go back to the jungle!" "Go home, Nigger!" "Monkey, go back to the jungle!" and other slurs. None of us could believe what we were hearing. Sammy told our driver, Arthur, to follow the van.

Little old Arthur was nervous, but he followed the vehicle as instructed. The van turned down a couple of streets, still blaring its filth. Suddenly, the sound went off. We followed, as it went down a dead end street. Now we were directly behind the van. It was obvious the people in the van knew someone was following them, but had no idea who it was.

Morty and I were so mad, Morty started out one side of the car and I started out the other. We wanted to confront these people. Not only were the epithets racial, but also anti-Semitic—Morty and I are both Jewish.

Sammy grabbed both of us by our coat collars and yanked us back into the car, "No! No, don't start anything here. We're on a dead end street, and we don't know how many people are in that van."

He told Arthur to get the hell out of there. Arthur was petrified, and only too happy to oblige. Sammy then asked Arthur, "Who in the hell are these people?"

"Those are Mosley's men."

"Who in the hell is Mosley?"

Arthur replied, "It's the Nazi Party."

I was stunned! "The Nazi Party in England? It's not that many years since the War."

"I didn't know there was any more Nazi Party around," exclaimed Sammy.

We pulled up in front of the club and all kinds of things were happening! People were picketing, screaming profanities with racial and ethnic slurs. However, around the club, and on both sides of the street, were Scotland Yard agents. They were dressed in the traditional trenchcoats—for which they are so famous—with the collars turned up. The agents were spaced pretty evenly apart for about a block or so. They just stood there, looking casual. Some were smoking pipes, some leaning up against the wall. Another read a newspaper with his foot up against a wall, leaning back on it. Oddly, a man lay in the gutter with his feet moving slightly.

We got out of the car fast, and ran downstairs. There was a big hubbub going on inside the club relating to what was happening upstairs on the street. The chorus girls were absolutely enraged. As we started through their dressing room to reach Sammy's, the girls bolted out the door past us yelling, "Let's go get the bloody bastards!"

Out they went, practically knocking us to the floor. In feathers, headdresses and very skimpy bottoms, they started up the back stairs toward the street. Along the side of this staircase, the champagne for the club was stored. As the girls ran up the steps, they each grabbed champagne bottles to use as weapons.

Al Burnett tried desperately to keep them from going out into the street. But a couple of them made it out, and rushed up to the picketers, hoping to do some serious damage. The Scotland Yard agents quickly stopped the girls from bashing in any heads.

We noticed something strange happening. Other people were quietly approaching the picketers, talking to them and walking beside them. They put their arms on the picketer's shoulders and looked like they must be friends. In reality, they were grabbing the picketers by the backs of their necks and pushing them up the street. Suddenly, a picketer would fall down or disappear—thus, the explanation about the man lying in the street.

We later learned that word had gotten out in the Soho District that the Nazis were picketing Sammy. Now, every major city has a Soho-type district, where the pushcarts and open-air marketplaces thrive in the daytime, but by night, the strip joints, hooker houses and criminal element survive. These people, as well as the rest of London, had really taken to Sammy. Some of the boys from Soho had come up to take care of the matter.

Scotland Yard never interfered during this incident. England is very big on free speech—perhaps even more so than the United States. Scotland Yard would not interfere unless there was violence. Of course, we didn't spend any time up on the street. I looked out from time to time to see what was happening, but Sammy didn't dare even stick his head out the door of the club. Finally, it ended as it had started, quietly. Bodies were lying here and there; but no one was dead, just moaning and groaning. Scotland Yard never lifted a hand.

After everything quieted down, Sammy sat in the dressing room looking into the mirror. He said to me, "So, my jaw's not tight, huh? I look relaxed, huh? I'm even handsome, huh? I think not! I don't need this kind of shit in my life!"

May arrived at the club; she had already been apprised of the situation. She came into the dressing room and sat down very quietly. Sammy asked her if what had happened bothered her.

She answered, "Yes, but to no great extent. Does it bother you?"

Sammy exclaimed, "Of course it bothers me! But it could have been a lot worse."

May became teary eyed; this was the first time she had run headlong into this kind of prejudice. It was one of the things that had concerned Sammy from the beginning. He had always worried about how May would take the awful things that would result from their relationship. However, May was not only a wonderful actress and a beautiful woman, but she had more grace, dignity and class than any woman I have ever met. Besides having the guts of ten people, she maintained the control of twenty. During their relationship, May

Al Hunt, Sam's publicist, with May Britt

walked with her head as high as she was tall, and never let any of this crap get to her. Except for my wife, I have more respect for that woman than virtually any woman I have ever known, because of the way May handled this situation, and the way she has handled the rest of her life.

The *Daily Mirror*, one of the biggest newspapers in London, had a very famous columnist by the name of Cassandra. The next morning she wrote, "Cassandra Writes a Letter to Sammy Davis, Jr.—Dear Mr. Davis, I don't know you. You don't know me. I have never seen your show, and I assume you have never seen mine. All I know is what I read about you in the papers.

"But this is just to tell you that the beastly racial abuse which you were subjected to outside the Pigalle Restaurant, when Mosley's louts followed you waving banners with the words, 'Go home Nigger,' has nothing to do with what the English people feel and think.

"I, and maybe I could speak for a few others (say 51,680,000 minus a hundred of the population of this country), feel revolted, angry and ashamed of what happened. Yours Sincerely, Cassandra."

That was just the beginning. Letters came from everywhere, from all over England. Telegrams arrived—hundreds of them, probably thousands—from people who were embarrassed, outraged by Mosley and his people. They were concerned about what America might think of the English people who truly had great affection for Sammy.

This affection developed very fast, and continued every place he went. In the streets and shops, people came up to him and May and apologized. Even the Bobbys asked for his autograph. It was a wonderful thing after such a distasteful and utterly repugnant event. From that night on and until we left, England seemed like a second home for us. Tensions really did leave us after the overwhelming show of support Sammy received from the English people. He actually thought seriously that perhaps we should move to England.

A few days after Cassandra's letter, Sammy commented to me that, since the English people had been so great to him, he wanted to give something back.

"Sam, what could you possibly 'give back' that you haven't already given? You've given them the greatest shows they've ever seen. The place is packed every night. The people love you; you love them. What else is there?"

"Call Al Hunt. I have an idea of something I want to do."

Al came right over and Sammy explained that he wanted to do two things before he left England. "I want to put on a show for the English and American troops—for the guys who can't come into London to see the show. I want to bring the whole show to them.

The other thing I want to do is go through the Black Museum of Scotland Yard with Arthur."

Al was surprised. "What do you know about the Black Museum?"

"Everything we could find out." Sam was serious. We've heard that it's very difficult to get into, but please see what you can do."

Al said he would do his best regarding the museum, but he would definitely work out a show for the troops. It didn't take very long. The next day Al had lined up a venue. We were to go to an air base to perform. The British Air Force would send a plane to pick us up, then deliver us back to London. May accompanied us a couple of days later, when we headed for a British Air Base. We were not told exactly where we were going, nor the name of the base.

As our plane landed we looked around, and there were no other airplanes to be seen! Not even a control tower—nothing to indicate we were on an air base. All we saw was a series of concrete runways going in every direction, and grassy knolls everywhere. No trees, just grass. We taxied up to the only visible building to deplane, and were greeted by so many people, it was absolutely unbelievable.

Some flatbed trucks had been set up to make a stage. On this make-shift stage, Sammy did a full performance for the troops, complete with chorus girls. The audience was thrilled. There were over two thousand people there with their families.

After the show, Sammy was asked to go down to the "ready room" and say a few words to the fellows who had not been able to see the show. We didn't know what a "ready room" was, but we went. This was the room where the Americans and English stayed on duty twenty-four hours a day. Airplanes were flight-ready at all times, and could actually take off about forty-five seconds after receiving their orders. This was where the U-2 spy planes were located and, at that time, where all the planes in Western Europe that carried atomic bombs were housed as well.

All those planes and bombs, and you could not see even one. They were all under the abutments, covered with grass. One push of a button, and the grassy knolls would open to reveal the planes. In fact, this is the same secret air base from which American, Gary Powers flew years later. His was a much publicized U-2 spy plane mission that was shot down over Russia.

A show for the troops

May and I watching Sammy

May & Sammy with base brass

Chorus Girls

Giving autographs

**Top to bottom:
Morty conducts,
Michael on drums,
while Sam sings
to May**

**Morty and Sam
share the stage**

**Base
Communications
interviews Sammy**

BASE COMM

Sammy did a short impromptu show for the men in the ready room. They had a piano, so Morty plunked out some tunes and Sammy performed. The guys were as anxious to see May as they were to see Sammy. May was, and still is, a very beautiful woman. Her movies were in theaters at that time, and she was an extremely popular star in Europe. The troops not only had Sammy, the world's greatest entertainer, but they also had world famous movie star, May Britt. They were delighted, and grateful that Sammy had come out to the middle of nowhere just to do a show for them.

Back in London, Al Hunt had arranged a visit for Sammy and me to the Black Museum of Scotland Yard. We were very excited. The New Scotland Yard Building was drab, painted an industrial green. We met the Chief Inspector of Scotland Yard and toured the main building. We were introduced to another inspector, our guide for the Black Museum, who took us into a section with a black enamel-painted door. The other doors were industrial green; this one was black.

Before we entered the door our guide asked us how much time we had, as private tours are based on how much time the guests wish to allot. Guides adjust the amount of information they give and how fast or slowly they move through the exhibits. We had about four hours so we got a very thorough tour.

The museum was unexpectedly small. Upon entering, one sees a large book on a pedestal that has the signatures of every reigning monarch since the inception of Scotland Yard. This is necessary because Scotland Yard is the detective force of London's Metropolitan Police, and must be signed into law by each new monarch. There was, also, every uniform used since the beginning of Scotland Yard— very impressive.

From that room, you immediately walked straight ahead into three more rooms that opened into one another. Three more rooms were to the left of each one of those rooms, full of glass cases and items hanging on the walls.

The items and stories were some we had never heard. We saw some of the evidence on Jack the Ripper. To this day, there is still speculation as to the identity of Jack the Ripper. Our guide told us a lot of inside stories about him, ones that had never been written in the papers or told to the public. It was very interesting.

Next to this exhibit there was an unusual bathtub which, I believe, was made out of brass. A very famous English murderer used to kill people and dissolve their bodies in acid in this bathtub. Some of the other stories were just as gruesome.

Houses of masochism are allowed in England, unless somebody complains to the police or Scotland Yard that they have been forced into masochism without their consent. At that point, Scotland Yard will close down the house without question. While we were in the city, Scotland Yard had closed down one of the biggest houses in London. Everything they had taken from the place had already been put into the Black Museum.

There was a huge wooden cross, the kind you would nail somebody to, or in this case, tie them to. It had four-by-fours and straps to hold arms and legs. At the bottom, instead of being narrow, it was wide so the person who hung on it would have his legs spread apart instead of together. A big black cabinet contained every type of sexual tool one could ever think of. It also had every kind of sex toy imaginable, and then some. There was a full-fledged stretching rack where a person could be tied on with buckles and straps. A turn of the handle would stretch them, and then the host would beat the person's body. An unusual pair of pants was used by some gay men. It had a fly in the front and a flap in the back that could be unbuttoned, for which you can use your imagination.

One interesting tool we saw was a piece of bamboo about three feet long wrapped in barbed wire all the way up, except for the handle. People used this tool to beat each other. The spikes still had blood on them. One of the most intriguing things to me was a little black satin Halloween mask, the kind you would buy in the dime store, lined in white. When the guide turned it over, around both eye holes we saw little tiny spots of blood, top and bottom. He explained that a female member of the Royal Family, from another time, had been involved in this activity, and this was her mask. He said when a person was beaten with the bamboo stick, they didn't scream or yell, but the pain was so intense the body actually dealt with the pain by releasing blood from the pores where the eyelashes go into the eyelids, top and bottom. We found that hard to believe, but he insisted it was true.

There was a saddle and bridle. The saddle goes around the body of one person. Another person sits on top, beating the person underneath all the while with a riding crop covered with barbed wire or with a cat-o-nine-tails. Two versions of the cat-o-nine-tails were displayed: one had leather thongs with knots tied in them, and the other had little beads on the ends. A metal bridle went into the saddled person's mouth, just like a horse, but it had little needles sticking out all around it. This museum was unbelievable! It had every means of torture known to humans.

Included were devices of a man who had murdered and dismembered nineteen or so people and had buried then in and around his house. In a little tin box, such as cough drops come in, the murderer carried tiny stacks of pubic hair from everyone he had killed. Very sick!

Sammy and I found the story of a famous English cat burglar very fascinating. He walked around town, very well dressed, complete with black cane; and no one ever suspected his trade. The cane was made of steel, and the bottom opened to reveal that the cane was made from sections of tubing, each one smaller than the other and fitting into each other. Inside the last tube was a series of little round steel bars that connected into holes in the sides of the tubing, forming a ladder. The top of the cane would hook over a balcony or window ledge, and he would climb up. When through, he would simply dismantle everything and once again have a simple walking cane. When he was caught, police found his diary. In it he explained how he found his victims by reading the society section of the newspapers, announcing who was going on a trip—and would not be home.

The museum had fountain pens that were really guns, and other simple everyday objects that were actually knives or other weapons. However, one of the most frightening things to us was a pair of binoculars that was sent to a member of the Royal Family—a female teenager; I do not remember who.

Our guide carefully handed the binoculars to Sammy, telling him not to put them up to his face. He said to turn the focus knob. When Sammy did, two needle-pointed pieces of steel came shooting out of both eyepieces. Most people, when picking up a pair of binoculars, turn the focus knob immediately. These daggers would have shot right through the eyes into the brain of the user and killed her immediately. It made Sammy and I cringe, just thinking about it.

Tragedy was averted because the butler felt there was something suspicious about the package when it was delivered. He had opened and examined it. Thankfully, because of his alertness, it never reached the intended victim.

This museum had every mode of torture, sexual deviation and tool of crime known. I could go on for hours relating the stories we were told. This was definitely one of the highlights of our trip to London.

Too soon, it was closing night at Club Pigalle. Sammy came out on stage for the final show; the club was full to the rafters. A number of additional tables had been put on stage to accommodate the overflow crowd; Sammy barely had room to work. Everyone employed at the club came to watch Sammy's act. It was informal, but everything else stopped while he did his show. People sat any place they could find a spot, or stood shoulder to shoulder. Instead of coming on stage wearing his customary tuxedo, Sammy wore an English suit with a vest and bowler hat; he carried his walking stick. (The English tailors are so good we all had suits made during our stay.)

I had asked Sammy why he decided to dress this way. He said, "Because, I feel like I am one of these people, and I want them to know and feel that I am one of them now. I am not just the little Black entertainer who came from the States. I feel that, in some way, I have also become British; and I want them to feel my love for them, as I have felt their love for me."

When Sam came on stage, the applause was beyond belief. He started to tear up, as did everyone else. He could barely get the show started, he was so emotional. But, as usual, he did a magnificent two-and-a-half hour show. At the end of it, Sammy began to sing a song one of the performers had done at the Royal Command Performance. The lyrics went, "We'll meet again, but who knows where or when."

At the airport, London

As he sang, the entire audience began singing with him, standing, singing, applauding, crying. It was a sad but glorious moment for Sammy, and for all of us who were with him—bittersweet. Sammy had to end the show right there; he could not go on. He bowed over and over again, then embraced them with his arms. It was a very touching and emotional moment to end our first trip to England.

Actress,
Alma Cogan,
me and
Lionel Blair,
choreographer

Sam with
vocalist,
Cilla Black

MAY FAIR
INTER·CONTINENTAL
LONDON

Sam at the Lincoln Memorial

Home Again

It was extremely sad for all of us, when we left for home the next day. We were flying to Washington, D.C. for our first show in the United States after Sammy's triumph in London.

The Lotus Club was located on the building's top floor. We went in the back entrance of the club. There we were joined by the rest of Sammy's people who had not gone to London. Among them was Sammy's bodyguard, Big John Hopkins, Sam Sr., Will Mastin and Nathan Crawford, Will's valet and good man Friday.

There seemed to be a lot of commotion going on around the outside of the club. When I asked about it Big John shook his head, "You don't want to know; it's terrible!"

Big John was a huge man, about six-foot-six, easily 350 pounds, with a very deep voice, and tough. He said, "Them dirty motherfuckers are downstairs walkin' out in front of this club. I want to go out there and kill me somebody!"

"John, what the hell is going on?" I asked.

"Go down there and look for yourself!" he answered.

I went down, looked through the glass doors and saw people picketing in front of the club. Crowds in the street were spitting and yelling at the picketers. Cops were everywhere. I was still standing behind the door when I pushed it open a little bit; the noise was deafening.

All of a sudden, a man walked toward me with a little black poodle on a leash. I'll never forget him. He wore brown slacks and a white shirt with the sleeves rolled up to mid-arm. A Nazi swastika was visible on his left arm. The little black dog had a swastika on a band around its belly. A sign was sewn to the top of the band that read: "I'm black, too; but I'm no Nigger!"

When I saw this man and his dog, I lost it! I bolted through the door to go after him. I was midstride when a big hand grabbed me, Large as I am, I was lifted by the back of my coat and yanked back inside.

It was Big John. "You ain't gonna go out there 'cause you're gonna get yourself killed!"

"No," I spat. "I'm gonna go out there and kill me somebody!"

"No you don't!" he commanded. "You're just gonna get yourself in trouble. The police have it all in hand."

"Who in the fuck are these people? What's going on?"

"Don't you recognize that man ?" John asked.

"Hell, no! I don't know who he is!" I was still livid.

"That's George Lincoln Rockwell."

"And who the fuck is George Lincoln Rockwell?"

Big John said, "He's the head of the Nazi party in the United States."

This demonstration was in response to Sammy's engagement announcement to May—to the fact that she was White and he was Black, and Jewish to boot. Unbelievable! Right in the capital of our country, the beacon of freedom and equality for the world. So much for "welcome home."

Big John (left)

Artist's idealization of Nazi party leader, George Lincoln Rockwell, and his banner

Sam and me at the Capitol Building, where Congress convenes

Center right: Sammy with NAACP Leader, Roy Wilkins

Right: Washington Monument in the distance

Counter-clockwise, starting above: Our guide to Washington D.C. the assistant to Adam Clayton Powell Jr.

Vice-President Nixon with Will

I sit at (then) Vice-President Richard M. Nixon's desk

Sam with Adam Clayton Powell Jr. one of the first Black Congressmen and a catalyst for racial equality

After the Lotus Club, we were scheduled to take Sammy's show to the Huntington Hartford Theater in Hollywood, one of the class venues of the time. The Sidewalk of the Stars was being built right in front of the theater, and there was a wooden walkway around the cement work, with handrails made of two-by-fours so people could walk safely.

It seemed everyone in Hollywood came on opening night to see Sammy. There had been lots of publicity about May and Sammy's engagement, as well as our Nazi reception in Washington, D.C.

I stood in front of the theater waiting for May to arrive. The limousine pulled up, a driver opened the door and May stepped out. The crowd started clapping their hands and shouting good wishes.

Everyone, that is, except one man. He yelled out, "There's that White bitch who's gonna' marry the Nigger!"

Instantly there was dead silence. Then, quick as you could blink your eyes, our very good friend, Steve Blouner, a big guy about six-foot-four, standing on the wooden sidewalk, grabbed a six-foot length of handrail and hit the bigot so hard he went sailing onto Vine Street and the middle of traffic. A roar of approval went up from the crowd, and the bigot took off running like hell down the middle of the street, never to be seen again. Funny—the police monitoring the crowd didn't see a thing; I guess they must have been looking at something else. Steve and I each took one of May's arms and escorted her into the theater to watch Sammy in another of his one-of-a-kind shows.

It was a very scary and intense time for all of us. We never knew where or when another threat or dangerous incident was going to happen.

May and I became life-long friends

Sam and me, best friends

We closed the Huntington Hartford and had another venue to play, the Curran Theater in San Francisco. Sam and May had been receiving so many death threats of late that everyone, including the William Morris Agency, wanted to put off the opening at the Curran for a while.

Sammy and I sat on the couch in his living room discussing this serious problem. "Silber, what do you think we ought to do?"

"What do you want me to say, Sam? That you should stay here, and never go there or anyplace else? We both know what you're gonna do. You knew what was coming when you asked May to marry you; at least you knew in your head. But now since all this scary shit has hit you in the face, you're starting to have doubts. On the other hand, we have the indomitable Sammy Davis Jr. who jumps into shit every day of his life and somehow manages to slosh through it and come out the other side—a little more battle worn, but smelling like the proverbial rose. No, Sammy Davis Jr. will go to San Francisco and face up to whatever happens. It's really simple. As I've always said to you, 'That's what makes Sammy run!'"

Sammy reached out and grabbed my hand with a little knowing squeeze, "Yeah, man, you're right. I guess you know me better than anyone."

"Well, at least a damn sight better than most! Remember, I am his majesty's blood brother; and I do know how you handle the sword. Not as good as I do, to be sure, but you're okay."

That broke the tension and we laughed. But never one to let me have the last word he replied, "Maybe on your one good day, Silber!"

A couple days later, we arrived in San Francisco, one of our favorite cities. Sammy had insisted May remain in Hollywood and made plenty of arrangements for a lot of eyes to be focused on her. At that time there was a well known Los Angeles private detective named Freddy O'Tash. You might say he was *Mike Hammer* to the stars. If you needed any kind of security help Freddy was your man, and he was a good friend of Sammy's, so Sammy felt safe leaving May under Freddy's watchful eyes and left for San Francisco.

At the Curran Theater, we were met by two San Francisco Police detectives. They were sent to keep an eye on Sammy and his people, as well as the theater. I must admit it was a little spooky to be standing there, just the four of us. Sammy said, "What are you guys doing here? Do we have some kind of a problem?"

"Actually, Mr. Davis," said one of the detectives, "we have had some nasty calls and a bomb threat."

"You know," I jumped in, "I'm getting a little fed up with all this shit! What in the hell is wrong with these people anyway?"

Sammy interjected, "Well, what's going to happen? I mean are we going to do a show or not?"

"Of course, Mr. Davis. We just don't want to take any chances. We get this kind of stuff all the time. It's some kook trying to cause trouble, but there very seldom turns out to be a real problem. We have already swept the theater and everything is okay. There will be someone with you the entire time you're here."

"I guess we should all be grateful," Sammy reflected. "But it's my ass out there on that stage. I'm sure you can understand what keeps running through my mind. I'm worried some damn crazy fool is gonna take a pot shot at me, or blow me up."

"Please Mr. Davis...."

"Call me Sammy."

"Okay, Sammy. Please try not to think too much about it. It's just some fool trying to make a statement."

"All right. Silber, you worry about it, and I'll get on with the show."

As usual, I got the hard job. Sammy and I always had a way of making a situation humorous with each other when things started to get too heavy. During the week we were at the Curran Theater nothing happened. The threats, thankfully, all turned out to be hollow.

Later—on November 13th, 1960—with Frank Sinatra and Peter Lawford standing by as best men, Sammy and May were married.

Lauren Bacall

Shirley MacLaine

Humphrey Bogart & Rat Pack women

Lana Turner

Angie Dickenson

(left to right)
The guys: Frank Sinatra, Dean Martin, Sammy, Peter Lawford, Joey Bishop

The Rat Pack
Magic or Myth

This chapter will explain that the media hype surrounding the Rat Pack was, and still is, just that: media hype. First of all, let's be clear about one thing. The original Rat Pack was actually started by Humphrey Bogart and his wife Lauren Bacall, Judy Garland and her husband Sid Luft, Swifty Lazar (a noted agent), actress Martha Hyer and a couple of others. By some quirk of fate, or the media looking for salacious headline stories, it was turned into a huge circus of make believe about Sinatra's "gang." Oh, please!

Originally, there was only Sammy, Frank Sinatra and Dean Martin in the Rat Pack. Joey Bishop and Peter Lawford were on the outer perimeter of the circle, as were Angie Dickenson and Shirley MacLaine, who had been in movies with them, Lana Turner and Marilyn Monroe. There were several more women, if you were to count all the relationships of each male person in the Pack. It was the press that made this group seem larger than life, and even now continues to build a mountain out of the only three shows the entire Rat Pack ever did together.

The first series of shows was the so-called "Summit at the Sands," during the *Ocean's Eleven* filming in Las Vegas in 1959. The second was shortly thereafter at the Fountainbleu Hotel on Miami Beach. That show only starred Sammy, Frank, Dean and Joey. The third and last event took place when Frank owned part of the Cal-Neva Lodge at Lake Tahoe; it starred only Sammy, Frank and Dean. Many years later, Sammy, Frank and Dean began a tour together; but Dean had to drop out shortly after the tour began, and Liza Minnelli finished the tour with Sammy and Frank. The Rat Pack made only three movies together as well: *Ocean's Eleven, Robin and the Seven Hoods* and *Sergeants Three*.

Since then, there have been television specials about the Rat Pack and Sammy which have compounded the myth. These were the megastars of their day, working hard to build their careers—they simply didn't have the time to hang out together, except when any or all of them happened to end up in one place at the same time. Then they would hang out and party, but not necessarily perform together. The press just kept making a big thing out of it. To my memory, there was never even a specific Rat Pack party.

The Rat Pack myth started when these stars opened at the Sands at the same time, while they were in Las Vegas to make *Ocean's Eleven*. No one ever knew which of the Rat Pack members would perform on any given night. It might be one or two of them or the whole group at once, but one of them would always be the star for the night. No matter who was starring that night, whoever else was there would make comments and remarks from an offstage microphone. For instance, when Sammy was in the middle of singing a ballad, one or more of the others walked across the stage behind Sammy wearing nothing but their underwear, not even looking at the audience. The place would get hysterical with laughter—and so much for the lovely ballad. This didn't happen only to Sammy. It didn't make much difference who was on stage. This was all in fun.

At that time the average cost of a dinner show at the Copa Room was approximately six dollars per person, plus the tip for the maitre d' and the doorman who seated you. This show became so popular, people were tipping the Maitre d' from one to twelve hundred dollars to get seats in front. It was sheer madness, that the power of their names made people go crazy. There were times, however, that the craziness on stage turned very sour, depending on how you took some of the comments that poured out.

Sammy knew he wasn't the best-looking guy in the world. He was only about five-feet-six, a hundred twenty-five to thirty pounds and had a nose that had been broken a couple of times and never set properly. He was ashamed that he had never attended school; he had met his share of racial bigots; and to top it all off, he had become Jewish. With all that going against him in his life, he managed to do pretty well for an ugly little Black man. I would think, also, that May Britt and Kim Novak, two of the most beautiful women in the world, falling in love with him ain't the worst thing that could happen. Obviously, they saw beneath the exterior to the inside of this dynamic little man. He had as many girls as Frank, Dean, Peter or Joey, and ones just as beautiful.

More than once during our private talks about it, he would say to me, "I just got to get bigger and better than anyone. I just got to keep pushing it to keep up!"

"Keep up with what?" I asked.

"Just have to keep up with Frank and Dean, and whoever else is out there."

"For Christ's sake, Sam! You're already as big or bigger than all of them."

"Nah, man. These guys got it all."

"Sam, what I keep telling you all the time, and will keep telling you till I die, I guess—you're full of shit!"

Many hurtful things happened with the Rat Pack—and I am sure the public didn't even realize what was happening. I must say they all treated me very well, especially Frank. But the things Frank and Dean said and did to Sammy under the guise of humor were painful, mean and infuriating. Not being Black, and not being Sammy, Frank and Dean may not have even realized just how hurtful they were to Sammy. The members of the Rat Pack were friends, and that made what they did hurt Sammy even more, right down to his very gut.

By then I spent most of my time working in our Hollywood office; but I ran over to Las Vegas two or three times a week, including opening night. That night there was not a seat to be had, not even for me, so I watched the show from the lighting booth. I had already spent half my life there, and it's the best seat in the house.

Beginning with opening night, the house lights would come down and the group would walk on stage, joking. Somebody called for the bar to be brought on stage, and they started. Dean picked Sammy up in his arms and said, "I'd like to thank the NAACP for this award."

The audience laughed, as did Sammy; and I started to simmer. Then from an offstage mike while Sammy was on stage by himself, Frank said, "Sing 'What Kind of Fool Am I,' but keep smiling, Smokey, so they can see you."

God, I got mad! There was no need for that! Sammy made a joke back, and kept going. Then came, "Hurry up, Sam; the watermelon's gettin' warm. Why don't you be yourself and eat some rind?"

I was so mad by this time, I was ready to kill someone. It was Frank and Dean who kept throwing the barbs at Sammy from off-stage. This went on every night.

After the show when Sammy and I were alone, I just had to say something. "You son-of-a-bitch. Why in the hell are you letting some of your best friends talk to you like that? It's not only that they're throwing every kind of indignity they can at you, but every person of color who sees it and hears it is demoralized too. I just want to slap you silly, you dumb son-of-a-bitch, for letting it happen!"

Sammy jumped right up. "Just cool it, Silber! I'm holding my own!"

"Oh, no, you aren't! The only thing you're holding are Frank and Dean's dicks. Can't you see what's going on?"

"Sure I can, but can't you see what I'm trying to do?"

"Oh, yeah, I can see what you're trying to do. You're trying to suck it up, just to stay up with the pack."

"Well, what's the harm in that?" he asked.

"You stupid motherfucker, you're giving up all the things you've spent your life trying to accomplish. You've always tried to break down the racial barriers. Now you're tossing it away just to suck up to Frank, Dean and the fucking so-called Pack. I tell you, Sam, I'm about as mad as I've ever been at what I've heard and seen tonight."

"Calm down, Arthur! Calm down, man; I know how you feel."

"You haven't a clue how I feel, seeing you degraded like that after all you've done, and still do, to lift up the image."

"I'm just trying to go along with it to get myself in tight with them. And I'm holding my own with them anyway."

"Oh, yeah, I could see that. That's why Frank and Dean sat on high black stools, and you sat on some kind of a little kid's white chair a foot high. Yeah, that's really holding your own! Just what do you think that Dad—I mean your dad—and Massey would think if they saw you right now, or saw this show?"

Sammy started to cry as he spoke. "Please, Arthur, get off my back for a while. I've gotta think."

"I'll get off your back, man, but just remember I'm on your side, and I have been all my life. I don't want to stand by and watch you become some kind of Black person sitting on a fence eating watermelon at the expense of every Black person in the world, lending yourself to that kind of racial humor for the sake of a cheap laugh. It ain't you, Sam. And ain't nothing you can say that will change my mind, so don't fucking try! You can't even fool yourself. And it's all for what? So the Chairman of the Board can make funnies at your expense? Shit, I better close my mouth for a while before you hit me with a chair or something."

"Thanks, man. Just let me be for a while."

He sat there staring at the floor, not moving, not saying a word. He knew I was right. I had just laid a very heavy burden on him. We both sat there for some time, not speaking. But he knew I wasn't finished yet. I would just save it for another day.

Early the next morning I was awakened by a little tapping on the door between our bedrooms. "That you, Sam?" I called out.

"Yeah, it's me. I wanted to pop in and say I'm sorry about last night. I guess I'm ashamed of it all. I'm really confused about all this stuff. I didn't really want to get so upset, but you were right about everything you said. You know how it pisses me off when you're right."

"Sam, God knows how much I love, respect and care for you. But what I don't think you know is what it does to me when I hear them talk down to you and make hurtful remarks. It's like they're doing it to me, and I just can't let it go down without saying something about it. I'm staying a few more days just to see how this plays out."

"Okay, man. I understand. I gotta be on the set in a few minutes, so…later."

"All right, go. But remember, I'm watching every move you make. So you go now, and get the hell out of my room before people start talking about me having another man in my room with me."

Later in the day, because nothing else was going on, I watched some of the filming. When the day's shooting was done, a few of us went to the steam room. On this day, Don Rickles was there, along with Sammy, Frank, me and a few others. It goes without saying that when you were anywhere with Don Rickles, you were in trouble. We weren't there more than a couple of minutes before Rickles started on Frank, and Frank went nuts laughing. Then out came the remarks. "Sammy, you can't wear white towels in here; we'll get some brown ones for you."

Sammy made some funny little retort, then bit the bullet. He turned around and looked at me and his eyes sent the message, "Don't say a word, Silber." I knew the look.

That night at the show, it was more of the same. It seemed to me that was the way these shows were going to be until the filming of the movie was over. It was Frank and Dean who loved to make Sammy the butt of their racial jokes, and Sammy who took the lashing. Sammy just kept slapping his knees, making believe he was laughing—but no sound came from his mouth. It was easy to tell what was going on.

At that point, there was nothing more I could say or do that would change a thing. Sammy did what he thought he had to, just to keep on the good side of Frank. It would not be fair of me to leave the impression that all the guys used Sammy as a whipping boy. Peter Lawford and Joey Bishop never lowered themselves to that kind of so-called humor.

There are many more things that could be said about the unpleasant words and gestures heaped on Sammy by Frank and Dean during those shows, but I believe my point has been made.

The Rat Pack, magic or myth—for some, it was and still is the Rat Pack. But to me and all those who were really on the inside, it was and always will be just a gigantic Hollywood myth.

Dean, Sammy (on child's stool) and Frank

Filming of final scene for Ocean's Eleven, *draws a crowd—background is present site of The Mirage*

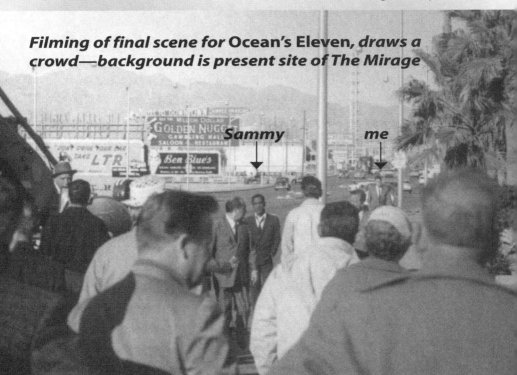

Below: (right) Sammy and Eartha Kitt in scene from Anna Lucasta, *Sammy's first starring film role* (left) Me, Sammy and David Landfield in front of Eartha Kitt's Hollywood dressing room

Alex Plasschaert

James Brown

Gina Lamyou

Clessia "Boots" Wade

David Toguri

Ellyn Brown

Nita Silber

Peppi Borza

HAL LOMAN DANCERS

Prince of Wales

an evening with

SAMMY DAVIS JR.

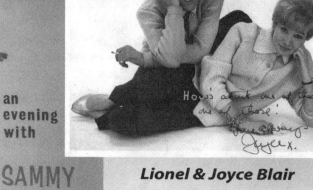

How's about some Mont Blanc Baby
Lionel

How's about one of those for one of those!
Love always,
Joyce x.

Lionel & Joyce Blair

Princess Grace and the Queen Mother Call —We Go Again

Our second trip to Europe was spurred by a request to perform at a Royal Command Performance for Princess Grace and Prince Rainier of Monaco. This was Princess Grace's annual benefit for the International Red Cross. After Monaco, Sammy would launch a three-month tour of England, beginning in London at the Prince of Wales Theatre, one of the premier theaters in England.

On this tour, Sammy was bringing his own dancers. He asked me to call our close friend, choreographer Hal Loman. Sammy decided to do something different and wanted to discuss it with Hal. He wanted eight of the best dancers available—he wanted them racially mixed, a novelty for that time. No major star had ever done it before, which, of course, was another first for Sammy.

Hal thought it was a wonderful idea, and said he would take care of the arrangements immediately. A couple days later, Hal called and asked Sammy and me to meet him at his rehearsal studio. To my surprise, Hal had selected my wife, Nita, and her brother, Peppi Borza, who were a well known acrobatic dance team. Hal had also chosen Alex Plasschaert and his wife, Ellyn Brown, Clessia "Boots" Wade, who was Black, Gina Lamyou, who was AmerAsian, James Brown (no relation to Ellyn), who was Black, and Asian, David Toguri.

Sammy had ordered a custom-made Rolls Royce Silver Cloud before we left the United States. I was to be the first one in our party going to London, so I could pick up this car and meet Sammy at the airport with it. I chose to fly on Air France this trip because I had never flown on that airline before, and had heard it was quite an experience. I hadn't paid any attention to my tickets and discovered upon check-in in Los Angeles that I was going to fly from Los Angeles to Paris, and then Paris to London. Not only would the plane stop in Paris, but my flight was into La Borge Airport, then out of Orly

Airport, on the opposite side of Paris. That didn't leave much time to make the connection, and I didn't know how to speak French.

It was too late to change anything. I carried a big shoulder bag full of clothes and, as always, my Roloflex camera, which hung around my neck. I managed to get on a shuttle bus going across Paris. Talk about crazy drivers—you ought to drive in Paris some time. Even on the shuttle bus it was nuts. The plane to London was already loaded and on the runway, but they had made arrangements for me to be picked up at the gate by a little tractor which usually pulled the planes around.

I ran like crazy across the airport's marble floor to make the plane. I was lugging my shoulder bag, with my camera bouncing around my neck and another bag in my hand. Running full bore, I tripped and fell face down in the middle of the airport lobby. My expensive Roloflex hit the marble first. To this day, I still have that camera and it still has the dent in it. Falling, I ripped a brand new pair of mohair slacks from my knee up to my crotch. But, I couldn't stop. I had to leap up and keep running or miss the plane. I made it, and thank God I had a shoulder bag with clothes in it. I was able to change clothes on the plane. The rest of my luggage was coming with Sammy.

After checking into the hotel, I called Rolls Royce, but not until I had called my travel agent to give him a piece of my mind about the lousy travel arrangements. He was going to have to buy me a new pair of mohair slacks, and fix my camera—if it could be fixed. That was the same camera I had used to take pictures of Sammy with Queen Elizabeth the previous year. Fortunately, I was able to have it repaired.

The driver from Rolls Royce arrived at our hotel with Sam's car. I was really impressed—the car was beautiful. What impressed me most though, was the extraordinary service. When you have a Rolls Royce made for you in London, a chauffeur comes with it for the break-in period, at no extra cost! Your Rolls chauffeur tells you all about the car and its features. So there I was for one whole day, with a Rolls Royce to ride around in on my own. Lionel Blair, his sister, Joyce, and Al Hunt spent that day with me.

Me on the beach at Monaco

Anthony Newley

Sammy and I went to the theater a lot during this stay in London. A week before we arrived, a new musical had opened which was the talk of the town. It was a smash hit called *Stop the World, I Want to Get Off!* Written by Anthony Newley and Leslie Brickus, it starred Anthony Newley, and was the most unique show anyone had seen. Tony was brilliant in the show. In England he was well known as an actor and a mime, but this was his first musical. Previously, he had not been considered a serious singer, or a musical star.

Sammy and I wanted to see the sold-out show, which was playing only about two blocks from Prince of Wales Theatre where Sammy was booked. We called Tony Newley, and he got us tickets. Tony and Sammy had developed a solid friendship during our first visit to London. This was a very unusual show with a unique set. It was the first time I had ever seen a theater with no curtain. The stage was exposed so the audience could see the set before the start of the show. It looked like the end of a circus tent. It is history now, that the show was a tremendous success.

Tony sang numbers in that show that blew Sammy away. In the course of a conversation with Tony, Sammy asked if he could sing one or two of these songs in his show. This is something that is never done. You just don't take songs out of a brand new hit and give them to somebody else who is performing two blocks down the street. Tony gave the songs to Sammy, a wonderful gesture on his part, and Sammy put them in his show. "Gonna Build a Mountain," "What Kind of Fool Am I?" and "Once in a Lifetime" became three of Sammy's biggest hits.

Sammy went into rehearsal with great earnest. He had a tremendous opening night, since he was so popular in England. We were the hottest ticket in town, next to *Stop the World, I Want to Get Off!*

Sammy and Anthony Newley share a stage

Tony's show finished each night before Sammy's. So Tony would come to the Prince of Wales Theatre to see Sammy's show. I don't think he ever missed a night of walking out on the stage during Sammy's show. Sometimes Tony would walk out alone, sometimes with somebody else. He pulled all kinds of stunts on Sammy. Sometimes they would sing a duet together, and sometimes Tony would do other things. This went on for the entire month we were there.

During the course of this engagement, every major star performing, living in, or visiting Europe at the time, came to see Sammy. They had to come through me first. Every night runners announced, "Sir Laurence Olivier would like to see Sammy," or "Maurice Chevalier would like to see Sammy," or "Christopher Lee…."

Sammy also performed for the Queen Mother, but it was nothing like the Royal Command Performance he had done for Queen Elizabeth II, on our first trip. Maurice Chevalier was the star of this show. Of course Sammy went out and drove the audience wild, having the same mesmerizing effect on them he always did.

Sammy greeted by the Queen Mother

My wife, Nita, and her brother Peppi Borza, acrobatic dancers

After the Royal Command Performance for the Queen Mother, we continued on to Monaco to perform for Princess Grace and Prince Rainier. We flew into the French town of Nice; from there it was a very dangerous drive to Monaco. People maneuvered their cars very fast on the narrow winding road. It was treacherous. Many people were killed on that road, including, later, Princess Grace herself.

This day, we were escorted to a helicopter, one of the first four-seater helicopters. The pilot, Sammy, Murphy and I filled that little helicopter. Our luggage came by car. We flew down the coast of the French Riviera, seeming to be about ten feet off the water. This helicopter was like a glass bubble, even the flooring. Sammy and Murphy sat in the back seat, scared to death.

I sat next to the pilot. I had done so much flying, in the Naval Air Reserve, as well as in my everyday life, that this didn't scare me at all. It was a unique experience to fly in a plane where you could look down between your legs and see the ground, or in this case the surface of the water. We flew along the beautiful Mediterranean coast until we reached our landing pad at the big casino in Monte Carlo.

Royal Performance in the presence of Her Majesty The Queen Mother on the Evening of Monday November 6th 1961 at The Prince of Wales Theatre, London.

Sam's photo of me in front of Monaco's royal palace, built in the 1600s—where we lunched with the Grimaldis

Lunch with Princess Grace and Prince Ranier

The next day was rainy, gray and funky. We went to rehearsal at the place where we were going to perform. It was an enormous veranda. Later we were told the show was going to be canceled due the weather. The performers were asked to stay over another day since this was to be a huge show, and there were major stars appearing, just as they did for Queen Elizabeth's Royal Command Performance. A number of actors were in the area filming *The Guns of Navarone*. That night Sammy, Murphy and I went partying with Douglas Fairbanks Jr., his daughter, David Niven and his wife, Gregory Peck, Anthony Quinn, and others who were not in show business.

The following day, the weather was still very iffy, but the show went on anyway. The last act to perform before Sammy was a world-famous dance team named Brascia and Tybee. They introduced him. When he came on, it started to rain. Sammy looked up at the sky and said, "Oh, God…Moses…whoever, I am one of you; please don't do this to me."

The minute he said that, the rain stopped instantly. That's the God's truth! He did his entire show and, as always, killed everybody. The instant he took his last bow, the skies opened up and the rain poured down. That story made the world press.

After the performance we were still enjoying the company of the same people with whom we had been partying the night before. Sammy was drinking a little Galliano. Two girls, who lived in Rome, were sitting at our table. One of them invited Sammy, Murphy and me to their house in Rome for dinner the next day. Sammy had just had enough Galliano to say "Okay."

I reminded him we had made reservations at the Georges Cinq Hotel in Paris—it was going to be our first visit to Paris—but that didn't seem to make any difference to him. He just kept raising his glass in the air and saying, "All roads lead to Rome; we're going to Rome." Of course, I didn't take him seriously.

Sammy was a person who stayed awake for sometimes two or three days at a time, burning up a lot of energy. When he finally went to sleep, the building could blow up and it wouldn't wake him up; he was dead to the world. You could not move him.

The next morning, there was a knock at the door that woke me. When I opened the door, a gentleman in a uniform stood there with two envelopes in his hand. He asked for Sammy Davis. I told him Sammy was sleeping. He flipped the envelopes over and asked if Mr. Arthur Silber was there. I identified myself and he handed me the envelope with my name on it. There was a royal seal on the top, and inside was a note inviting me to lunch at the royal palace that afternoon at one o'clock. The note was signed, "Princess Grace Grimaldi."

I asked the courier if I could call to R.S.V.P. He said, "No, sir. I have to take the answer back with me." Off I went to Sammy's bedroom to try and wake him up. I did everything I could think of, wondering all the time how Princess Grace knew who I was. I had never been introduced to her and, in fact, neither had Sammy. There had been no receiving line after the show.

Finally, I woke Sammy up by turning the mattress over and rolling him onto the floor. Boy was he mad! "What the hell are you doing?" he demanded to know. "Are you crazy?"

I tried to show him the invitation to the palace, over his protests, finally just reading it to him myself. That woke him up, and got him excited. "Oh, my God! Oh, my God; what are we gonna to do?"

"Well, are we going to go?" I asked.

"Of course!" he answered.

Back at the door, I told the messenger that we would accept the invitations, and asked directions. He said to just take a cab; any cab would take us to the palace, which was up on the hill.

Suddenly Sammy was a crazy man. "What are we gonna wear?" he was frantic; we hadn't brought many clothes, since we thought we were only going to be gone from London for two days. We didn't even know what we should wear, or how we were supposed to act. This socializing with royalty was a totally new experience for us. I suggested we call the concierge at our hotel, which we did. He explained to us that the Grimaldis were very gracious hosts. Also, he said that since it was an afternoon function, we should dress casually, in sports wear with an ascot.

"What the hell is an ascot?" Sammy wondered, so we asked the concierge. He pointed us toward a men's shop and we got outfitted.

Our cab left us on the hilltop before a most beautiful palace. It had a wonderful view, overlooking the bay. The palace had two entrances, each with guards marching in front of them. We didn't know which entrance to use. While we were standing there trying to decide, people began to recognize Sammy. They started asking him for autographs and pictures. In no time, a crowd had gathered around Sammy. He was becoming a little frustrated.

Just then, a car came around the corner beeping its horn. It was David Niven and his wife in their little convertible. He was one of the nicest men I have ever met in my life. He was also one of the funniest, with a great sense of humor, yet, at the same time, very dignified. He was extremely close friends with Princess Grace and visited the palace often. He and his wife were invited to lunch as well. So they invited us to ride the rest of the way with them—good thing, too, because Sammy and I were headed for the wrong entrance.

The palace doors were huge. As they opened, we saw the palace wall to our right side, extending a long way back. On our left side was the cliff. Between the wall and the cliff a flat lawn stretched into the distance. On that lawn, running towards us, was Princess Grace—Grace Kelly, as we knew her. She was wearing a powder blue, chiffon gown. It was strapless, with a scarf about twenty feet long around her neck, that was blowing in the breeze like in a TV commercial or a movie. She threw her arms around David Niven—gave him a big hug and kiss—greeted his wife the same way, then put her arms around Sammy smiling. "Welcome to our home." She called me by name and welcomed me as well.

We walked to the "back yard." Another famous movie star, Tony Franciosa, was there with his wife, along with a Count from Turkey, a Princess from Greece, and Prince Rainier. That was the party for lunch.

Prince Rainier sat in a wooden chair wearing blue denim pants, white deck shoes, and a blue and white striped T-shirt. We were introduced, and I found him to be a very pleasant man. He and I talked for an extremely long time. He had just bought a new boat, made in the United States, which was anchored in the harbor below us. It was a little Glasbar fishing boat, about an eighteen footer. He was so proud of that boat. We both love to fish, so we talked at great length about boats and fishing. It was very nice and comfortable.

They had a beautiful swimming pool, huge and done in mosaic tile. They also had bathing suits in every conceivable size so everyone could swim, even if they did not come prepared. We swam, then went to eat lunch. Tables were set up overlooking the cliff. The waiters were dressed in white, with white cotton gloves. The cooks wore tall white hats. As you proceeded along the buffet line to get your food, it was all served and cut with gloved hands. We had huge beautiful, napkins decorated with the royal crest in gold. I was able to figure out how to get two of them into my pockets for a souvenir, but to this day I don't know what happened to them. They just disappeared.

During the meal Sammy turned to me. Out of the blue he said, "Did you make the reservations for Rome?"

"What?" I said.

"Did you make the reservations for Rome where we're going to dinner?"

"No, I didn't." I hadn't a clue he even remembered Rome. I reminded him we still had reservations in Paris, but he said we were going to Rome instead, to have dinner. "With whom?" I asked.

"We're going to go to Rome and have dinner over at this girl's house."

"Does Murphy know we're doing this?" I asked. Murphy was back at the hotel waiting for us. Sammy told me to call Murphy and have him make reservations for us in Rome.

I asked Princess Grace if there was a phone I could use. I must admit, I felt pretty good walking along with her in the Palace all alone as she ushered me into her private office. She took me through a courtyard where they had the royal carriages parked around the quadrangle. There was also a section where they held concerts for their friends in the evenings, sometimes under the stars. Princess Grace was extremely polite and exceedingly beautiful.

She asked me who I needed to call, because she spoke French and I do not. First, I needed to call an airline to get us to Rome, so she called Air Italia for me. I had to make reservations for a specific flight because one of the girls had already left to go back to Rome, but the other one was still in Monaco and we were supposed to go on the flight with her. We didn't know anyone in Rome, and she was to be our guide. I called the hotel and told Murphy we were definitely going to Rome. He was surprised, but agreed to call the Georges Cinq Hotel in Paris and cancel our reservations. I told him to call the rest of the troupe in London and tell them we were going to Rome, but I didn't know where we would be staying. Princess Grace gave me the name of a good hotel in Rome and I made a reservation.

On location of The Robe, *first film shot in Cinemascope, Sammy chats with Jean Simmons who starred with Richard Burton*

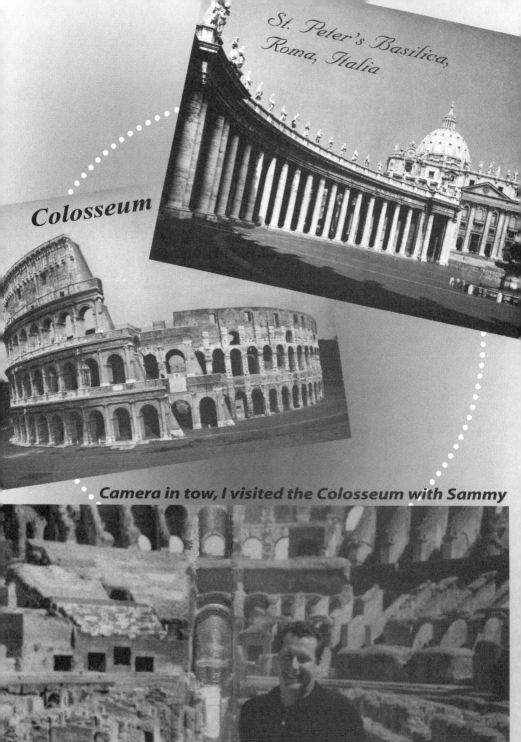

St. Peter's Basilica,
Roma, Italia

Colosseum

Camera in tow, I visited the Colosseum with Sammy

We Walk Where the Caesars Walked

Sammy had a thing he did with some people, me in particular. You had three chances to get something right. If you made a mistake, he would say, "That's one!" Next, "That's two!" and finally, "That's three!" After number three, you were dead. That's it! He was mad, really pissed off!

Princess Grace gave us a car with a chauffeur. He took us back to our hotel after lunch, waiting for us while we picked up our bags and Murphy. Then he took all of us to the airport. At the counter I picked up our tickets and met the girl who was waiting for us to accompany her to Rome. When our flight was called, she told us to come with her. We went through the passport line. At the end of this line, people were sent to the right or the left. The girl was in front of us and was sent to the right. We were sent to the left. I tried to protest, "Rome! Rome!" In very broken English, an official told us our plane would go to Rome. We figured the other plane was overloaded, so they were sending two planes to Rome. We went on the flight to which we were directed, while our girl guide took the other flight.

We got on the plane and were seated in coach. As I said before, Sammy never flew coach, only first-class. After boarding the plane, Sammy observed, "We're in coach."

I said, "I know; this is all I could get. I don't speak French or Italian. These are the seats they gave me."

Sammy turned to me, saying, "That's one!"

The plane took off. After flying for a while, an announcement was made to fasten our safety belts, we were going to be landing in Sicily. I called the stewardess over and asked why we were landing in Sicily. I explained we were supposed to be going to Rome. She answered that this flight would stop in Sicily, then go on to Rome.

Sammy asked the stewardess, "So this plane going to stop in Sicily?"

"Yes," she replied

"Then we're going to fly on to Rome, right?"

It was "Yes," again. But from Sammy I heard, "That's two!"

We had to get off the plane in Sicily and go through Customs. Sammy was not too thrilled about standing in the Customs line. As we got closer to the Customs official we could hear that he only spoke Italian. Sammy told me to make damn sure we changed our seats and flew the rest of the way to Rome in first-class. I told him I would do the best I could. A man about two people behind us stepped up and said, "Mr. Davis, my name is Bill; maybe I can help you. I speak fluent Italian." Bill helped us through Customs, but told us we could not change our seats.

We learned, as the evening progressed, that Bill was a pilot for the Mob. He flew planes all over Europe, running errands. Bill was a very nice guy who was also flying to Rome. When we left to return to our plane, we were now to board a different airplane—different seats, but still in coach.

"Well, dat's three!" Sammy was so angry he was talking Colored to me now. "When we get to Rome, I's goin' to the hotel. You 'n' Murphy's gonna pick up the bags 'n' youse gonna find a hotel by yo' damn self!"

When we landed, Sammy, as threatened, just took off. In fact, he left with Bill, who had, by now, joined our little group, making us a four-some. It was my job to contact the girl whose house we were going to for the dinner party, and tell her we were bringing a fourth. She had given us a phone number, but we didn't know where she lived.

Murphy and I got the luggage, and on the way into town, we went by the Colosseum. It was magnificent! This meant a lot to me, as I knew it would to Sammy. It brought back memories of our youth when we would sword fight and pretend to be gladiators. I asked the driver if all cars coming from the airport had to pass the Colosseum. He said, "Yes." I turned to Murphy smiling, "Don't worry, Murphy. As soon as Sammy sees this Colosseum, it's all over; he won't be mad any more."

As we entered the hotel lobby, Sammy was going up in the elevator—one of those open ones, so I could see him. We checked in, and went to our suite. The minute we opened the door, Sammy yelled at me, "Did you see it? Did you see it?" and all his anger was gone.

Now we called the girl to whose house we were going. We agreed to meet downstairs at 8:00 P.M., and I told her we had another friend with us. She said to bring anyone we wanted. It turned out Bill had an American girlfriend who happened to be in Rome. Our party of four was now a party of five. Downstairs, three taxicabs pulled up to get us. Murphy got into one, Sammy boarded the second, and I got into the third. By now, our party of five had grown to eleven and the party at the house had transformed into dinner at a well-known restaurant. The cabs took off in different directions to visit various sites of interest. Sammy was taken to one of the Seven Hills of Rome; I went to the Vatican; and Murphy visited yet another historical site.

The Vatican is huge. It was designed by Michelangelo and is absolutely incredible. Outside, there are many, many rows of columns in in a sort of semi-circle—that's all you see—columns. If you stand on the concrete disk in the center, all the columns appear to merge, becoming one. If you stand one foot off the disk, you are back to seeing row after row of columns, maybe ten or twelve deep. Back on the circle, they're one again; just amazing.

People in Italy drive just as wildly as they do in France. Cars and motor scooters are going every which way, and all yelling at each other. We pulled up to the restaurant which was on a little cobblestone side street. Sitting in front was a donkey-drawn cart, hay piled in the back, spilling out. In fact, there was hay all over the street. The donkey was tied there, and chickens pecked through the hay. We couldn't imagine what kind of a restaurant we were going to.

We were guided down a very narrow staircase to the restaurant door. Inside it felt humid. It was very hot in Rome, and you could smell the dank, moss-covered walls. We wondered where we were being taken. We kept descending until we were in a huge room, the walls hidden by wine casks, fifteen to eighteen feet in diameter. This room had once been in the sewers of Rome. Just six weeks before we arrived, this room had been discovered during some excavation. Since it was right below the restaurant, it belonged to the restaurant.

There was no air conditioning; people were smoking, and you could hardly breathe. We sat around a big table with wine decanters. Europeans drink wine like we drink water. A fat, bald-headed little man approached our table. His face was red and a shock of red hair decorated the middle of his head. He could speak no English at all. But he did say, "Sammy Davis! Sammy Davis!" and he kept bowing.

An Italian band played at the other end of the room. The five band members wore old-time green stocking caps hanging off to the side with big red balls on the ends. They played Italian music with mandolins. It actually turned out that we had a ball. There was so much smoke and it was so hot down there, that Sammy had a glass or two of wine. He was getting plowed just because of the heat in the room.

We learned, through our new Italian-speaking acquaintances, that the bald proprietor wanted Sammy to perform with the band. Sammy didn't know what to sing. He didn't know Italian, and was sure the band didn't know how to play any of his music. But, eventually he gave in and went up to the bandstand. He shook hands with the musicians and began to count off a beat, snapping his fingers like he always did, "Cachink, cachink." Well, the band picked up on it; he started, and kept going for twenty-five minutes—in English. It was really fun.

We had made arrangements for a driver to pick us up the next day to take us sight-seeing. Sammy and I wanted to go to the Colosseum, Trevi Fountain and any other places that we could see during the day. The Colosseum was thrilling, and our driver was an excellent guide. He took us to a round building with no lights inside, but a hole in the top of the dome roof. Inside were beautiful paintings on the walls. As the sun moves across the sky, it shines down through the opening onto each of the exquisite paintings, one at a time. It was very interesting, and a wonderful thing to see.

That evening we all went to a restaurant called Bricktops, named after and owned by a Black, American woman, a famous jazz singer at the time who had been living in Europe for many years. Sammy and I rode in the same car we had used for sight-seeing earlier. Murphy rode in a different car. Our group was still eleven or twelve people. We traveled on a highway, built by Mussolini during World War II. It was his answer to Hitler's Autobahn in Germany.

Murphy got to the restaurant before us and stood outside in the driveway of the nightclub waiting for us to arrive. There was a little mound of grass and a decorative wire fence about ten inches high that kind of looped at the top. Our driver had a sense of humor and kidded us that he was going to run Murphy down. It was a joke, but he headed the car in that direction like he was actually going to do it. Murphy of course, jumped back, and as he did, he caught his foot in this little wire fence and fell to the ground. He hurt himself badly and was in a lot of pain. The driver was extremely apologetic and upset as he never meant to hurt Murphy.

We went in just as the show started. It was already dark. Murphy sat next to me. Someone sat between him and Sammy. As the show began I looked at Murphy and saw tears streaming down his cheeks. I leaned over and asked if he was okay. He said, "No, man, I'm dying. The pain in my foot is just killing me. I'm really hurting."

I went to Sammy and told him Murphy was really hurt. Sammy looked over and saw Murphy crying quietly. At that point, I said Murphy had to see a doctor. We made arrangements for our driver to take him to the nearest emergency room. Murphy went off with the driver to the local hospital. When they saw him they determined it was a broken foot. The hospital wanted to keep Murphy overnight and set the foot, but he would have no part of that. He was so scared all he could think of was being in a hospital in a foreign country; and the only one who speaks any English is the guy who tried to run him down and got him into this condition.

The driver came back to the restaurant and told us what happened. I told Sammy I would go get Murphy and take him back to the hotel. Sammy said he'd watch the rest of the show, then return to the hotel. The hospital had wrapped Murphy's foot, but he was in such pain he was beside himself. They had given him some pain killers that were suppositories. Murphy had no clue what a suppository was, let alone what to do with it. He took one out of the package and asked me, "How the hell do you swallow this damn thing?"

"You don't swallow it," I said. "You stick it up your butt."

"I ain't stickin' nothin' up my ass!"

"If you want to stop the pain, you'd better stick it up your ass, or wherever else you've got to stick it." He asked me to do it for him. I said "No way!"

He managed to do it himself, and it did help him. The pain subsided, but he couldn't walk. He tried to help me pack his luggage and Sammy's, since we had to catch an early morning plane.

**Murphy Bennett,
Sammy's loyal valet**

Sammy came waltzing in about six o'clock in the morning, just about the time we had to leave. Sammy had been up all night. By the time we arrived at the airport, he was dragging butt. We checked in and tried to get to our plane, me helping Murphy, who was hanging on to my shoulder because he had no crutches. I carried Murphy's shoulder bag and mine.

At this time, to the best of my recollection, the only jet airplane made was British and was called the Comet. They had three or four crashes in that plane when they first got it in the air, but that was the type of aircraft on which we were returning to London. You had to go out on to the tarmac and enter the plane through a very small door in the front, almost as small as a pilot's door.

Somehow, I got Murphy up the stairs and onto the plane. We took the closest seats in first-class. They faced one another. Sammy sat next to Murphy and I sat facing them. A woman sat next to me reading a book. She looked like an old hag and was smoking like a chimney. Her fingers were stained with nicotine, and she was drinking a Bloody Mary. As we took off Murphy sat there with tears running down his face. The woman, in a heavy British accent, spoke to me, "Excuse me, but your friend seems to be having some sort of difficulty. Is there anything I can do?"

I explained what had happened to Murphy, and that we were trying to get him back to London, that he was not going to stay in Italy by himself. She was friendly, even while reading her book, drinking one Bloody Mary after another and smoking like a train. She and Sam struck up a conversation. She was really very funny. After a few minutes, she and Sammy ended up exchanging dirty jokes—not real vulgar, but cute. This lady acted like an old hooker; she was a character.

At one point the pilot appeared. The woman stopped him and said something to him I couldn't hear. He went on about his business. Finally Sammy said, "Please excuse me, I haven't introduced myself. I'm Sammy Davis Jr. and I'm very pleased to meet you."

"I know who you are," she replied.

Sammy offered, "I'd like very much for you and your husband to come to my opening night show. Just tell Arthur your name, and he'll make all the arrangements."

I reminded Sammy that we had been sold out three months before we even arrived in Europe. There were no seats. He glared at me, "Just get the seats!"

She handed me her card, and I thought to myself, "Oh, God, we're in trouble!" Sammy went on and on talking with her, but she still had not introduced herself. She just kept drinking her Bloody Marys, and she and Sam were having a hell of a time. After a few minutes he asked if I had all the information I needed to get her tickets for the show. I said I did. Then I told him I wanted to introduce him to the lady he'd been talking to all this time. "Sammy, I'd like you to meet Lady Douglas of Kirkleside."

"Oh, shit!" he exclaimed. "I did it again! Talking to somebody I don't know and making a complete fool out of myself."

Well, Lady Douglas got a big kick out of this. She thought it was the funniest thing in the world. She said, "Oh, don't pay any attention to that shit!"

When we landed in London the doors of the plane opened, and in came four paramedics with a stretcher. They stopped by us, wanting to put Murphy on the stretcher. We asked what was happening and Lady Douglas said, "Don't worry; I've taken care of everything. They're going to take you to the hospital."

They couldn't put him on the stretcher, since the door to the plane was too small to get him through lying down. He looked at Sammy, and Sammy told him to just go. They got Murphy down the steps and into the waiting ambulance; off he went to the hospital.

Lady Douglas of Kirkleside, was married to Lord Douglas of Kirkleside, who had been the head of the British Air Ministry during the Second World War, working directly with Sir Winston Churchill. Now, he happened to be the president of British Overseas Airways, whose airline we were on. When she had talked to the pilot, she told him to radio ahead for an ambulance to take Murphy straight to the hospital when we landed. Murphy found out he was going to the room that had just been vacated by Elizabeth Taylor (when she had her tracheotomy). He just loved being in "Elizabeth Taylor's room."

Lord and Lady Douglas of Kirkleside came to opening night. She was decked out in a beautiful ball gown and diamonds. She became a close friend of Sammy's and mine. She invited us, and the rest of the troupe, to visit her castle at Kirkleside. The entire troupe went, except me; I had become ill with the flu. Lord and Lady Douglas took everyone first on a tour of a church, then to the oldest pub in all of England, and finally on a tour of their castle. It was an interesting trip, full of English history.

Lady Carolyn Townsend with me and Murphy Bennett

Singer, Cilla Black, Sammy and Elvera (Sam's mother)

Back to London
Back to Work

Back in London, we rehearsed our show for the Prince of Wales Theatre, which was to open on July 20, 1961. It would run for four weeks. It was a very big show that had to be perfect.

I had taken an apartment in Kensington with my wife and her brother. Sammy stayed at a hotel. This meant I had to find my own way to and from the theater every night. So did Alex Plasschaert and his wife. Another friend of ours, Lady Carolyn Townsend, had done some modeling in Wimbledon for an Italian motor scooter company called Lambretta. She arranged for Alex and me to purchase Lambretta motor scooters, to ride back and forth to work. At that time it was the best motor scooter in the world,

Alex and I had never driven in England before, except when I picked up Sammy's Rolls Royce. It was the wrong side of the road for us. We went to Wimbledon on the train to pick up our motor scooters. Now we had to find our way back from Wimbledon into London, quite a long drive, especially when you don't know the way and have to navigate on the wrong side of the road.

At that time, a new company called Hammer Productions had started a film studio in London. They had acquired rights to major horror films which Universal Studios had put out through the years. They had *Frankenstein*, *The Mummy* series, all the *Dracula* pictures, *The Werewolf* films and many more. These horror pictures later became actor Christopher Lee's forte; he was the ultimate Dracula. Hammer Productions remade them all in color. Of course Sammy and I, being the big movie buffs that we were, wanted to go out to Hammer Productions and watch them shoot something, which we did.

One day, while we were there walking through the studios, they were in the middle of shooting one of the *Dracula* pictures. There are lots of ensemble casts in England, and these horror pictures were no exception. We went through the makeup room, and on the shelves were the masks that were used in the previous films. We were particularly taken by the mask of *The Mummy* which, even sitting on its own stand, was very frightening. Of course, someone had painted eyes on the dummy's head, so even with no one wearing the mask, there were eyes staring down at you. It was a very tight fitting mask with a tiny little zipper in the back. Sammy commented he'd love to take a couple of the masks home.

Meanwhile, Sammy was thrilling audiences every night with his show, which was the talk of London. The mini-cabs were on strike at the time. They would circle the block on which the Prince of Wales Theatre stood. People could not drive in or out. We played to a packed house every night anyway. Somehow, people dealt with the inconvenience of transportation to the theater.

When Sammy came out of the theater, he had to walk fifteen yards to his Rolls Royce. Someone took a photo from overhead, four or five stories up, down onto that street when Sammy was walking to his car. You couldn't see Sam or his car—there were so many people. Every night was like that, oceans of people wanting to get his autograph, or just to see him. It was unbelievable. I was raised in show business, and all my life had been around some of the biggest stars in the business; but I had never seen anything quite like this.

Every night Sammy would take the whole troupe to dinner and hang out with Tony Newley and Joan Collins, his wife at the time, as well as with Lionel Blair and his sister, and other famous English stars. We'd go to places like the White Elephant or Les Ambassadeurs.

After we finished our engagement at the Prince of Wales Theatre, we were going to tour England; so we wanted to make the most of enjoying London. One time when we went to dinner at the White Elephant, our dancers were with us—the girls, of course, were quite attractive. The waiters brought water and bread to our table and started talking about each of the girls in Italian as they took their orders. They started at the far end of the table. By the time they reached my wife, who was at the near end of the table, they had said plenty of things they didn't think we could understand. My wife, Nita, who is fluent in Italian and Spanish, ordered her meal in Italian. The waiters were very embarrassed. They didn't know what to do. They had thought no one could understand them, and they had been saying some fairly vulgar things about the girls. The next person to order was my brother-in-law, Peppi, also fluent in Italian and Spanish. He too, ordered in Italian. Later when we left the restaurant, Peppi said to the manager in Italian, "You'd better tell your waiters to be careful what they say because a lot of people do speak their language."

As the end of the first four weeks drew near, Sammy had an idea. The theatrical performers who worked in London did their shows at the same hour Sam did his, so none of them were able to see Sammy's show. They were clamoring to see Sammy, but it seemed there was no way for that to be possible. Sammy came up with the idea that on our last night in town, he would do a special show for London performers only. We had to get special clearances; this meant our theater was going to have a very late performance, after the regular show. The theater would need to be emptied after our show and then filled again with these performers. The publicist got the necessary clearances in regard to traffic and permits for the theater to stay open late.

When word got out about that special performance, it sold out immediately—even the standing room. At the end of every show Sammy would ask for the house lights to be turned on, and he finished his show by talking with the audience. This closing night something was going to happen that Sammy knew nothing about. In fact, only two of us knew about it, the publicist and me. The stagehands at the theater wanted to give Sammy an award—something unheard of before. They had a plaque created, to be presented to Sammy by Tony Newley at this special performance.

Sammy was scared to death about doing this performance because, it's one thing to perform for the public, but quite another to perform for your peers—an entire audience of show people. In all my years with Sammy, the thousands of shows I saw him do, I never saw him do a show like this. He did stuff he had not done in ten years. He did every trick he knew. He danced until he could hardly move his legs; I had never seen him dance any better. He did impersonations he had not done in years. He did it all.

Sammy gives his all

Of course, the audience was absolutely flabbergasted and couldn't stop applauding. To this day, I don't think there is a dancer who could touch Sammy, except perhaps for Gregory Hines or Savion Glover. I don't think anyone who ever saw Sammy dance would dispute that.

At the end of the show, when Sammy asked for the house lights to come up, I was not standing where I normally did, off to the side of the stage. I had changed positions. When the house lights did not come up, Sam looked around to the wings for me; but I was stage right, out of his line of sight. At this point, Tony Newley walked on stage with a parchment plaque. He made a beautiful speech about how he had never seen anything like this done in the theater before, then handed the plaque to Sammy. I was standing behind Sammy, who still did not see me.

Sammy had on a pair of gray slacks and a gray silk shirt. By this time, he had taken off his jacket and tie. He started to read the plaque, but was overcome by emotion. I saw his shoulders tighten up. He clutched the plaque to his chest. He just could not say another word. Tony Newley walked back onto the stage saying, "Sammy cannot read this to you. Please, Sam, let me read this to the audience."

Beautifully written on parchment paper in embossed script, it read: "To the greatest performer who ever trod the boards of the illustrious Prince of Wales Theatre…." There were other words I can't remember, and it was signed by every member of the stage crew, and all the other employees of the theater.

Sammy took the plaque from Tony Newley and clutched it to his chest again. As he did, he continued to cry—something Sammy never did on stage. A tear ran down his face and fell on this beautiful document. When the document was finally laminated, that tear stain remained. It hung in Sammy's house for years. To this day, wherever that document might be, that tear stain still stands testament to this most touching moment.

Tony walked off the stage leaving Sammy speechless. He tried to talk, to thank the audience and the crew, and tell them what a great experience it had been for him to do this show for his peers. But he simply could not talk any more. He finally just walked off the stage. Being Sammy, however, he realized he couldn't just leave the show like that. All the stage lights were still up, so he composed himself and, still clutching his award, went back on stage.

We had gotten a call before the show was to close that the Scotch Royal Grenadier Guards, the group who plays the bagpipes and drums, was on tour. World famous and quite impressive with leopard skins, tall furry hats, and full regalia, they had said they wanted to come and pay tribute to Sammy. That day they had driven almost five hundred miles to get to the theater just for this final show. Earlier, when Sammy had been looking around for me and asking for house lights that did not come on, the entire group of about one hundred and fifty people had come into the theater and lined up across the back of it. What is truly amazing is that there were about a hundred bagpipers. It is literally impossible to blow up a bagpipe without making any noise, but they did it without Sammy being aware of their presence. The drummers had huge drums, and drumsticks about a foot-and-a-half long attached to their wrists by tethers, so they could swing them and twirl them as they beat their drums. By then I had moved to the back of the room so I could watch.

While Sammy was on stage, all of a sudden, from nowhere came the noise of a single drum. It was immense! The drum must have been five feet in diameter—a huge drum that went "Kaboom! Kaboom!" Sammy looked all over for where this noise was coming from. All the audience turned around in their seats. The Guards had come into the theater and set up unnoticed, except by people in the very last rows. Then the bagpipes started. The noise was unbelievable! They started marching down every aisle in the theater. That's when I brought up the house lights.

The audience started yelling and screaming. Anthony Newley walked out on the stage with May. I have been in this business over fifty years, and this was probably the most emotional, breathtaking, heart-stopping moment of my life. Nothing I have ever done or seen since could equal this moment. It was a moment in time when the world just stopped.

The Guards marched down the aisles to the beat of their music. The leader turned around, blew his whistle, and they started playing "Auld Lang Syne." The audience chimed in singing. Sammy completely lost it on stage, as we all did, even as I am tearing up now, reliving it for this book. Everyone cried. It was intense and magnificent! At that moment standing there, I felt I had just shared a few moments with a king!

*Sam with Vikki Carr &
Burt Bacharach (above)*

Sam with actor, Kenneth More

*Sam with drummer, Michael Silva,
& Murphy Bennett (in hat)*

On the Road in England

We set out on a show tour that included Liverpool, Birmingham and Manchester; Sammy traveled mainly by train. One of our first stops, after leaving London, was the Palace Theatre in Manchester. This is a huge theater, with the dressing rooms stretched out upstairs, one floor above the stage.

Michael Silva, Sammy's drummer, was easily scared, so much so that he and Sammy used to have a thing going to see who could scare who the worst. It began in Boston, when the movie *Psycho* first came out, and we all went to see it. Sammy would hide in Michael's shower. When Michael walked in and pulled back the shower curtain, Sammy would jump out at him, giving him a good fright. Once when Sam was hiding in Michael's shower, Michael managed to sneak up, throw back the curtain and scare the hell out of Sammy. When Sammy asked how Michael knew he was there, he replied, "If you ever want to do that again, don't put on cologne first."

While we were at the Palace Theatre, one of the lesser-known actors from Hammer Productions stole *The Mummy* mask which Sammy had liked so much. He came to Manchester and gave it to Sammy as a gift. Sam didn't know it had been stolen. He accepted it, and loved it.

Sammy decided to play a prank on Michael and put the mask on. Let me tell you that when someone put that mask on, it was one scary sight. Sammy took his glass eye and turned it around. When he did this, all you could see was the white part of the eye. There was no color or pupil, a scary thing in itself, especially with his black skin. But this mask, it was frightening even with the lights turned on. Sammy put on his trenchcoat, pulling it up around his collar so you couldn't see him at all. There was only this horrible mummy face above the coat.

He went into Michael's dressing room and climbed onto the shelf above the dressing table. Small as he was, he could do that easily.

The rest of us knew what was happening, but couldn't say anything. We had to stay in our own dressing rooms waiting for Michael to arrive at his. When he did enter, Sammy made a low groan. Michael looked around. He had not switched on the light yet. Sammy stuck his head out from the shelf and made a horrible sound. You could hear Michael scream a mile away. He raced down two flights of stairs and left the theater, running down the street. We did not see him again for about twenty minutes. A few days later Sammy promised Michael he would never scare him like that again.

During the show, Sammy used to do a drum stunt with Michael in which they would play the floor, the chairs, the music stands, everything—kind of like a drum challenge. Then, Sammy would walk off and let Michael play a solo. During Michael's drum solo, this same night Sammy had given Michael such a scare, Sammy walked off the stage, and when he came back, he was wearing the mask. He walked behind Michael, who had no idea he was there. People yelled and screamed, but Michael didn't know why. He thought it was because he was playing so well. Sammy just stood behind him with the mask on, his hands across his chest while watching him play. Michael finished his drum solo, stood up, bowed, then turned around and saw Sammy standing there. Sammy didn't even have his eye turned around that time. Michael still got so scared he threw his sticks down, ran off the stage and never did come back on stage.

Not more than two days later, the newspaper reported that the Hammer Productions studio had been robbed and one of their most valuable masks had been stolen. It was, in fact, this mask that had been given to Sammy as a gift. Of course, Sammy returned it to the studio and feared that the actor who gave it to him, a member of the ensemble cast, might lose his job. He asked the studio to downplay the incident, and said he did not want anyone fired. The papers later reported that it was taken and returned anonymously.

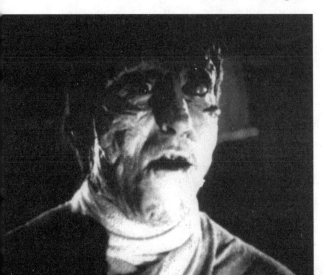

Mask from The Mummy

Sammy drums up a storm

Life's a party —Sam with English actress, Alma Cogan

Alma and Sam offer a cake—right of Sam: Lionel Blair, Diana Dors, Murphy Bennett, Hal Loman

"MR. WONDERFU
A New Musical Comedy
The WILL MASTIN TRIO
STARRING
SAMMY DAVIS, JR.
KAY MEDFORD
OLGA JAMES
with CHITA RIVERA
JACK CARTER
Book by JOSEPH STEIN & WILL GLICKMAN   Music & Lyrics by JERRY BOCK, LARRY HOLOFCENER & GEO
Entire Production Staged by JACK DONOHUE

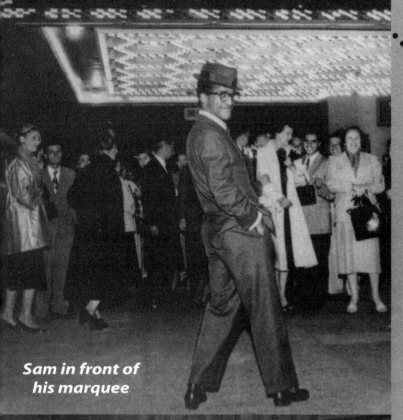

*Sam in front of
his marquee*

*Sam and me
in rented
New York
office*

Arthur Goes Bye Bye

As I knew it might happen, the Chicago bookkeepers and attorneys came to Hollywood. Our office suite had to get bigger to accommodate the expanding number of people. In 1959 we acquired a new larger office right in the middle of Sunset Strip. It was a great location, but a bitch to find a parking space; in the middle of the Strip there just isn't any place to park. We were just down the hill from Sammy's house and a couple of blocks from Ciro's. This, too, felt like good luck, but I figured someday the good luck would run out; that's exactly what happened a few years down the line.

We were all in the suite of offices trying to do our things: bookkeepers, attorneys, secretaries, both personal and general office, and me. I still diligently tried to get some meaningful projects going for Samart Enterprises. At this time I was mostly glued to the office for many reasons. The main one was that by now Nita and I had started a family. Also, Sammy wanted me to keep an eye on what was really going on. He didn't trust the Chicago people. This was one of his few smart ideas; it didn't last too long. These people were much to slick to get caught in anything big.

I was still plodding along when two more great opportunities came our way, in the form of two movie scripts. One terrific script was brought to me by a very good friend, Gilbert L. Kay, a film writer and director. The script was titled *Fame*—not the musical or the television series of later years by the same name. I worked for months with the writer, rewriting the script so the lead character was a Black man. We then put together a production company named Tauries Productions, a combination of my Taurus birth sign and Gilbert's Aries birth sign. We had pre-production shooting layouts, and we were starting to cast people and get others to commit to the project. We even raised the money we needed twice. I really felt this was going to be the big one. But alas, it was not to be. Sammy was getting ready to begin rehearsals for his

starring role in *Mr. Wonderful* on Broadway. He didn't have time to spend on the movie that we were preparing. All he could think of was his first Broadway show. If he had just been able to commit to doing the movie, we could have locked up the deal and began filming when he was available. But, in his usual Samart judgment, he just couldn't see it at that moment. The script was sold to some other people. This made me mad as hell because so many people were involved. It made Sammy and me look really stupid.

When that axe fell, I picked up the phone and really started in on him. "Sam, what in the hell is going on with you? Every time I come up with a good thing for Samart, you won't get off your ass. You just take all the air out of the balloon. Why in the hell did we start this business if we don't ever do anything with it?"

"Yeah, Silber, you're right. But with this show and all, I can't think of much else right now."

"It ain't a matter of money this time, Sam. It's just a commitment to do a movie from a script you love. I've brought a lot of our friends in on this thing, and I'm the one who's taking the heat."

"I'm sorry as hell about them; but tell them to hold on, and we'll do it."

"I can't, Sam. The writer-director has to live and eat just like the rest of us. He had no choice but to sell off the property to someone else."

"Then what can I say?" he asked.

"Not much, but I can say something. You just did it again. You've got some kind of a death-wish about doing something that would make us a lot of money. It's money that these guys sitting in the rest of our offices can't get hold of. Shit! I've had it for today. Later, man."

I slammed down the phone and left the office in a storm of rage. I simply did not understand why every time I came up with a good deal, Sammy either couldn't see it or was busy doing something else.

A few weeks later a man came into my office with an undeveloped idea for a movie, but he didn't know the first thing about the business. This was typical. I met a lot of these people; but their ideas never turned out to be much. A lot of people even came in asking "How do I get into show business?" Lots!

However, this day I felt that the little guy in front of me had a good idea for a movie that would be a natural for Sammy, remembering that Sammy's big dream was to be a movie star. I kept opening the door for him and he, in his wisdom, kept slamming it shut. He had done a lot of movies and television shows, but now we were talking about a big movie, that he and he alone would star in—without the help of Frank Sinatra. You can't be a big movie star playing a garbage truck driver, or playing second fiddle in a gang of others.

The gentleman in my office had an idea about a man who made special custom saddles. Some guys broke out of prison and robbed and killed an old man, stealing some of his saddles to make their getaway while his son watched the whole thing. Sammy would play the part of the son who later went after the gang.

"God," I thought to myself, "Sammy's got to do this one."

I called Sammy and told him about the idea, and he actually jumped on the idea, too. "What's the name of the script, and when can you send it to me?" he asked.

"Slow down a bit, Sam. The story has no name yet, and there's no script. So far, it's only an idea."

"Then why tell me about it now?"

"Because I already came up with a name: *Seven Saddles From Socorro*."

"That's a great title."

"The man wants me to help him develop it. I told him I would, if you like the idea."

"Damn right," he said. "I love the idea, Silber. Go to work on it, and keep in touch with me."

"I will. But we're back to the same old problem."

"And that would be what?" he asked.

"You need to commit to doing it, if you like the script."

"Okay, Silber, you got the commitment, if I like the script."

"Can I give this guy a letter stating that you are committed to the project, providing the script meets with your approval?"

"Yes, you can."

"Thanks, Sam. This may be one of the ideas that makes it."

When I got off the phone, the little guy's face lit up as I told him he had Sammy's commitment. I gave him his letter and set up the times that we could work on the script. We worked for many weeks. When finished, it was really good.

But behind my back there were other things going on in the office—things that were about to drastically change my life. One day in 1971, one of the Chicago lawyers called me into his office and started asking questions about Samart Enterprises. He wanted to know what it was all about. I explained the whole idea behind it, and told him some of the big things that had gone by the wayside due to Sammy's stupidity, such as the clip-on tie, and the Fizzies, and the guy just couldn't believe it.

The lawyer kept asking me how I could justify the cost of running Samart. I said there was nothing much to justify, as that is what Sammy and I wanted to do. "Furthermore," I asked, "why do I have to justify anything to you? You have nothing to do with Samart."

He took a different road and tried to explain that, due to Sammy's overhead, they could no longer justify paying me or the cost of Samart. I couldn't believe my ears! Here was the Chicago Mob lawyer telling me they couldn't justify me and Samart.

I started to get louder, as I got madder. I could see what was coming. The only reason they were supposed to be out here was to help Sammy with his IRS problems. Now they wanted to get rid of me. If they were successful, Sammy wouldn't have anybody here to keep an eye on his office.

By that time I didn't care who I was talking to. "Who in the hell do you think you are talking to here?" I yelled. "I've been around taking care of Sammy and his many personal problems for over twenty years, and in you march and tell me to be gone."

"Well," said the lawyer, "I'm afraid that's the way it has to be for now."

"Does Sammy know about this?"

"Yes, he does."

"Then why didn't he tell me himself?"

"To be honest, he got very emotional when we told him he had to cut down on his office staff. You aren't the only one who's leaving; there are others."

"Others, my ass," I yelled. "I'm not just 'others,' you shit-face. I'm Sammy's best friend and his goddamn blood brother."

At that point, I didn't care who these guys were. They had just fucked me up and my family's life as well, and they did it only so they could get control of Sammy's money. I jumped up and said, "You and your whole fucking group can go to hell!"

I slammed his door and went into my office to call Sammy. When Sammy answered the phone, I was steaming mad. "Do you know what the fuck just went down here with me and Samart?"

Sammy was actually crying. "Yeah, man, I do. What can I say?"

"Well, you can start by saying you're sorry."

"Oh, shit! I am so very sorry. I just don't have the words to tell you what's in my heart."

I shot back, "I have some words from my heart about what you and the assholes from Chicago have come up with. The first question is why in God's name couldn't you have told me yourself? After all these years, and everything we've shared and done together! Why? Remember the swords and the blood? What's that mean now? My God, Sammy! The pain's piercing into my head from my heart right now. I just can't think about this any more. What's worse, I can't believe it!"

"Christ, Arthur, please forgive me! You are, and always will be my right arm. You mean more to me than words could ever tell. You'll always be my shadow watching over me, a job which was given to you many years ago. That cannot, and will not ever change. My heart and all my doors will be open to you as long as I live. But, man, at this point in my life, I don't have any choice if I'm to survive."

"Then, if I must go, Samart Enterprises goes with me. Of course, it'll always be ours, and you'll always be the big guy in charge."

"I love you, Arthur! You're the most special person in my life. May God and Moses always smile upon you and the family. Someday you'll be back. I promise you that from my heart. So long for awhile, my friend."

"So long, Sam."

To my pal <u>Art</u>, The Best Always—Sammy

Arthur Comes Back

Leaving Sammy was one of the hardest things I have ever done. It took a very long time to get over it. I guess God and Moses were looking down on me, because I was able to make the transition to another job fairly soon. Of course, I wasn't sitting in my nice office on the Sunset Strip, but it paid the bills. Sammy came to town a few months later and called me up to his house, where we had one of our long talks. We cried a little, but, all in all, it went well. I guess you can't stay too pissed off at someone with whom you have spent two-thirds of your life.

We chatted about how things were going with him, but he wasn't too thrilled. "Not much has changed, man," he said. "I still can't figure out what's going on with this IRS thing, and where the hell my money is going."

"Damn, Sam, that's an easy question to answer. It's going into someone else's pocket. You just can't find out how or who."

"Well, I guess you're right again. But at least they're keeping the IRS off my back for now. These government guys just keep coming after my money. Enough of that, though. How are you and your family doing?"

"We're making it. But life ain't the same. It's been a major change, that's for sure."

We continued talking for some time, then said our goodbyes. We kept in touch. But as the years went by, I started hearing things about Sammy's health, his drinking, and more. To my bitter dismay, May had been forced to get a divorce, mostly due to the fact that Sammy just couldn't change his life-style enough to be a real father to their biological daughter, Tracy, and their two adopted sons, Mark and Jeff. They were all raised by the wonder of a woman who is their mother. Mama had passed. So had Massey, Peewee and Sam Sr.

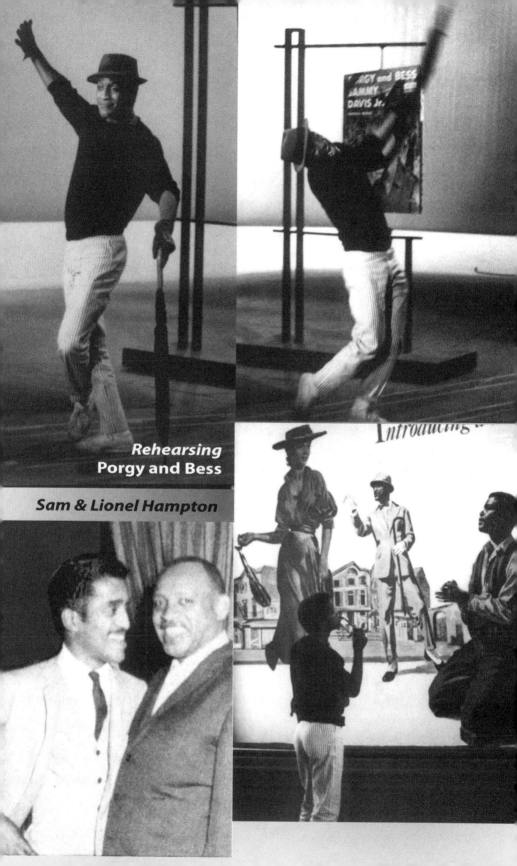

**Rehearsing
Porgy and Bess**

Sam & Lionel Hampton

I enjoy good friends Barbara Constantino (later Crosby) and Bill Miller—manager of the Flamingo in Las Vegas and owner of the Riviera in New Jersey, where I first went with Sam

Then Nita and I were invited to a wedding reception for Sammy's next wife. That is when Sammy's world really started to change. In came the love beads, Nehru jackets, bell-bottom pants and, of course, drugs, sex and rock 'n' roll. Years passed, as they quickly do, and I continued to hear bad things about Sammy's life.

About six years later, one of the lead guys on my current job came to me saying, "There's some guy on the outside line saying he's Sammy Davis Jr. He's asking to speak to you. I think the guy's nuts. Do you want to take the call?"

If someone says he's Sammy Davis Jr. and is asking for me, you can bet your life that's who it is!"

"No shit?" he questioned.

"No shit!"

As I walked to the phone, I wondered why in the world Sammy would be calling me after all this time. I picked up the phone with a small amount of trepidation. Then I put on my happy voice. "Hi, Sam. What's going on that's so important you have to call me at work? God, don't tell me that someone else has died!"

In his best happy voice, Sam said, "No...no, nothing like that. I just wanted to talk to you. Could you come to the house tomorrow?"

"Hey, man, remember? I'm working. I can't just take off whenever I want to. But, maybe I can get off for half a day."

"That's great! So, tomorrow about two...we'll have lunch. Anything in particular you want to eat?"

"Yeah, some of Mama's fried chicken."

That caught Sammy a little bit by surprise. "Don't we all wish that! God rest her soul."

"I don't care what we eat, Sam. Anything will do."

"Okay, I'll tell the cook to fix up a nice lunch. And I'll see you tomorrow."

"Hold on, my man!" I said. "Since you became the big superstar and bought a new house in Bel Air, I don't know how to get to your place." Sam gave me directions.

The lead manager was still in somewhat of a state of shock. He could not believe he had answered the phone and Sammy Davis Jr. had been on the other end of the line.

"So...Mr. Silber!" He said, "I guess that's how all of us have to address you now that Sammy Davis Jr. is calling you here to chat."

"Okay, whatever makes you happy, but I do need a favor."

"And what would that be, Mr. Silber?"

"I need to take off tomorrow at noon. Is that okay?"

Sarcastically he answered, "Sure, Mr. Silber; anything for you." He was having a little fun with me.

Sammy's new house was quite a place. I pressed a button on the gate and the security guards opened it for me electronically. There were guards and cameras everywhere. I parked my car and went to the door. Sammy came bursting through and jumped into my arms.

"Okay, Sam, I get the idea. You're glad to see the jolly old Jew."

"Damn sure am; come on in." He gave me a cook's tour of the house, especially his bedroom which had three huge televisions built into the wall—one for each network. Next we went to his private office, which had three smaller televisions, a whole bunch of electronics and all the security monitors. I was impressed.

"Sit down, Silber," he pointed to a chair. "I'll have lunch brought in here."

"Okay, little man," I smiled. "You've impressed me, so now tell me what all this is really about."

As we ate, he explained. "Do you remember, a long time ago I promised that you would someday be back with me? Well, this is that day."

I was genuinely taken by surprise—so many years had gone by. "Of course, I remember. That was, and still is, a hard day to forget."

Sam went on. "I'm changing my whole office setup…and I want you to come back and work with me again."

"Do my ears hear you right?" I asked. "You want me to come back and work for you? Is that really what you're saying?"

"Not quite," he answered. "I not only want you to come back, I need you to return."

"You need me?"

"Yes, my brother, I need you. It's been much too long, and I missed your cute face."

I heard all these new words, but the hairs on the back of my neck told me there was more to this than a simple request to return. And the hairs on the back of my neck are never wrong. "Okay, Sam, spit it all out!"

"It's really simple. During the past few years, I've been through so much shit that I should be dead by now."

"Yeah, I know. I've heard a lot about you."

"Well, I want a semblance of what used to be. I want my friends, and people I can trust to sort of circle around me once again."

"Christ, I told you this years ago!" I blurted.

"I know, I know! But let's not go there now. That has to be the proverbial water under the bridge."

"All right, water under the bridge. I get it. So, go on. Let's hear it all."

"I have an office manager," he began, "who has been traveling with me on the road, taking care of the production staff as well as the office business. I have another guy named Jay Brown who is my stage manager, but he doesn't have much of a background in show business. He's done a little acting in movies, and used to be a janitor at the Hollywood Park Race Track, cleaning the stalls. The office manager is coming off the road, and I've hired my secretary's boyfriend, Billy, to do my lighting. He, too, has never done this kind of work. I need you to take over being my Production Manager, overseeing the others, making sure my lighting and staging is all done right. You know how I am about all that."

"Yeah, I know. That's why it doesn't make sense that you've hired people who don't have any experience in these jobs."

"Well," he said, "I'm doing my secretary a favor because she and Billy are getting married, and he needs a decent job. And the stage manager...."

"Stop right there. Let's talk about Billy, the lighting guy. Sammy, I've been learning and doing lighting all my life. Lighting design and direction isn't learned overnight. You're a big star—you know a person with no experience can't walk onto the stage in a major club with highly professional union lighting technicians. He wouldn't speak their language. It would make you look like a fool."

"That's why I need you."

"So you want me to be the front guy and go through all the technical stuff with Billy, then let him call the lighting cues. Is that about it?"

"Well, yeah."

"Okay. Now let's talk about the stage manager, Jay Brown. What's his real job?"

"He makes sure all the equipment gets shipped to the venue, then unpacked and set up on the stage."

"No problem there," I said.

"Well, can you do it?" he asked.

"Wait a minute Sam. It's not a question of can I do it. You know I can do it, or you wouldn't have called me here. But I have to talk to my wife, and I have to know about the money and other things."

"Okay, let's talk about the money. How much do you need, or should I say want?"

I told him, and he agreed. "So, now that the money's agreed to, go talk to Nita. But make your decision as quickly as you can, because I need you right away. I have a television show coming up real fast, in Paris. Then in three weeks I'm beginning a tour of Australia."

"I'll give you an answer tomorrow."

The next day I called Sammy and told him I'd take the job. But I had to give one week's notice on my other job first. When the week passed, I had a meeting with the office manager, whose job I was taking, with the stage manager, Jay Brown, and with Billy, the new lighting guy. It went pretty well. But I knew right off the bat that Jay Brown was going to be a problem. Boy, did I turn out to be right about that! The other two guys were very nice, and I foresaw no problems there.

However, it was a little strange coming back into Sammy's organization as the top dog, when Sammy was in Europe. I had no one to break the ice for me. But I was really glad to see old friends again, such as Sammy's conductor, George Rhodes, whose wife, Shirley, was now Sammy's administrative assistant. Even so, we worked out everything we could, and made plans to meet in San Francisco to catch the plane to Australia. The office manager would be coming along on this trip until Sammy arrived, and the rest of us settled in.

Once in Australia, we had a production meeting with the television production staff. It took place in a rather small room in our hotel. The door was in one corner of the room. There were tables in the middle of the room with the production drawings spread out all over them. I stood in the far corner of the room. To get to me, anyone had to pass by all the other people there.

In the middle of the meeting there was a knock at the door, and in came Sammy from his Paris trip, with Murphy Bennett right behind him. Sammy walked around the room introducing himself to the television people and shaking their hands. He completely ignored the fact that I was in the room. He didn't even look my way until after greeting everyone else. Then he walked over to me and said, "And this one is family." He put his arm around me, and kissed me smack on the lips. It was a warm and heartfelt gesture, but one glance at Sammy's two other guys, and I knew that no matter how nice the gesture, Sammy had just burned them and made me king for sure. I knew I was in for a lot of resentment, especially from Jay Brown. This had really gotten his goat, since he didn't like White people too much anyway.

That night Sammy and I stayed up talking, and talking, like we used to, until the sun started to rise. I noticed something sad. This was not the same Sam I had known most of my life. He seemed a little sullen, and some of the spark wasn't there any more. I thought it might be just me, since we hadn't hung out together for so long. Trying to get a rise out of him I said, "How's your golf game, guy?"

"Oh, pretty good. I have the clubs with me all the time. But I don't get to play much."

"Yeah, I can understand that, at your advanced age, and not being able to move like you used to."

That did it! Just like always, I baited him, and he took it. He screamed out to Murphy to find the nearest golf course and get us a tee time at our first break in the schedule. "You think I'm too old, and have lost some of my stuff? Well, Silber, as always I can beat your ass any time, and for the same money."

"You're gonna beat my ass?" I asked. "And that will be on what day?"

"Any day!"

"Okay…if you can still hold a club."

For that short moment, we had gone back all those years; and for that short moment, the spark was there. "Well, Sam, I know you need to start getting your rest, so I will bid you a good night 'til there be the 'morrow."

"Yeah, the 'morrow," he said, "when I will kick your ass!"

We didn't have a day off for another couple of days, but Sammy was always ready to go. I kept baiting him until we got on the course. For years we had a standing bet of fifty cents a hole. That was a given. And it was one of Sammy's reasons for living—to win that fifty cents off me—providing, that is, that he could beat me. On this day though, I beat him by four holes, which of course meant he had to pay me two dollars. Lord, he hated to pay me, and couldn't wait until the next time we would play, and he had another chance to beat me. We played golf as much as we could, while touring all over Australia. Sammy won a couple of times; but, for the most part, I had him by a couple of holes each time we played.

The tour went well. But, as I had thought from the time I met him, Jay Brown would never work out. Talk about attitude! He invented the word! However, Billy worked out much better. He was a great guy and really had a strong desire to learn as much as he could. Given that attitude, I taught him as much as I was able. It takes years and lots of training to become a lighting tech. I gave him a crash course.

There was one night, however, when I had to take over and actually run the lighting control board. Sammy closed the show with "Mr. Bojangles." At the very end of the song is an important lighting cue. There was a light shining straight down on Sammy at that point. When he raised his hand, the light had to go out immediately; that was the cue. I missed it by one beat, since it was the first time I had done that song.

Singing "Mr. Bojangles"

Sammy never said a word to me about it, because it wasn't even noticeable to the audience. But Sammy did notice. I turned to Billy and said, "I guess there's one thing I haven't told you about yet. Sammy gives out certain signals, and it's going to take you a while to learn them all. You're allowed to make some mistakes on opening night, no matter what you're doing: lighting, sound or music. However, if the mistake is made any time after the second show, Sammy will—right on the stage—go into Amos and Andy character. Making a joke out of it, he'll say, 'There'll be a meetin' in the town hall tonight.' That signals to all his employees that there will be a meeting in the dressing room after the show, to discuss what happened and why.

"There is also another thing that may take you quite a while to learn. After the first two or three songs, Sammy has a unique way of knowing how his audience is, and what kind of a show he wants to give them. He will leave his show set list, and take the orchestra down whatever path he feels appropriate to please the audience, but will almost never tell George what song he is going to do next. Sammy will start to tell a story to the audience and that story will cue the conductor on what song he is going to do next—the audience never realizes.

"I guess I should tell you something, before Sammy has to. He is a little man of five-foot-six standing on a stage that may be fifty or sixty feet wide. No more than ten or twelve feet of the stage area on which he is performing should ever be lit. He feels that the audience did not come to see a whole stage lit up, when someone his size is standing in the middle of it. It's not an egotistical matter; it's a way of directing the eyes of the audience onto the person who is doing the performing. We don't need extraneous lighting all over the place. Learn that lesson well, man. It will stand you in good stead with whoever you work with in this business; and if you have any questions about what I've just told you, don't be afraid to ask."

The last place we played in Australia was a town called Perth. Australia is a larger country than the United States, and Perth is farther away from Sydney than New York is from Los Angeles. We left the next morning for the long flight back to Sydney, finally arriving at our hotel about nine-thirty in the evening.

Everyone was starved. Sammy wanted to get Chinese food for the whole group, so he had Murphy call the best Chinese restaurant in Sydney. They were closing up for the night and didn't want to take our order. When Murphy told us, Sammy ordered him to get back on the phone, and he would speak to the manager himself.

Sammy was soon talking to the owner. He said, "Hello. This is Sammy Davis Jr., and my people and I have flown all the way from Perth. We need to eat, but all the places around our hotel are closed. Let me ask you—how much do you pay your cooks per week?"

The owner told him, and Sammy responded, "Well, sir, I will pay all of you twice your weekly salary, and pay for the food as well, if you'll please bring us something to eat."

The owner asked what we wanted. A while later the food arrived— on silver serving dishes, brought by the owner and three chefs, complete with all the works. It was quite a meal, not to be forgotten by us, or those people either.

The next order of business for Sammy was to find out which two movies Quantas would be showing on the long flight back to the United States. He told Murphy to call Quantas. It was so late at night Murphy could talk to no one higher than the night manager, who said he did not know what movies would be showing.

Sammy took the phone again. "Good evening. This is Sammy Davis Jr. It's very important that I find out what movies you're going to show on the flight to Los Angeles tomorrow. I've seen so many of the movies you are showing, I really want to know. Could you please try and get in touch with someone who knows this information and call me back?"

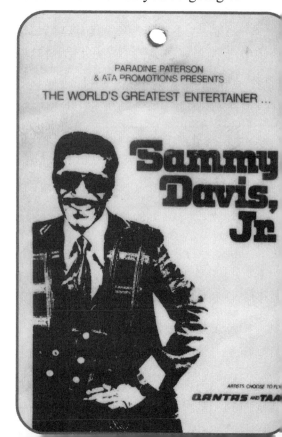

The night manager complied. Sure enough, Sammy had seen both of the movies on his flight from Paris. He asked what other movies they had available. He picked two of them, and—are you surprised—the ones he chose, were shown during our flight. That's the power of a real superstar.

Sam was a hit in Australia

Sammy had quite a remarkable memory. We were all checked in for the flight home, and Sammy was doing his usual shopping. As I sat in my chair reading, he came over and threw a small box in my lap. Then he said, "Maybe next time, you won't miss a light cue by one beat!" Inside the box was an Omega Chronograph, one of the most expensive watches in the world.

Our next engagement was a tour of Canada, beginning in Toronto. When we arrived and had unpacked, I gave Sammy a call, saying "What's going on?"

"Nothing," he answered. "Why don't you come up?"

As I entered his room, the pungent smell of garlic damn near knocked me out. There Sammy sat, on the floor chopping garlic on the coffee table. "What in the hell are you doing?" I asked.

"I'm cooking dinner."

"You're planning to cook dinner?"

"Yeah. I forgot; you don't know that I started to learn gourmet cooking, and this suite has a kitchen."

"Sammy Davis Jr., a gourmet cook. Now I've heard it all!"

We talked, and he chopped garlic until I couldn't take the smell any more, and went back to my room. About seven-thirty the whole group showed up at Sammy's suite. There, laid out before us, was a full meal. The main course was his specialty, chicken cacciatore. Funny thing about his cooking, he never ate it himself. He might pick on it a little, but he would not eat a full plate of anything he cooked. I never asked why.

Back in my room after dinner, some things started to become clear to me, as other things had in Australia. This was a very lonely man, who took up cooking in his room because he had nothing else to do, and no place to go except to work. No more sword fights, fast draw practice or fake fighting. I didn't even see any cameras around. My heart really dropped.

Our next show was in Montreal, where Canadian French is spoken. We had two opening acts on this show, and we had to make an announcement before the show. This announcement had to be in Canadian French as well as English. I don't speak French at all, so I had to learn. The first act on the show was from Montreal, and the performers said they would help me out. I sat in the theater lobby and wrote the announcement out phonetically, then practiced it over and over until I thought it was perfect. Our sound man recorded it on tape to be played each night we were there.

When it played on the sound system, a man poked his head out from behind the curtain and said my pronunciation was wrong. He told me his "correct way," and I went back to the lobby to practice again. Our sound man recorded it a second time, and someone else said it was wrong. This happened four times before it came out to everyone's satisfaction.

During the rest of that tour, I could see Sammy getting more withdrawn and more unhappy, all the time. He drank much more than he should, and this was not a good thing. It really started to get to me. But there didn't seem to be anything I could do about it.

Upon completing our Canadian tour, we started some one-nighters. On a Sunday night in Denver, as we were setting up, we discovered the piano was no good. Sammy told me to "get a new piano."

"You mean get another piano, don't you?" I asked.

"No, I want a new one."

"But, Sam, it's Sunday afternoon. Where in the hell am I going to find a new piano?"

He was in a very strange, bad mood that day. When he was like that, no one could reason with him. "Okay," I said, "I'll see what I can do."

I got together with the promoter, and presented the problem to him. Of course, he would not buy the theater a new piano, and had no ideas. But I did. "Get me the owner of a local piano store on the phone, right now!" I said.

"But it's Sunday!"

"I don't care what day it is. If you want a show here tonight, then find him for me."

It took some doing, but the promoter got someone on the phone. I told the guy we needed a piano there immediately. He said the only piano he currently had in his store was a forty-thousand dollar Steinway. I told him to get it over to the theater right away, along with a piano tuner.

"Yes, sir," he said, "but who's going to pay for all this?"

"Sammy Davis, Jr." I put the store owner back on the phone with the promoter so the promoter could tell him I was authorized to make this transaction. I knew Sammy well enough to know he wanted the piano at any cost. Sammy bought the piano; and when the show was over, he donated it to the theater. That was Sammy!

When I saw him later, I asked, "What was that piano thing all about? We could have gotten another piano without you spending forty grand buying it, and you know it. What in the hell is going on with you, Sam—and what can I do to help?"

"Nothing, man. I'm just in a rotten mood lately."

"Nah, Sam. It's more than that. You forget who you're talking to. It's me, and I know you like I know the back of my hand. There's something more going on."

"I promise, Arthur. That's all it is."

"Okay, I'll let that go for now. But there are other things I have to make you aware of. Do you really know what's going on in your group?"

"What do you mean?"

"For one thing, do you know how Jay Brown talks to people? Remember, when he barks orders. It's you that's in back of him, and it's you who will take the heat after we leave. Besides, the guy thinks he can order me around, too; and you know I don't take that shit from anyone."

"Oh, he's just testing you to see how far he can go before you take a bite out of him. Then he'll stop."

"Well, it won't be long before I do. I'm fed up with him."

"I'm aware of what goes on around me."

"Okay, as long as you know."

"Don't worry too much. But, continue to keep an eye out...and don't worry too much about me"

"Yeah, don't worry about you. That's a laugh! Remember, that's part of my job description; or have you forgotten that part?"

"No, I haven't forgotten. You're just a worry wart."

"Yeah, we'll see."

It wasn't too long before I took a big bite out of this asshole of a so-called stage manager. Sammy was going to do a special three-night show at Radio City Music Hall in New York City. The show also starred Buddy Rich and Nancy Wilson.

Singer, Nancy Wilson
Drummer, Buddy Rich

*Sammy rocks
Radio City Music Hall*

Technically, it was a gigantic feat to handle; our forty-eight piece orchestra had to be split in half during the performance. One half had to be moved to each side of the stage, because Buddy Rich and his orchestra had to come down the middle of the stage, to play their part of the show. Then Buddy's orchestra would be moved out, and our orchestra would be united again. We would have to move all these musicians without unplugging any microphones, lights, wires or anything else.

It took me a week to draw the production plans, then two staff meetings with all the head technical people at Radio City. These people are the best of the best, and are all members of Stagehands Local One International. This is the top and most controlling theater union local of them all. As I am a member of that Local, the Radio City stagehands and technicians all looked to me as a brother, just as all our union members do, no matter where you are in this country. If I had not been a member of this union, I would have had a hard time of it.

I had done all the groundwork. We had it down pat. After we pulled apart the forty-eight piece orchestra, we had to move Buddy Rich's orchestra into place with one move. We did this by using two fork-lifts. Then we had to put our orchestra back together for the second half of our show. It became a matter of personal pride for the stage-hands, as it often does, to see how fast they could make all these maneuvers with the musicians and equipment. They took seconds off each time they tried it.

On the day of the first show, our almighty "stage manager" came on stage and started telling the men they weren't moving fast enough. The head stage manager of Radio City called me over and said, "Who is this asshole who's trying to tell my crew to move faster?"

"I know, I know!" I apologized. "The guy knows absolutely nothing about anything in show business."

The stage manager continued, "If he mouths off one more time, I'll pull my crew off the stage."

"Don't worry. I'll take care of him." Of course, it happened again. Sammy was sitting down in the front row, along with all our people. Sammy started to stand up because he wasn't happy with what was going on. I put up my hand, gesturing for him to sit.

I was livid, and the big bite was coming. At the top of my voice, I yelled at Jay, "You big, fat asshole. Shut your fucking mouth! Don't you say one more word to anyone, or you're off the stage! As a matter of fact, you can get your ass off this stage now! You're not a member of any union, and damn sure not this union! You can't move a thing—not a wire, not a piece of string! You can't so much as pick up a stick, or I'll have this crew pulled off this stage; and there will be no show at all! Now get your ass gone! This is no joke! You've pulled your last attitude on me, and on anyone we work with."

Needless to say, he was in shock. He looked at Sammy. Sammy gestured for Jay to leave the stage. Sammy looked at me and gave me a subtle clapping of hands. Then this whole, huge stage crew started clapping hard. Their stage manager came over and shook my hand. They all knew, I was one very mad son-of-a-bitch. Mr. Jay Brown never crossed me again!

As time went by, things got worse with Sammy. He kept digging himself deeper into a black hole of depression. His health was bad; drinking was destroying his liver. He'd had a second mild heart attack, and there was no way I could get through to him. It got so I couldn't even bait him any more. That spoke volumes to me.

We were playing Harrah's at Lake Tahoe, Nevada. I sat in my room looking out over the lake and could not stop thinking of all that was going on.

Bill Harrah, owner of Harrah's chain, shows Sammy a model of Harrah's, Lake Tahoe, before it was built—unique at the time for blending so harmoniously into its surroundings

Harrah's Hotel & Casino Lake Tahoe, Nevada

Then I made the hardest decision of my life. I had to go to Sammy and tell him what was tearing me apart. I walked over to his room, knocked on the door, and let myself in. As always, I had a key to his room. He was sitting on the couch watching TV. I walked over and turned it off.

"What in the hell are you doing, Silber?" I had his attention.

"Sam, I have to talk to you, without anything interrupting what I have to say."

"So get it out then, if you must."

I sat down on the couch next to him. "Sam, I just can't sit around any longer, watching what's going on with you, and around you. It's getting to be too much for me. Your god-damn stage manager is 'borrowing' your x-rated tapes, and charging the hotel employees to come to his room and watch them. Can't you see that everyone is stealing you blind?"

"Yeah, man, I know. But it really don't bother me that much. It's only money."

"No, it's more than money. They're taking everything from you. Sam, if you let this go on, they will take not only your money, but more important, your pride and your dignity. Before I see that happen, I have to get out of here."

Wearing a face he would only show to me, he asked, "What in the hell are you talking about?"

"Sam, I've just got to go. In my heart, I know that you know I'm right. I love you, man, and I just can't take it any more. It's tearing me apart, so I'm out of here. You are, and will always be, part of my heart and my being."

As the door closed behind me, the tears came easily—a day I will never forget, as long as I live.

Beautiful Lake Tahoe, Nevada

DAVIS

WILL MASTIN, SR.

HE WAS A VAUDEVILLIAN

SAMMY DAVIS SR.

DADDY SAM

DEC. 12, 1900 – MAY 21, 1988

Epilogue

Writing this book was not an easy thing for me to do. Living one's life over again brings back so many of the good times, and also many of the bad times. But this is a story that had to be told. Many have tried but never gotten it quite right. I can only hope that what I have written of my life with Sammy, will shed a warm light over the life of this little giant.

During his life, Sammy was many things to many people. To some, he was just another Black man trying to get ahead in a White man's world. To others, he was the greatest meal ticket in the world—to be taken from, where and when they could. To most, he was the greatest entertainer who ever lived! Not many who saw him perform could ever say any different. When he passed away, Las Vegas turned out all the lights on the Strip. They have never done that for another person.

Sammy was bigger than he thought he could ever be. But he never felt in himself that he was as big as he really was, and as powerful a person as he really was. If it hadn't been for his courageous efforts to open doors—not just for Black entertainers, but for all Black people—it would have taken much longer for those doors to open at all. He lived life to the fullest, and sometimes to the very edge.

But for me, he was my best friend, my family, and my brother.

God really did bless you, Sam! Rest in peace.

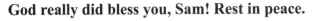

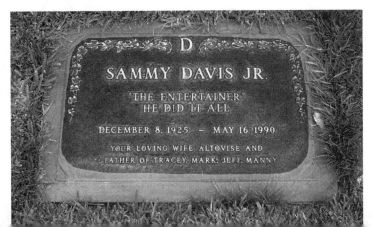

Photo Credits:

All photographs in this book are from the Arthur Silber Jr. personal library, Arthur Silber Jr. family archives, and the archives of Samart Enterprises. Additional photo credits:
  back cover, Mel Garza.
  page 13, Oahu, HI, and page 304, St. Peter's Basilica and Colosseum
    –Donald M. Witte, *Photo Archive of Famous Places of the World*, Dover Publications, Inc., New York.
  page 160, Sammy deals Blackjack–Dr. & Mrs. Bob Bailey CDA-Culturally Diverse Advertising/Media Relations.
  page 248, Paul Robeson–Rutgers University Archives.
  page 344–Harrah's Archives, UNLV Special Collection.

Index